EMPLOYEE ENGAGEMENT IN CORPORATE SOCIAL RESPONSIBILITY

Sara Miller McCune founded SAGE Publishing in 1965 to support the dissemination of usable knowledge and educate a global community. SAGE publishes more than 1000 journals and over 800 new books each year, spanning a wide range of subject areas. Our growing selection of library products includes archives, data, case studies and video. SAGE remains majority owned by our founder and after her lifetime will become owned by a charitable trust that secures the company's continued independence.

Los Angeles | London | New Delhi | Singapore | Washington DC | Melbourne

Edited by Debbie Haski-Leventhal,
Lonneke Roza & Stephen Brammer

EMPLOYEE ENGAGEMENT IN CORPORATE SOCIAL RESPONSIBILITY

⑤SAGE

Los Angeles I London I New Delhi
Singapore I Washington DC I Melbourne

Los Angeles | London | New Delhi
Singapore | Washington DC | Melbourne

SAGE Publications Ltd
1 Oliver's Yard
55 City Road
London EC1Y 1SP

SAGE Publications Inc.
2455 Teller Road
Thousand Oaks, California 91320

SAGE Publications India Pvt Ltd
B 1/I 1 Mohan Cooperative Industrial Area
Mathura Road
New Delhi 110 044

SAGE Publications Asia-Pacific Pte Ltd
3 Church Street
#10-04 Samsung Hub
Singapore 049483

Editor: Matthew Waters
Assistant editor: Jasleen Kaur
Assistant editor, digital: Sunita Patel
Production editor: Sarah Cooke
Marketing manager: Abigail Sparks
Cover design: Francis Kenney
Typeset by: Cenveo Publisher Services
Printed in the UK

First published 2020

Library of Congress Control Number: 2020937190

British Library Cataloguing in Publication data

A catalogue record for this book is available from the
British Library

ISBN 978-1-5264-5264-5
ISBN 978-1-5264-9650-8 (pbk)

At SAGE we take sustainability seriously. Most of our products are printed in the UK using FSC papers
and boards. When we print overseas we ensure sustainable papers are used as measured by the PREPS
grading system. We undertake an annual audit to monitor our sustainability.

To the pioneers, frontrunners and gamechangers in CSR,
who inspired us to write this book
And to all the conscious business students, the future makers,
whom this book is for

Contents

About the Editors and Contributors

Editors

Debbie Haski-Leventhal is Professor of Management at Macquarie Business School and an expert on corporate social responsibility (CSR), responsible management education (RME) and volunteerism. Together with the United Nations Principles for Responsible Management Education, she conducts international studies on business students around the world and their attitudes towards responsible management. She has published over 50 academic papers on CSR, RME, volunteering and social entrepreneurship in *Human Relations, Journal of Business Ethics, MIT Sloan Management Review*, NVSQ and other journals. Her work has been covered many times by the media, including in the *New York Times* and the *Financial Review*. She is the author of *Strategic Corporate Social Responsibility: Tools and Theories for Responsible Management* (SAGE, 2018), with a foreword by David Cooperrider, and of an upcoming book, *The Purpose-Driven University* (Emerald, 2020).

Lonneke Roza, PhD, is an assistant professor at Rotterdam School of Management and specialises in (employee engagement in) impact-first and impact-only strategies to create positive social change, including corporate citizenship. philanthropy and social responsibility. Lonneke teaches courses and conducts training for master's students, MBA students and professionals on social entrepreneurship, (employee engagement in) corporate social responsibility and cross-sector partnerships. As well as her position at the university, Lonneke is a consultant for companies, corporate foundations and charitable organisations and works with (international) platforms, such as the European Venture Philanthropy Association and the RW Institute. She serves on three boards of corporate foundations and on the board of the umbrella organisation for community foundations.

Stephen Brammer is a professor and an experienced academic leader, having held senior roles in three research-intensive universities in the United Kingdom (the Universities of Bath, Warwick and Birmingham), before taking up his current role at Macquarie University in Sydney, Australia. As Executive Dean of Macquarie Business School, he is responsible for the strategic direction of one of Australia's leading centres of business research and education. He is a leading scholar in the fields of business ethics, corporate social responsibility, and sustainability. Specifically, his research explores firm–stakeholder relationships, the strategic management of these and the corresponding impacts on company performance and reputation. He continues to serve as an associate editor of the *British Journal of Management*, as a member of a number of journal editorial boards, and as a member of the scientific committee of the Chartered Association of Business Schools' Academic Journal Guide.

Contributors

Cassondra Batz-Barbarich is Assistant Professor of Business at Lake Forest College in Lake Forest, Illinois. She earned her PhD and MS in Industrial-Organisational Psychology at Purdue University, and her BS in psychology at Loyola University, Chicago. She is actively engaged as a researcher, practitioner and educator in her field. Her research on well-being and gender challenges in the workplace has been featured in top scientific journals, including *Psychological Science*, and she has worked for Fortune 500 companies in the areas of human resources and human capital management.

Jacqueline M. Cramer, PhD, is Professor in Sustainable Innovations at Utrecht University and Strategic Advisor of the Utrecht Sustainability Institute. Her research interest is primarily related to industry, working on the implementation of sustainable entrepreneurship, corporate social responsibility and circular economy. She was and still is a member of various (inter-) national advisory boards of the government, industry and non-profit organisations. From 2007 to 2010, she was Minister of Housing, Spatial Planning and the Environment for the Dutch Labour Party.

Tanya Gapeka serves as Director of Impact and Learning at PYXERA Global. In this role, she leads a team of technical specialists and global programme staff in planning for, measuring and demonstrating the impact of complex social good partnerships. She oversees PYXERA Global's efforts in monitoring, evaluation and learning. This includes helping PYXERA Global identify and scale up innovative approaches in Global Pro Bono and Enterprise & Community Development practices that address global challenges and maximise programming impact.

Ante Glavas' research focuses on the intersection of Corporate Social Responsibility and Sustainability (CSR) and employee engagement. His research has been covered in media outlets such as CBS, CNN, Fast Company, Fortune, GeekWire, GreenBiz, *USA Today* and *The Wall Street Journal*. His professional experience is in driving change for CSR which includes the founding of three social/sustainable enterprises, a senior executive role in a Fortune 500 company, and numerous consulting engagements. For his contribution to society, he received the Medal of Honor from the President of Croatia.

Zoë Godfrey is a PhD candidate at Drexel University's LeBow College of Business. Her research explores consumer identity, corporate political activism and consumer interactions with music. Zoë received a BS in Marketing and a BA in Music from La Sierra University, and an MBA from Claremont Graduate University's Drucker School of Management.

Femida Handy is Professor of Nonprofit Studies at the School of Social Policy and Practice, University of Pennsylvania, and Director of its PhD programme in Social Welfare. She recently completed her six-year term as the editor-in-chief of the *Nonprofit and Voluntary Sector Quarterly*, the leading journal in the field. Dr Handy's research is collaborative and interdisciplinary. It has been widely published on a wide range of topics that focus on the economics of the nonprofit sector, and she has won multiple awards for her publications. Her most recent work is a co-authored book, *Ethics for Social Impact* (with Allison R. Russell, Springer, 2018).

Howard Harris is an associate professor at the University of South Australia in Adelaide. After obtaining his PhD, he taught ethics in the business school for many years. He is secretary of the International Society for Business, Economics and Ethics (ISBEE) and a former president of the Australian Association of Professional and Applied Ethics. As a chemical engineer, he worked in industry before commencing his PhD studies. He has a particular interest in virtue ethics.

Lesley Hustinx is Associate Professor in the Department of Sociology at Ghent University. Her primary research fields are social theory, political sociology and the third sector. Her research focuses on the consequences of late-modern social change for citizenship and voluntary solidarity. Lesley received her PhD from the University of Leuven and was a visiting fellow at the London School of Economics, the University of Pennsylvania and the University of Southern California.

Andrew Kidd is a tutor at the University of South Australia in the School of Management. His recent PhD covered the recognition and respect received by employees who engage with CSR policies, procedures and practices, the conditions that allow this and the enhanced sense of dignity that results. Andrew has prior experience in senior management roles in manufacturing, and a teaching involvement with vocational education, supporting lower and middle management employees motivated to improve their careers through management training. He retains an interest in the enhancement of dignity through engagement with work and with CSR.

Daniel Korschun is Associate Professor of Marketing at Drexel University's LeBow College of Business. His research examines how consumers and employees react when companies get involved in social, environmental or political issues. He has published in journals such as *Academy of Management Review, Journal of Marketing, MIT-Sloan Management Review, Journal of Public Policy & Marketing* and *Journal of Business Ethics*. He is the co-author of two books, *Leveraging Corporate Responsibility: The Stakeholder Route to Business and Social Value* (with C. B. Bhattacharya and Sankar Sen, Cambridge University Press, 2011) and *We Are Market Basket: The Story of the Unlikely Grassroots Movement that Saved a Beloved Business* (with Grant Welker, AMACOM/HarperCollins Leadership, 2015).

Thomas Maak is Director, Centre for Workplace Leadership and Resident Professor of Leadership at the University of Melbourne. He is a global authority in the field of responsible and values-based leadership. He uses a multi-level lens to research leadership at the individual, group and organisational levels, linking ethical theory, political philosophy, relational thinking and stakeholder theory. Thomas has extensive experience in leadership development and has worked for several years with PricewaterhouseCoopers on their award-winning senior executive program 'Ulysses'. Beyond leadership research, his interests include ethical decision-making, political CSR and organisational neuroscience. Through his work with leading social entrepreneurs, he is also interested in social innovation and the advancement of human dignity in a connected world.

Amanda MacArthur is Chief Program Officer at PYXERA Global and leads the organisation's Global Pro Bono and Enterprise and Community Development practices. In this role, she provides strategic leadership for the programme team and oversees design, development and delivery for $30 million in programming. As a member of the executive team, she leads a programmatic strategy that supports the organisation's mission of reinventing how public, private and social interests engage to solve complex global challenges and ensure that maximum value is provided to the organisations' partners, be they locally owned and operated small businesses, NGOs or Fortune 500 companies.

Philip Mirvis is an organisational psychologist whose studies and private practice concern large-scale organisational change, the workforce and workplace, and business leadership in society. An advisor to companies and

NGOs on five continents, he has authored, co-authored or edited 12 books, including *The Cynical Americans* (on social trends; Jossey-Bass, 1989), *Building the Competitive Workforce* (on human capital investments; Wiley, 1993), *Joining Forces* (on the human dynamics of mergers; Wiley, 2010), *To the Desert and Back* (on business transformation; Wiley, 2010) and *Beyond Good Company* (on CSR; Palgrave Macmillan, 2007). He received a career achievement award as Distinguished Scholar-Practitioner from the Academy of Management and teaches executive education in business schools and firms worldwide.

Nicola Pless is Professor of Management, Chair in Positive Business and Director of the Centre of Business Ethics and Responsible Leadership at UniSA Business School. She has served on the faculties of ESADE, University of St Gallen and INSEAD. She has held the Honorary Jef Van Gerwen Chair (University of Antwerp) for pioneering work in the field of Responsible Leadership, and has received the Aspen Faculty Pioneer Award for teaching innovation and excellence. Her work has been published in journals such as *Academy of Management Learning and Education, Human Resource Management, Journal of Business Ethics, Journal of Management Studies* and *Organisational Research Methods*. Her mission is to advance the practice of responsible global leadership and its development through research and teaching innovation.

Deborah E. Rupp, PhD, is Professor of Psychology at George Mason University. She was formally Professor and Byham Chair in Industrial-Organisational Psychology at Purdue University and Associate Professor of Psychology, Labour/Employment Relations, and Law at the University of Illinois. Her research focuses on EEO-related legal issues; organisational justice and CSR; as well as behavioural assessment within organisations. Her research has been cited in US Supreme Court proceedings, and she has consulted many organisations around the world. She has published six books and 100+ papers, sits on the editorial boards of five journals and is the former editor of the *Journal of Management*.

Katharina Spraul is Professor and the Chair of Business Administration, in particular Sustainability Management, in the Department of Business Studies and Economics at Technische Universität Kaiserslautern (TUK), Germany. She graduated with a Master's degree, PhD and post-doctoral studies in business administration from the University of Mannheim. Her research deals with sustainability management and CSR and has been published in scientific outlets such as *Business & Society, International Journal of Public Administration, Journal of Business Ethics* and *Nonprofit & Voluntary Sector Quarterly*.

Nicole Strah is a graduate student in Purdue University's Industrial-Organisational Psychology doctoral program. She earned her MS from Purdue University in 2018. Her main research interests revolve around gender equality in the workforce, diversity, organisational justice, and the intersection between psychology and the law.

Angela van der Heijden, PhD, has pursued her interest in the role of business in society, through her work as a researcher and project manager at Erasmus University Rotterdam, and subsequently though the Copernicus Institute of Sustainable Development at Utrecht. Her recent work focuses on long-term collaborative processes to implement sustainability in companies and business chains. Her aim is to answer practice-based questions by gaining insights into the translation of sustainability into the going concern of the organisation. She currently works as a programme director at the Centre of Expertise Social Innovation, Rotterdam University of Applied Sciences.

Riccardo Wagner is professor for digital brand management and communication at Macromedia University of Applied Sciences in Stuttgart, Germany. He has 20 years of practical experience in journalism, public relations and marketing, and he has been working intensively on questions of corporate sustainability for more than 13 years. Riccardo is the editor of several books and studies on CSR and CSR communication, and he is head of the CSR Communication Working Group of the German Public Relations Association and the German Business Ethics Network, which is also the organiser of the German CSR Communication Congress.

Marieka Walsh is a program manager at PYXERA Global where she provides programmatic support to clients in the Global Pro Bono (GPB) practice area. She manages various aspects of GPB programmes, from programme development and implementation to monitoring and evaluation. Marieka also manages Global Pro Bono LEAD, an exclusive community of corporations advancing the field of GPB. Global Pro Bono LEAD provides members with a networking opportunity to Learn, Exchange, Adapt and Deliver knowledge and tools to advance GPB within their company.

Chelsea Willness, PhD, is a professor in the Edwards School of Business and is currently Chief Governance Officer of the University of Saskatchewan. Dr Willness is a passionate champion of community-engaged scholarship. She has held national research grants for her research on how stakeholders (job seekers, employees, consumers) respond to organisations' environmental practices and community involvement. She has published this work in top journals and book chapters, and presented to academic and professional audiences locally, nationally and internationally. She has consulted for a wide variety of organisations in areas such as corporate social responsibility, governance, strategy and stakeholder engagement.

Acknowledgements

As the editors of *Employee Engagement in Corporate Social Responsibility*, we would like to thank all the authors who contributed their time, effort, wisdom and talent to this book. We also thank them for peer reviewing other chapters and for working closely with us on perfecting each chapter. Together, their outstanding and multidisciplinary knowledge has contributed to this book and to global knowledge on CSR and employee engagement.

We would also like to thank the wonderful team at SAGE UK, who worked with us tirelessly on bringing this book to print: Matthew Waters, our editor, Jasleen Kaur and Sarah Cooke. Thank you for sharing our enthusiasm for this book and for all your great support. We would also like to thank Sharon Cawood for copyediting the text.

We thank our universities for supporting us and allowing us to spend the needed time on creating this book: Macquarie University in Sydney and Erasmus University in Rotterdam. We are grateful to our academic and other colleagues who create CSR knowledge for us and for others to use, in this book and in many other endeavours. We would also like to express our appreciation to the many industry colleagues and friends with whom we work. Your ongoing efforts to make the world a better place provide us with inspiration and knowledge.

Moreover, we would like to thank all our past and present students, who demonstrated an eager interest in CSR and inspired us to create more knowledge – for them, and for scholars and practitioners in the field.

Finally, we would each like to thank our families and friends for their superb support, patience and appreciation.

Part 1
Introduction

1 Introduction

Lonneke Roza, Debbie Haski-Leventhal, and Stephen Brammer

Business as usual is no longer a viable option. It is estimated that if we aim to resolve the social issues detailed in the Sustainable Development Goals (SDGs), we have an annual funding gap of more than 2.5 trillion dollars (Garroway & Carpentier, 2019). Consequently, we see an increasing interest in new ways of organising individuals and institutions to create and scale social impact.

Subsequently, businesses worldwide increasingly recognise the urgency of transforming their organisations towards sustainability and responsibility. They do so to maintain their competitive advantage in the market, ensure their social license to operate and secure the future of this planet (Haski-Leventhal, 2018). For many businesses, this transition is extremely challenging, as the full integration of CSR is a process that takes a vast amount of time and effort. It implies a profound shift from a focus on profits and shareholders to taking a broader view on creating value and considering all stakeholders. For this to occur, businesses need to shift from short-termism to long-termism (Bansal & DesJardine, 2014). Many fail in this attempt as they underestimate the role of their employees in this transition process. Indeed, to be able to scale these socially responsible practices, it is important that CSR is not embraced by a select few, but by every person in every organisation.

To create this much needed systemic change to resolve social issues and create positive social change, changing the underlying mental models is key (Werhane, 2008). Stimulating employee engagement in CSR is therefore of the utmost importance and can contribute to the redirection of mental models into more sustainable ones. Indeed, employee engagement in CSR has a positive influence on employees' socially responsible behaviour and identity (Haski-Leventhal, Roza, & Meijs, 2017), both inside as well as outside the workplace. If employees are stimulated at work to be more socially responsible, they start to apply those attitudes and behaviours in their private life as well (Grant, 2012; Rodell, Breitsohl, Schröder, & Keating, 2016).

Employee engagement is often perceived as both a state of mind and a behaviour that link employees and employers beyond formalised role requirements. Yet, formalised within these roles, employee engagement in CSR initiatives can lead to organisation-wide impacts, encourage sustainability-related innovation, and create radical and systematic change across the supply chain of business (Kennedy, Whiteman, & Williams, 2015).

Employee engagement in CSR does not only help to facilitate change within an organisation at the start of a transition process, but it can also sustain the transformation and further diffuse its positive effects in the long run (Schein, 1996). It is oftentimes not the initiation of change that is most difficult, but rather it is that difficulties often come after the change begins (Kanter, 2007). Engagement in CSR increases employees' 'buy-in' to environmental and social challenges (Kitazawa & Sarkis, 2000) and facilitates a morality and an empathy that stimulate collective engagement (Muller, Pfarrer, & Little, 2014; Zutshi & Sohal, 2004). As such, employee engagement in CSR has the potential to become a collective action closely aligned with the organisational culture (Chen & Hung-Baesecke, 2014). To further strengthen alignment with corporate culture, companies can support organisational change towards sustainability by instituting systems that promote desired behaviours, including socialisation and training, incentive and reward programmes, recruitment and selection, communication and employee empowerment to take action (Mandip, 2012; Ramus, 2001).

Yet, in many cases, top managers announce a plan for change and simply expect people to start implementing the new ideas, which is usually not the case (Cameron & Green, 2009). Here, a significant challenge is employee non-engagement or even disengagement. Although researchers have identified numerous drivers of employee engagement, still, it is challenging to get employees on board and create a strong impetus for CSR (Wickert & De Bakker, 2019). One explanation might relate to the very nature of the oft-used CSR definition and interpretation. In general, CSR examines the role of business in society and its responsibility towards all stakeholders, not just shareholders; the importance of ethical behaviour; and the impact of business on society and the environment (Aguinis & Glavas, 2012; Haski-Leventhal, 2018). Yet, in many cases, CSR is defined as being voluntary (e.g., Van Marrewijk, 2003). Hence, this voluntary nature of CSR implies that employees have the right to choose whether they want to participate or to what extent they want to involve themselves in CSR (Hejjas, Miller, & Scarles, 2019).

However, whilst our knowledge about CSR has increased in coverage and popularity, it is mostly composed from studies adopting a corporate-level perspective on CSR, thus leaving a void on the micro-level of CSR, and, in particular, on the ways individuals are involved in, and respond to, these activities (Aguinis & Glavas, 2012). Filling this void is vital as employees execute the implementation of CSR strategies and carry out the responsibility of making sustainable decisions in their daily lives (Collier & Esteban, 2007). Moreover, involving employees at all levels can help sustainability to shift from a top-management agenda to a collectively embraced movement for positive social and environmental change, and lead to a holistic approach (Haski-Leventhal, 2018). To clarify what we talk about in this book, we define employee engagement in CSR as in-role and extra-role attitudes and behaviours related to their employer's CSR.

At the same time, CSR also plays an important role in employee engagement with the company (Brammer, Millington, & Rayton, 2007). Employee engagement with the company is a desirable condition, with an organisational purpose, indicating employee involvement, commitment, enthusiasm, focused effort and energy (Macey & Schneider, 2008). CSR can be a powerful way of engaging employees and creating impact.

It is to the above described urgency of employee engagement in CSR that this book aims to contribute. By focusing on the micro-level of CSR, the book portrays organisational dynamics and processes of how CSR is developed, implemented and practised (see also Costas & Kärreman, 2013). Specifically, this book focuses on the antecedents, processes and impacts of employees' attitudes and behaviours towards CSR. We do touch on employee engagement as the psychological outcome, also referred to as employee engagement through CSR, as that is claimed to be an important part of the business case of CSR, but that is not the primary aim of the book.

The book is built on the latest insights from academic research and gives readers a better understanding of the complexity of employee engagement in CSR. In each chapter, we include practical implications, so those who are practising CSR or want to stimulate employee engagement in CSR within their own organisation, have some practical suggestions on how to get started with it or further develop it.

This book integrates various perspectives on the topic, from organisational behaviour, change management and human resource management to the behavioural and organisational psychology perspective, thereby offering a multidisciplinary view on the complexity of employee engagement in CSR. This book not only serves as a basis for current knowledge, it also offers academic researchers a fruitful ground for building future research.

Overview of the book

The book consists of three main sections: Antecedents of Employee Engagement in CSR; Processes of Employee Engagement in CSR; and Impacts of Employee Engagement in CSR. Figure 1.1 summarises the three parts and the topics included in each. By integrating these three parts, this book offers a comprehensive view of the current knowledge on employee engagement in CSR, and a combination of theory, literature, empirical findings and implications for practice.

Following this introduction, Part 1 of the book discusses the antecedents of employee engagement in CSR, covering organisational and individual

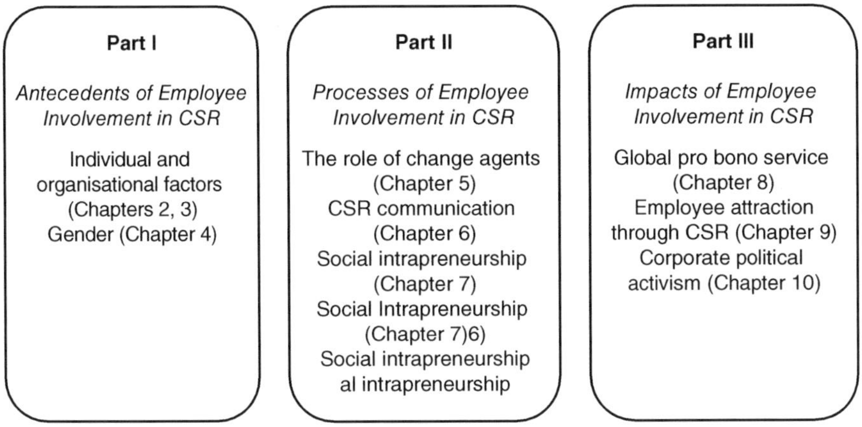

Part I	Part II	Part III
Antecedents of Employee Involvement in CSR	Processes of Employee Involvement in CSR	Impacts of Employee Involvement in CSR
Individual and organisational factors (Chapters 2, 3) Gender (Chapter 4)	The role of change agents (Chapter 5) CSR communication (Chapter 6) Social intrapreneurship (Chapter 7) Social Intrapreneurship (Chapter 7)6) Social intrapreneurship al intrapreneurship	Global pro bono service (Chapter 8) Employee attraction through CSR (Chapter 9) Corporate political activism (Chapter 10)

Figure 1.1. The structure of the book

factors related to employee engagement in CSR. It begins with Chapter 2, by Glavas and Willness, which provides an overview of what we know and do not know about employee (dis)engagement in CSR. Chapter 3, by Kidd et al., sheds light on employee engagement through CSR. Chapter 4, by Strah et al., discusses the intersections between corporate social responsibility and gender.

The second part of the book – Processes of Employee Engagement in CSR – contains three chapters which focus on innovative ways in which companies may involve their employees in their CSR. Chapter 5, by Van der Heijden and Cramer, shows that CSR managers, as organisational change agents, use different strategies to spread CSR initiatives within their organisation. Chapter 6, by Wagner et al., examines the role of CSR communication in engaging employees in sustainable initiatives. Using a sensemaking approach for internal CSR communication, they show that people construct different realities based on information and experience. The last chapter in this part, by Haski-Leventhal et al., examines the recent development of social intrapreneurship and how employees use social innovation to address societal and environmental problems within existing organisations.

Finally, the third part of the book explores the potential outcomes of employee engagement in CSR. Chapter 8, by Mirvis et al., details the impact of the global pro bono service (also known as international, skill-based corporate volunteering) on employees. To see how CSR can help to attract talent, Handy et al. (Chapter 9) discuss how CSR affects the job choice decisions of (Indian) business and engineering students. The chapter shows that young people are attracted to responsible employers to the point of being willing to sacrifice future income to work for such employers. We conclude this part with an excellent chapter by Korschun and Godfrey (Chapter 10), focusing on employee engagement in corporate political activism, where companies actively take a stand on political issues. While this is not without consequences for the consumer brand image, an increasing number of companies now involve their employees in political activism.

The book concludes with Chapter 11 – a comprehensive discussion, providing the narrative of the book, connecting its various aspects and offering overall insights on employee engagement in CSR, with a call to further accumulate and curate knowledge on this important topic.

Who is the book for?

This book is aimed at researchers and academics who are interested in CSR, employee engagement and, in particular, the integration of the two. Scholars who are interested in CSR in general will find new definitions and approaches to this important concept, and innovative ways of capturing and executing responsibility and sustainability. In doing so, it explores the meso-level of CSR, or the organisational level. The book also sheds light on employee engagement in general, but, more specifically, on how to engage employees in the company's CSR activities. It examines the determinants, processes and outcomes of the micro-level of CSR. Furthermore, some chapters also discuss the work that employees do for society and with the community, and, as such, they will interest scholars who are focused on the macro-level of CSR. The book is written by and for scholars from various disciplines, from management to psychology, and would be useful for researchers from different fields.

In addition, the book is aimed at teachers and students of CSR. It offers a broad overview of the antecedents, processes and impacts of employee engagement in CSR and can complement more macro- or meso-level books on CSR or organisational behaviour. With each chapter opening with learning outcomes and ending with questions for students, the book may be widely used in CSR classes, as a textbook or as a supplementary text to books such as *Strategic CSR* (Haski-Leventhal, 2018) or *Business Ethics* (Crane et al., 2019). The book is designed to be used in a variety of settings, such as a module, minor, elective or core course within a bachelor or master's programme. Because of the international setting of the book, it is widely useable in various countries around the world.

Lastly, but equally important, the book is aimed at supporting CSR practitioners who wish to develop programmes and involve employees in such initiatives. If we consider the transformation that we still need to undergo to resolve the most pressing problems in contemporary society, CSR managers, organisational leaders and other practitioners are vital to achieving these goals. We hope that managers and practitioners will find the academic literature and implications for practice in this book, useful and helpful in their journey towards employee engagement in CSR.

References

Aguinis, H., & Glavas, A. (2012). What we know and don't know about corporate social responsibility: A review and research agenda. *Journal of Management, 38*(4), 932–968.

Bansal, P., & DesJardine, M. (2014). Business sustainability: It is about time. *Strategic Organization, 12*(1), 70–78.

Brammer, S., Millington, A., & Rayton, B. (2007) The contribution of corporate social responsibility to organizational commitment. *The International Journal of Human Resource Management, 18*(10), 1701–1719.

Cameron, E., & Green, M. (2009). *Making sense of change management* (2nd edition). London: Kogan Page.

Chen, Y. R. R., & Hung-Baesecke, C. J. F. (2014). Examining the internal aspect of corporate social responsibility (CSR): Leader behavior and employee CSR participation. *Communication Research Reports, 31*(2), 210–220.

Collier, J., & Esteban, R. (2007). Corporate social responsibility and employee commitment. *Business Ethics: A European Review, 16*(1), 19–33.

Costas, J., & Kärreman, D. (2013). Conscience as control: Managing employees through CSR. *Organization, 20*(3), 394–415.

Crane, A., Matten, D., Glozer, S., & Spence, L. (2019) *Business Ethics.* Oxford: Oxford University Press.

Garroway, C., & Carpentier, C. L. (2019). Why are we behind on SDG finance and what can we do about it? *UNCTAD.* Retrieved from https://unctad.org/en/pages/newsdetails.aspx?OriginalVersionID=2204.

Grant, A. M. (2012). Giving time, time after time: Work design and sustained employee participation in corporate volunteering. *Academy of Management Review, 37*(4), 589–615.

Haski-Leventhal, D. (2018). *Strategic corporate social responsibility: Tools and theories for responsible management.* London: Sage.

Haski-Leventhal, D., Roza, L., & Meijs, L. C. (2017). Congruence in corporate social responsibility: Connecting the identity and behavior of employers and employees. *Journal of Business Ethics, 143*(1), 35–51.

Hejjas, K., Miller, G., & Scarles, C. (2019). 'It's like hating puppies!': Employee disengagement and corporate social responsibility. *Journal of Business Ethics, 157*(3), 319–337.

Kanter, R. (2007). The enduring skills of change leaders. *NHRD Network Journal, 65* (special issue), 53–59.

Kennedy, S. P., Whiteman, G. M., & Williams, A. (2015). Sustainable innovation at interface: Workplace pro-environmental behavior as a collective driver for continuous improvement. In J. L. Robertson & J. Barling (Eds.), *The psychology of green organizations* (pp. 351–377). Oxford: Oxford University Press.

Kitazawa, S., & Sarkis, J. (2000). The relationship between ISO 14001 and continuous source reduction programs. *International Journal of Operations & Production Management, 20*(2), 225–248.

Macey, W. H., & Schneider, B. (2008). The meaning of employee engagement. *Industrial and Organizational Psychology, 1*(1), 3–30.

Mandip, G. (2012). Green HRM: People management commitment to environmental sustainability. *Research Journal of Recent Sciences*, ISSN 2277 2502. Retrieved from 38.ISCA-ISC-2011-18CLM-Com-03.pdf.

Muller, A. R., Pfarrer, M. D., & Little, L. D. (2014). A theory of collective empathy in corporate philanthropy decisions. *Academy of Management Review, 31*(1), 1–21.

Ramus, C. A. (2001). Organizational support for employees: Encouraging creative ideas for environmental sustainability. *California Management Review, 43*(3), 85–105.

Rodell, J. B., Breitsohl, H., Schröder, M., & Keating, D. J. (2016). Employee volunteering: A review and framework for future research. *Journal of Management, 42*(1), 55–84.

Schein, E. H. (1996). Culture: The missing concept in organization studies. *Administrative Science Quarterly, 41*(2), 229–240.

Van Marrewijk, M. (2003). Concepts and definitions of CSR and corporate sustainability: Between agency and communion. *Journal of Business Ethics, 44*(2), 95–105.

Werhane, P. H. (2008). Mental models, moral imagination and system thinking in the age of globalization. *Journal of Business Ethics, 78*(3), 463–474.

Wickert, C., & De Bakker, F. (2019). How CSR managers can inspire other leaders to act on sustainability. *Harvard Business Review*. Retrieved from: https://hbr.org/2019/01/how-csr-managers-can-inspire-other-leaders-to-act-on-sustainability.

Zutshi, A., & Sohal, A. S. (2004). Adoption and maintenance of environmental management systems: Critical success factors. *Management of Environmental Quality: An International Journal, 15*(4), 399–419.

Part 2
Antecedents

2

Employee (Dis)Engagement in Corporate Social Responsibility

Ante Glavas and Chelsea Willness

Overview

Despite the increased focus of firms on corporate social responsibility (CSR), most initiatives remain either at the level of top management and/or on the periphery of business. This is problematic because although CSR is an organisational-level construct, it influences and is influenced by individuals such as employees, investors, customers and other stakeholders. Without the engagement of individuals at all levels of the organisation, CSR initiatives may simply become symbolic. Thus, there has been growing scholarly interest in exploring how to engage employees in CSR. We briefly review this burgeoning literature, focusing especially on how individual and organisational factors influence employee engagement. In addition, we assert that exploring the factors that lead to disengagement is likewise important. Prior literature has often treated CSR as an organisational construct that affects all individuals in the organisation in a uniform way. However, individuals do vary – so not only will different factors influence their engagement in CSR, but some may actually be disengaged in (or by) CSR. We build from this foundation to develop a prescriptive framework for engaging employees in CSR, with the aim of advancing future research. In addition, our framework provides general guidelines as well as examples of specific recommendations for practice. We conclude with recommendations for future research, questions for applying learnings from the chapter, and recommended reading.

Learning objectives

By the end of this chapter, readers should be able to:

- detail the literature on engaging in CSR
- explain the individual and organisational factors that lead to either engagement or disengagement in CSR
- apply the included framework to one's job (CSR in work) and at the organisational level (CSR at work)
- gain access to sources supplied via online tables that summarise the literature, recommendations for future research, questions to apply one's learning, as well as recommended reading.

Introduction

This chapter provides an overview of factors that lead to employee engagement and/or disengagement in corporate social responsibility (CSR), which we define as firms' involvement in addressing social and environmental issues while also benefitting the business and its stakeholders. To do so, we build on four foundational premises. First, environmental (e.g., climate change) and social challenges (e.g., health, poverty, education) are among the most pressing issues in the world today (see Hawken, 2017). Second, the involvement of firms (i.e., CSR) is critical to successfully addressing these challenges (Margolis & Walsh, 2003). Third, CSR is enacted through individuals in firms (Aguinis & Glavas, 2012). And, finally, it is not enough for a few individuals in a firm to be engaged in CSR; rather, individuals at all levels need to be engaged if CSR is to be substantively, and not just symbolically, implemented (Aguinis & Glavas, 2013). Thus, in order to address today's pressing global challenges, it is essential that we understand the factors that enable (or inhibit) employees at all levels – not just top management – to engage in CSR. Therefore, the focus of our chapter is primarily on what engages frontline employees. At the same time, we acknowledge the multilevel nature of CSR, such that frontline employees are also influenced by other employees at all levels, and that there might be similarities and differences across levels.

Another, equally important focus of our chapter is what leads to employee *dis*engagement in CSR. By understanding the differences between employees who engage and/or disengage, and the organisational contexts and actions that contribute to engagement versus disengagement, we learn about the key leverage points for implementing CSR.

This is critical for firms to understand, as there are conditions under which CSR is implemented (e.g., how and with whom) that may lead to negative consequences for the firm. Importantly, our examination of disengagement is based on a 'do no harm' assumption in terms of the organisation's CSR practices. As we describe in more detail later – and to provide some much-needed conceptual clarity – we focus on employees' positive, negative and neutral responses to CSR, as opposed to reactions to CSiR (corporate social *irresponsibility*) or intentions to mislead or misrepresent the nature or impact of CSR initiatives.

Although it is not easy, in an ideal scenario, CSR would be implemented such that the firm flourishes while also substantively addressing environmental and social issues that impact the greater good. Towards this goal, we provide a review of the factors that influence engagement or disengagement, and we build from this foundation to develop a prescriptive guiding framework for engaging employees in CSR that we hope will advance future research and practice.

Our review is not exhaustive but was intended to assess key patterns in the literature (e.g., past and current trends, gaps, opportunities for future research and practice) and to provide some representative journal articles. Nonetheless, we applied a rigour to our review that is equivalent to a systematic review as seen through: (a) conducting searches through ProQuest using multiple combinations of terms such as 'engagement', 'employees', 'corporate social responsibility' and/or 'sustainability'; (b) a review of reviews in CSR and especially micro-CSR, as well as the articles cited in those reviews; and (c) a review of the most-cited articles in the general engagement literature (i.e., often not related to CSR).

Individual factors that influence employee engagement in CSR

In the psychology literature, 'engagement' represents a body of literature that is related to an employee's general motivation at work (see Kahn, 1990; Rich, LePine, & Crawford, 2010). We build on Kahn's (1990) definitions of engagement and disengagement by applying them to (dis)engagement in CSR. Thus, personal engagement in CSR is defined 'as the harnessing of organisation members' selves to their work roles; in engagement, people employ and express themselves physically, cognitively, and emotionally during role performances' (1990, p. 694) in CSR. As for disengagement in CSR, it is 'the uncoupling of selves from work roles; in disengagement, people withdraw and defend themselves physically, cognitively, or emotionally during role performances' (1990, p. 694) in CSR. We also clarify that, while involvement in CSR activities might lead to more overall engagement in the firm, we focus more on what influences employee involvement or engagement in CSR. To that end, we distinguish engagement *in* CSR (the latter) from engagement *through* CSR (the former). However, as we write later, we do build on the extant literature on engagement *through* CSR because this provides insight into the potential factors that might influence why an employee engages *in* CSR.

We build on the 'micro' CSR literature – the study of CSR that includes, but is not limited to, the individual level of analysis (for reviews, see Glavas, 2016b; Gond, El Akremi, Swaen, & Babu, 2017; Jones & Rupp, 2018; Rupp & Mallory, 2015). The majority of this literature has positioned engagement in CSR as an antecedent rather than an outcome (Glavas, 2016b; Opoku-Dakwa, Chen, & Rupp, in press). Therefore, we know much less about why, when and how individuals might engage in CSR.

As such, we expand our review to go beyond the extant literature on engagement in CSR to include learnings from the broader engagement literature on factors that influence why an individual might be engaged in general. We then apply these learnings to engagement in CSR throughout this chapter. Prior scholars, such as Rupp and Mallory (2015), suggested that engagement theory helps to explain employees' CSR involvement, and examining the roots of this theory reveals why this is the case (Glavas, 2016b). According to engagement theory, the more employees express their whole selves, the more they are engaged at work (Kahn, 1990). Prior research has supported the idea that CSR enables employees to bring more of their whole selves to work (see Glavas, 2016b), especially when the following aspects of themselves can be found at work (Kahn, 1990): (a) *contributing to a higher purpose and finding meaningfulness at work*, (b) *values*, (c) *psychological availability/self-concept*, and (d) *psychological safety/organisational support*.

Purpose/meaningfulness: engaging in CSR can be a source of work *meaningfulness* – many employees find that helping improve the world (i.e., CSR) gives them a *sense of purpose* in their work (for an overview, see Aguinis & Glavas, 2019).

Values: CSR expands the nature of work beyond only short-term profits because CSR includes caring for the well-being of stakeholders. As such, CSR enables work to be more aligned with an individual's *values* – which are enduring beliefs regarding desirable modes of conduct and goals in life – such as caring for others, respect, equality, justice, helpfulness, love, harmony, security, a world of beauty, a world at peace, and so forth (for literature on values in general, see Rokeach, 1973; Schwartz, 1992). Indeed, numerous studies have found that employees engage in CSR due to the values that it embodies (e.g., Evans, Davis, & Frink, 2011; Vlachos, Panago-poulos & Rapp, 2013).

Psychological availability/self-concept: a major stream of research on CSR engagement builds on the Theory of Planned Behaviour (TPB), the critical element of which is the perception that one can control and achieve a certain behaviour (for a review, see Ones & Dilchert, 2012). Similarly, Sonenshein, DeCelles, and Dutton (2014) found that individuals were more likely to engage in CSR when they had higher *core self-evaluations* (i.e., positive, confident beliefs in their own abilities). However, they found that this relationship was not necessarily straightforward, which we later describe regarding factors that may lead to engagement and/or disengagement.

Psychological safety/organisational support: scholars have asserted that social exchange theory helps explain why employees engage in CSR (see Rupp & Mallory, 2015). According to this theory, employees will reciprocate when the organisation treats them well. Organisations high in CSR have been found to provide greater *support* for employees – and as employees perceive greater support, they become more engaged (e.g., Farooq, Payaud, Merunka, & Valette-Florence, 2014; Shen & Benson, 2016).

The factors noted above are derived from engagement theory in general, but we apply them to engagement in CSR. In addition, there has been some research on the micro-level of CSR, namely on individual factors that lead to engagement. This literature is fragmented, but there have been two areas that have also been studied in more detail: *organisational identification* and the *multiple needs model of justice*. Specifically, the justice literature frames CSR as a form of justice that is directed towards external stakeholders (Rupp, 2011; Rupp & Bell, 2010). As such, those employees for whom justice is important will be positively affected when the firm is involved in CSR: they will feel that, because the firm is fair to external stakeholders, they can expect the firm to treat them fairly, which in turn results in employees reciprocating by giving back to the firm. Using a similar logic, we expect employees to be drawn to CSR for these same reasons, and thus want to engage in CSR.

One of the most studied areas in the micro-level CSR literature is that on organisational identification (OI). Employees also tend to identify more with firms that engage in CSR (De Roeck, El Akremi, & Swaen, 2016; De Roeck & Farooq, 2018; El Akremi, Gond, Swaen, De Roeck, & Igalens, 2018; Farooq et al., 2014) because it is aligned with how those employees perceive their own identity, such as 'being a good person'. Also, scholars have found that employees are positively affected by CSR because it increases organisational prestige and pride (De Roeck et al., 2016) and trust (De Roeck & Delobbe, 2012). These studies suggest that prior research on how employees are affected through engagement in CSR might also work in the reverse, thus revealing factors that influence these employees to engage in CSR in the first place. Similarly, employees might want to engage in CSR because it will increase their identification with the firm. That is, there could be a reinforcing positive feedback loop in which employees engage in CSR which increases employee identification with the firm, which in turn influences employees' desire to increase their engagement in CSR because they identify with the firm.

Three other areas in the micro-level CSR literature that are less studied but growing in attention are *individual differences, benefits of engaging in*

CSR and *perceptions of CSR*. As for individual differences, two findings stand out. The first is that *age* is slightly positively correlated with engagement in CSR (for a meta-analysis, see Wiernik, Ones, & Dilchert, 2013), which may be contrary to widely held beliefs. One reason might be that youth are passionate about the issues and more outspoken, but, as people get older, they still remain concerned about CSR (albeit maybe for different reasons). For example, someone in the later stages of their career might be concerned about legacy and leaving the planet and society better than they found it (e.g., for their children and future generations). The second aspect is *gender*, with females tending to be more positively influenced by CSR. These areas and others related to individual differences offer fruitful ground for future research.

As for the other individual factors, we do not discuss perceived benefits in detail here because there is extensive literature that covers the positive effect on employees of the benefits resulting from CSR (e.g., Bode & Singh, 2018; Hejjas, Miller, & Scarles, 2019; Merriman, Sen, Felo, & Litzky, 2016). As for *perceptions of CSR*, Jones (2019) asserted that this is one of the most important areas for future CSR research. We still know very little about how employees become aware of CSR and how perceptions are formed. Research to date has mostly focused on CSR *attributions* (see Donia & Tetrault Sirsly, 2016; Donia, Ronen, Tetrault Sirsly, & Bonaccio, 2019; Vlachos et al., 2013). For example, employees who consider their organisation's motives for CSR to be substantive, and not symbolic (i.e., inauthentic, greenwashing), find a greater person–organisation (P–O) fit with the organisation in addition to other positive work attitudes.

Organisational factors that influence employee engagement in CSR

A few key themes underlie the major organisational factors that influence employees to engage in CSR. The first of these are the *values of the organisation and its leaders* (e.g., Agle, Mitchell, & Sonnenfeld, 1999; Bansal, 2003), because of what those values signal to employees, and because CSR may be perceived as more authentic if employees feel the organisation is 'walking the talk' (i.e., leaders embody the values). Moreover, it also leads to an alignment of values between the employee and the organisation, which in turn affects engagement (Vlachos et al., 2013).

Second, employees engage more in CSR as a result of *organisational practices* such as training (Stevens, Steensma, Harrison, & Cochran, 2005), sending employees to CSR conferences (Johnson & Greening, 1999; Weaver, Treviño, & Cochran, 1999a, 1999b), and communication around CSR (Ramus & Steger, 2000). However, it is important that employees feel they have the autonomy to engage in CSR and it is not forced upon them (Hejjas et al., 2019; Rupp, Shao, Skarlicki, Paddock, Kim, & Nadisic, 2018).

The third and final key theme – and perhaps the most studied under organisational factors – is the important role of *support for CSR from supervisors and the organisation*. Employees are more likely to be engaged if their supervisor supports CSR (Ramus & Steger, 2000). While this might seem obvious, many organisations overlook this point and instead focus their strategy on communicating to the whole firm in a uniform manner. Prior research suggests that the organisation should specifically target and train their leaders, because leaders' behaviours signal support of CSR and thus influence engagement (Robertson & Barling, 2013). It is critical that leaders do more than talk about supporting CSR by showing authentic support through their own actions.

Individual factors that influence employee disengagement in CSR

As we noted, our focus is on the factors that are associated with employee disengagement in presumably well-intentioned CSR initiatives, or employee disengagement in the organisation more broadly, as a result of its CSR initiatives. Under this lens, disengagement would be among a variety of potential, unintended negative consequences of CSR, or 'CSR backfire effects' (Willness, 2019). Thus, we focus on those firms that are *not* purposefully misleading or expressing disingenuous CSR claims – or what we might colloquially refer to as the 'dark side' of CSR (e.g., greenwashing – Lyon & Montgomery, 2015; decoupling – Crilly, Hansen, & Zollo, 2016). We base these parameters of our review on the premise that regardless of the perceived reasons for, or nature of, an organisation's specific CSR initiatives, employee disengagement is not a desirable outcome for most firms (hence our framing of disengagement as an *unintended negative consequence of CSR*). Although there are firms that might participate in irresponsible CSR, that is a distinct topic beyond the current scope of this chapter.

In a related field, consumer behaviour scholars have been well ahead of the Human Resources field in examining the potential negative responses to CSR, compared to the CSR literature on employees or job-seekers that is relatively less developed (Willness, 2019). Thus, we adopt a fairly wide view of disengagement (encompassing aspects of organisational citizenship behaviours (OCBs), identification, trust, etc.), in order to describe and hopefully draw insights from the scant literature on the topic to date. Nonetheless, some studies have begun to examine – or at least uncover – the phenomenon.

There are different motives that individual stakeholders (e.g., employees, job-seekers, consumers) might ascribe to an organisation's CSR, including, at the broadest level, self-serving versus other-serving motives. Despite some studies finding that people react differently depending on which motives they attribute to CSR (e.g., Donia et al., 2019; Vlachos, Theotokis, & Panagopoulos, 2010), some have suggested that stakeholders can be accepting of even self-serving motives, as long as the organisation is honest and transparent about them (e.g., Du, Bhattacharya & Sen, 2010).

Nearly all of the studies we could locate examined individual factors that influence employee disengagement through (i.e., *because of*) CSR; that is, negative responses to an organisation's CSR practices (as opposed to disengagement *in* CSR). For instance, corporate citizenship was found to have a negative influence on aspects of employees' OCBs (Lin, Lyau, Tsai, Chen, & Chiu, 2010), particularly among employees with lower levels of other-regarding value orientation (Evans et al., 2011). In another study, when employees felt that CSR is important in principle, it magnified the negative effects of 'symbolic CSR' (i.e., the firm just trying to 'look good') on outcomes like work attitudes and self-reported performance (Donia et al., 2019). An individual difference called social cynicism (i.e., the belief that institutions or people who hold power cannot be trusted) has been associated with positivity towards firm practices that benefit the employee rather than CSR that benefitted other stakeholders (West, Hillenbrand, & Money, 2015). For those who were lower in social cynicism, CSR was associated with increased employee trust and decreased distrust (West et al., 2015). Also relating to cynicism, one study found that a small percentage of job-seekers was either unaffected by, or reacted negatively towards, CSR for reasons that suggested scepticism or cynicism towards CSR (Jones, Willness, & Heller, 2016; for two other studies that focus on job-seekers, see Bridoux, Stofberg, & Den Hartog, 2016; Rupp, Shao, Thornton, & Skarlicki, 2013).

In an interview-based study in a firm, Rodrigo and Arenas (2008) found that some employees – particularly those without a permanent contract – viewed work as an economic exchange without broader social responsibilities, thus questioning why the organisation would invest in 'intangibles' like CSR rather than employee incentives or salaries. When the organisation implemented CSR policies, such workers experienced frustration, a lack of identification, and sometimes even became less productive. The study suggests that non-permanent workers, and employees at the lowest hierarchical levels, may resist accepting CSR practices or the needs of the broader society when they are preoccupied with their own personal needs, or because it may be counter to their worldview.

Regarding lack of engagement or indifference towards CSR, several individual factors may play a role, such as (perhaps especially) employees' lack of awareness or knowledge of firm CSR initiatives (Slack, Corlett, & Morris, 2015; see Jones, 2019 for a review and research agenda). Other factors that influence disengagement include attaching low importance to work in general, low organisational identification, or lack of clarity about the role of the organisation within broader society (Rodrigo & Arenas, 2008).

Organisational factors that influence employee disengagement in (or as a result of) CSR

Relative to research on individual factors, there is slightly more published work on how organisational factors may influence employees' disengagement, which can be grouped into a few key themes. With respect to how CSR initiatives are planned and/or implemented, there are implications regarding *how CSR is aligned and integrated into the firm, and into employees' work.* For instance, when CSR is not adequately embedded in core business practices (Aguinis & Glavas, 2013), it may lead to the perception that the organisation is not treating others fairly, which, according to social exchange theory, may influence employees to reciprocate by disengaging (Paillé & Mejía-Morelos, 2014). Similarly, when there is a lack of strategic alignment of CSR to business and personal objectives, or CSR is seen to be at odds with the operational aspects of the business, it can impede engagement in CSR (Slack et al., 2015). One study found that when CSR is extra-role, it negatively affects employees (Glavas, 2016a), and another study concluded that when employees feel pressured to be involved in CSR, it can actually drive disengagement (Hejjas et al., 2019). In other words, when employees have to spend time on CSR outside of their daily work and are forced to do so, they become more disengaged.

Perceptions of CSR as authentic is a key element, and research suggests that employees can (and do) distinguish between authentic and inauthentic CSR practices (McShane & Cunningham, 2012). As noted earlier, while substantive CSR initiatives can lead to positive outcomes, like enhanced perceptions of P–O fit, symbolic CSR can have the opposite effect (Donia et al., 2019).

There also seems to be potential for tension *when CSR is viewed as the firm supporting or prioritising 'others' over its employees.* Perceptions of the organisation's care for its public image versus care for its staff can seed frustration and disillusionment among employees (Brunton, Eweje, & Taskin, 2015). CSR strategies that favour external versus internal (employee-directed) CSR have been linked to emotional exhaustion and perceptions of corporate hypocrisy among employees, and subsequent turnover (Scheidler, Edinger-Schons, Spanjol, & Wieseke, 2019). The pursuit of external legitimacy through CSR (i.e., trying to 'look good') in the absence of commensurate internal legitimacy (i.e., CSR being supported by colleagues and managers) can have a 'negative net effect' on organisational identification and attachment (Lee & Yoon, 2018, p. 628).

Overall, there is relatively little research on employee disengagement resulting from CSR, and even less on disengagement in CSR. Most studies to date have examined organisational factors, as opposed to individual factors, leaving ample opportunity for future research. We refer readers to Willness (2019) for future research suggestions regarding CSR backfire effects more broadly, including employee disengagement.

Framework for engaging employees in CSR

In our review of the literature, an unanswered question is whether employees are willing to directly engage in CSR because it might meet perceived personal needs and motives (e.g., OI, values, justice), or whether they are simply willing to reap the benefits of CSR while not engaging directly in it. The factors that lead to the former (clearly more beneficial for both the organisation and the employee) versus the latter (arguably less so) remain unexplored. To answer this question, we have put forward a guiding framework of CSR in and at work (Figure 2.1) that builds on Glavas (2012) and Pratt and Ashforth (2003): *CSR in work refers to CSR that is embedded in an employee's job; CSR at work refers to CSR that takes place at the organisational level.* Through this framework, we provide guidance on how to successfully engage employees both *in* and *at* work, as well as how to navigate the potential backfire effects. Our intent is to provide a general framework from which scholars and practitioners may develop specific strategies, and we outline that framework next. In the section on 'Implications for Practice', we expand on these guidelines with examples of specific recommendations.

Many firms utilise a uniform strategy for engaging employees; however, the literature suggests that employees vary in what attracts them to CSR, thus different strategies should be used for different employees (Aguinis & Glavas, 2019). Based on these differences, we recommend that organisations intentionally target individuals who might be suited to four different combinations of low versus high CSR in work (i.e., in one's job) and/or CSR at work (i.e., at the organisational level), shown in Figure 2.1:

1. *Low CSR in Work/Low CSR at Work*: in this quadrant, employees are not engaged in CSR at all. This may be a recommended strategy where the organisation does not have a substantive CSR programme and/or does not have employees who care about CSR. As an example of why this is important, some organisations do not have the culture, values and leadership that embody CSR – nor employees who do – yet they try to carry out symbolic CSR programmes. As noted, this can lead to employee disengagement.

2. *High CSR in Work/Low CSR at Work*: according to the Job Characteristics Model (Hackman & Oldham, 1975), individuals are primarily concerned with finding meaningfulness in their jobs. Many employees do not have an awareness or interest in what happens at the organisational level. If they are personally concerned about CSR, they are willing to be engaged in CSR primarily through their own job. Conversely, there might be employees who care about what the organisation does, which can lead to a situation where you have employees who are happy with their own job but dissatisfied that their organisation is low in CSR. This

Figure 2.1. Guiding framework for engaging employees in CSR

	Low CSR at Work (i.e., organisational level)	High CSR at Work (i.e., organisational level)
Low CSR in Work (i.e., in their job)	Employees are not engaged in CSR at all. CSR is not found in one's job or at the organisational level. In this scenario, employees are not engaged in CSR because they are philosophically opposed to CSR (e.g., they believe that CSR should not be part of a business), or they may be sceptical of the organisation's motives for CSR.	CSR is not found in one's job but is found at the organisational level. Employees prefer not to be personally engaged in CSR in their work but do favour the organisation being involved. This results in increased organisational identification, prestige and other benefits of CSR. Usually, these employees are self-oriented and low on altruism.
High CSR in Work (i.e., in their job)	Employees are primarily concerned with CSR being part of their own job, while not being aware and/ or as concerned with CSR at the organisational level. Such employees place an importance on personally having an impact on others through their job (e.g., thus finding meaningfulness in their work).	Employees care about the external image of the organisation and also want to be personally involved in CSR. In addition, these employees want CSR both at and in work because the authenticity of CSR initiatives is important to them (i.e., they might feel it is inauthentic if they have CSR in their work but the organisation is not substantively focused on CSR) or vice versa.

scenario illustrates why it is important for organisations to understand employees' views of CSR, and their expectations of the employer in that regard.

3. *Low CSR in Work/High CSR at Work*: there are some employees who want the organisation to engage in CSR but do not want to personally engage in CSR – possibly because they have a self-orientation (Bridoux et al., 2016). As such, they find personal gain from improved organisational prestige, greater support for employees, and other benefits. These employees are happy with the organisation engaging in CSR, as long as they do not have to personally engage – and, as we noted, pressuring employees to be involved in CSR can actually have negative effects. In this scenario, employees have a lack of engagement in CSR, which is different from disengagement in CSR. It could become disengagement, however, if they feel pushed to be involved in CSR.

4. *High CSR in Work/High CSR at Work*: here, employees want to be personally involved in CSR through their work while also wanting the organisation to engage in CSR. Such employees place high importance on the organisation being authentic, which means that CSR must be embedded in firm strategy and practice, rather than simply on the periphery or 'bolted on' to existing practices and objectives (Aguinis & Glavas, 2013).

Implications for practice

This chapter outlines some key leverage points that both scholars and practitioners can immediately apply, and that may guide future learnings on employee (dis)engagement in CSR. Most notably, *we recommend that a 'whole person' approach is taken in which CSR is not seen as just another task to be performed, but rather is a pathway through which employees can show more of their whole selves through work (e.g., values, purpose, meaningfulness)*. Towards that end, an important organisational factor is support shown by an employee's supervisor and by leaders. Leaders can therefore use the information in this chapter to create conditions for engagement. For example, if we know that alignment with values and/or finding meaningfulness at work is important to an employee, supervisors can promote CSR as a source and means for this to occur.

In this chapter, we do not distinguish among whether engagement is in pre-existing CSR, whether employees are engaging in new CSR initiatives they create, or whether CSR is initiated by top management, middle managers, or bottom up. We cover factors that influence engagement, but not the type, source or direction of engagement. Nonetheless, we assert that the individual and organisational factors listed in this chapter can be used not only to engage employees in pre-existing initiatives, but also as factors that influence bottom-up CSR. For example, there is a growing literature on 'social intrapreneurship' (for a review, see Alt & Geradts, 2019), which is employee-led and discretionary CSR that also contributes to business objectives. It is entrepreneurial in nature, but within a firm. There are also other bottom-up strategies, such as influencing CSR in work through job crafting (see Wrzesniewski & Dutton, 2001), for instance when an employee changes their work to include more CSR. Employees can also engage in social issue selling (Wickert & De Bakker, 2018), or attempts to influence CSR by trying to change firm strategies, policies and initiatives. Combining such bottom-up strategies with pre-existing programmes, along with what we have outlined in this chapter, we provide examples of recommendations for each four of the quadrants (High vs. Low CSR in Work (i.e., in one's job) and High vs. Low CSR at Work (i.e., at the organisational level) in Figure 2.1:

1. *Recommendations for Low CSR in Work/Low CSR in Work Contexts*: because employees are not engaged at all, supervisors could try to engage employees through increased CSR at work by more openly describing their own values related to CSR, engaging personally in CSR, and by providing training and communication about existing CSR. For CSR in work, leaders could work with employees to craft jobs that include more CSR, or employees might themselves (without waiting for supervisor input) engage in social intrapreneurship, job crafting and/or issue selling.

2. *Recommendations for High CSR in Work/Low CSR in Work Contexts*: some employees may be engaged as long as CSR is part of their job. But for those whom it is important that CSR is also at work (i.e., present at the organisational level), we recommend that they engage in issue selling, social intrapreneurship and/or activism (Wickert & De Bakker, 2018) – such as the internal activists shaping a Danish pharmaceutical firm's CSR practices (Girschik, 2020). Especially important in this process is how issues are framed and 'sold', which should be done while also keeping in mind the context and what is important for the business (for a framework, see Alt & Craig, 2016).

3. *Recommendations for Low CSR in Work/High CSR in Work Contexts*: trying to involve employees in CSR when they are content to benefit from the organisational-level CSR impact on prestige and reputation, while not engaging in CSR personally, might lead to disengagement. On the other hand, other employees could become disengaged in CSR in this scenario because they *do* want CSR in their jobs in addition to high CSR at work (Aguinis & Glavas, 2013). For them, supervisors might engage in role expansion to include CSR. Employees could themselves initiate involvement in CSR through job crafting (see Wrzesniewsk & Dutton, 2001) and/or social intrapreneurship (see Alt & Geradts, 2019). One common example is an employee in operations working on implementing sustainable energy that is also more cost-effective. Another example is a marketing employee working on a programme to influence the well-being of consumers (e.g., Base of the Pyramid programmes; for a roadmap, see London, Sheth, & Hart, 2014).

4. *Recommendations for High CSR in Work/High CSR in Work Contexts*: here, the prior two conditions are combined – an employee is involved in CSR in their work and there is high CSR at the organisational level. For those who want to be engaged in CSR, this is ideal. However, we also recommend caution in involving all employees in the same manner. As our earlier discussions about disengagement in CSR show, some employees might not be interested in CSR due to, for example, lower, other-regarding value orientations (Evans et al., 2011). Thus, it is important to first understand the orientations and values of employees, and only then to connect to CSR in and/or at work.

There are also important implications for staffing practices more broadly. For instance, recruitment and selection processes might include values and/or personality assessments, to strengthen CSR-related fit and the likelihood of future engagement. During onboarding, supervisors should ensure that the 'big picture' of the organisation's CSR strategy and practices is made salient to new hires, who may be (understandably) focused on their particular department or function and may lack awareness of their employer's CSR and its positive impacts. For career development, employees should be encouraged to express their whole selves at work, and supervisors and leaders will need to ensure that the conditions exist to facilitate this.

Conclusion

Research on employee (dis)engagement in CSR is still in its nascent phase and we need to learn much more about factors that influence employees' engagement in CSR – and the conditions under which such efforts can backfire and lead to disengagement. Also, little is known about the influence of external factors on employees (although there are studies at the organisational level). In general, the interplay of factors at all levels (individual, organisational, societal) is a promising area of future research, as is studying what leads to *successful* employee engagement in CSR, because not all engagement may be impactful.

Moreover, not all employees need to be engaged all the time. However, for CSR to be successfully implemented, a sufficient number of employees need to be engaged, to reach a tipping point where the culture and practices shift, and CSR is truly embedded throughout the organisation – from firm strategy to daily tasks. Ultimately, CSR is enacted by individuals and thus should not be a 'one size fits all' endeavour, but rather tailored to meet the needs, values and other factors important to each individual.

Questions for students

1. What are the most important individual/organisational factors that lead to employee engagement in CSR?
2. What are the most important individual/organisational factors that lead to employee disengagement in CSR?
3. What is the difference between CSR in and at work, and for which employees might it be important?
4. What do you think are some reasons why you might, or might not, be engaged in CSR?
5. How might you encourage and support others around you to be more engaged in CSR, and to bring more of their whole selves to work each day?

References

Agle, B. R., Mitchell, R. K., & Sonnenfeld, J. A. (1999). Who matters to CEOs? An investigation of stakeholder attributes and salience, corporate performance, and CEO values. *Academy of Management Journal, 42*, 507–525.

Aguinis, H., & Glavas, A. (2012). What we know and don't know about corporate social responsibility: A review and research agenda. *Journal of Management, 38*, 932–968.

Aguinis, H., & Glavas, A. (2013). Embedded versus peripheral corporate social responsibility: Psychological foundations. *Industrial and Organizational Psychology: Perspectives on Science and Practice, 6*, 314–332.

Aguinis, H., & Glavas, A. (2019). On corporate social responsibility, sensemaking, and the search for meaningfulness through work. *Journal of Management, 45,* 1057–1086.

Alt, E., & Craig, J. B. (2016). Selling issues with solutions: Igniting social intrapreneurship in for-profit organizations. *Journal of Management Studies, 53,* 794–820.

Alt, E., & Geradts, T. (2019). *Social intrapreneurship: Unique challenges and opportunities for future research.* Paper presented at the 79th annual meeting of the Academy of Management, Boston, USA, July. Retrieved from https://journals.aom.org/doi/pdf/10.5465/AMBPP.2019.188.

Bansal, P. (2003). From issues to actions: The importance of individual concerns and organizational values in responding to natural environmental issues. *Organization Science, 14,* 510–527.

Bode, C., & Singh, J. (2018). Taking a hit to save the world? Employee participation in a corporate social initiative. *Strategic Management Journal, 39,* 1003–1030.

Bridoux, F., Stofberg, N., & Den Hartog, D. (2016). Stakeholders' responses to CSR tradeoffs: When other-orientation and trust trump material self-interest. In A. Glavas, C. R. Willness, & D. A. Jones (Eds.), *Corporate social responsibility and organizational psychology: Quid pro quo* (pp. 40–57). Lausanne: Frontiers Media.

Brunton, M., Eweje, G., & Taskin, N. (2015). Communicating corporate social responsibility to internal stakeholders: Walking the walk or just talking the talk? *Business Strategy and the Environment, 26,* 31–48.

Crilly, D., Hansen, M., & Zollo, M. (2016). The grammar of decoupling: A cognitive-linguistic perspective on firms' sustainability claims and stakeholders' interpretation. *Academy of Management Journal, 59,* 705–729.

De Roeck, K., & Delobbe, N. (2012). Do environmental CSR initiatives serve organizations' legitimacy in the oil industry? Exploring employees' reactions through organizational identification. *Journal of Business Ethics, 110,* 397–412.

De Roeck, K., & Farooq, O. (2018). Corporate social responsibility and ethical leadership: Investigating their interactive effect on employees' socially responsible behaviors. *Journal of Business Ethics, 151,* 923–939.

De Roeck, K., El Akremi, A., & Swaen, V. (2016). Consistency matters! How and when does corporate social responsibility affect employees' organizational identification? *Journal of Management Studies, 53,* 1141–1168.

Donia, M. B. L., Ronen, S., Tetrault Sirsly, C. A., & Bonaccio, S. (2019). CSR by any other name? The differential impact of substantive and symbolic CSR attributions on employee outcomes. *Journal of Business Ethics, 157,* 503–523.

Donia, M. B. L., & Tetrault Sirsly, C. A. (2016). Determinants and consequences of employee attributions of corporate social responsibility. *European Management Journal, 34,* 232–242.

Du, S., Bhattacharya, C. B., & Sen, S. (2010). Maximizing business returns to corporate social responsibility (CSR): The role of CSR communication. *International Journal of Management Review, 12,* 8–19.

El Akremi, A., Gond, J. P., Swaen, V., De Roeck, K., & Igalens, J. (2018). How do employees perceive corporate responsibility? Development and validation of a multidimensional corporate stakeholder responsibility scale. *Journal of Management, 44,* 619–657.

Evans, W. R., Davis, W. D., & Frink, D. D. (2011). An examination of employee reactions to perceived corporate citizenship. *Journal of Applied Social Psychology*, *41*, 938–64.

Farooq, O., Payaud, M., Merunka, D., & Valette-Florence, P. (2014). The impact of corporate social responsibility on organizational commitment: Exploring multiple mediation mechanisms. *Journal of Business Ethics*, *125*, 563–580.

Girschik, V. (2020). Shared responsibility for societal problems: The role of internal activists in reframing corporate responsibility. *Business & Society*, *59*(1), 34–66.

Glavas, A. (2012). Employee engagement and sustainability: A model for implementing meaningfulness at and in work. *Journal of Corporate Citizenship*, *46*, 13–29.

Glavas, A. (2016a). Corporate social responsibility and employee engagement: Enabling employees to employ more of their whole selves at work. *Frontiers in Psychology*, *7*(796), 1–10.

Glavas, A. (2016b). Corporate social responsibility and organizational psychology: An integrative review. *Frontiers in Psychology*, *7*(144), 1–13.

Gond, J. P., El Akremi, A., Swaen, V., & Babu, N. (2017). The psychological microfoundations of corporate social responsibility: A person-centric systematic review. *Journal of Organizational Behavior*, *38*, 225–246.

Hackman, J. R., & Oldham, G. R. (1975). Development of the job diagnostic survey. *Journal of Applied Psychology*, *60*, 159–170.

Hawken, P. (2017). *Drawdown: The most comprehensive plan ever proposed to reverse global warming*. New York: Penguin Books.

Hejjas, K., Miller, G., & Scarles, C. (2019). 'It's like hating puppies!': Employee disengagement and corporate social responsibility. *Journal of Business Ethics*, *157*, 319–337.

Johnson, R. A., & Greening, D. W. (1999). The effects of corporate governance and institutional ownership types on corporate social performance. *Academy of Management Journal*, *42*, 564–576.

Jones, D. A. (2019). The psychology of CSR. In A. McWilliams, D. E. Rupp, D. S. Siegel, G. Stahl, & D. A. Waldman (Eds.), *The Oxford handbook of corporate social responsibility: Psychological and organizational perspectives* (pp. 19–47). Oxford: Oxford University Press.

Jones, D. A., & Rupp, D. E. (2018). Social responsibility in and of organizations: The psychology of corporate social responsibility among organizational members. In N. Anderson, D. S. Ones, H. K. Sinangil, & C. Viswesvaran (Eds.), *Handbook of industrial, work, and organizational psychology* (2nd edition, pp. 333–350). London: Sage.

Jones, D. A., Willness, C. R., & Heller, K. (2016). Illuminating the signals job seekers receive from an employer's community involvement and environmental sustainability practices: Insights into why most job seekers are attracted, others are indifferent, and a few are repelled. *Frontiers in Psychology*, *7*(426), 1–16.

Kahn, W. A. (1990). Psychological conditions of personal engagement and disengagement at work. *Academy of Management Journal*, *33*, 692–724.

Lee, S., & Yoon, J. (2018). Does the authenticity of corporate social responsibility affect employee commitment? *Social Behavior & Personality: An International Journal*, *46*(4), 617–632.

Lin, C. P., Lyau, N. M., Tsai, Y. H., Chen, W. Y., & Chiu, C. K. (2010). Modeling corporate citizenship and its relationship with organizational citizenship behaviors. *Journal of Business Ethics*, *95*, 357–372.

London, T., Sheth, S., & Hart, S. (2014). *A roadmap for the base of the pyramid domain: Re-energizing for the next decade.* Retrieved from https://wdi.umich.edu/wp-content/uploads/BoP-Roadmap.pdf.

Lyon, T. P., & Montgomery, A. W. (2015). The means and end of greenwash. *Organization & Environment, 28,* 223–249.

Margolis, J. D., & Walsh, J. P. (2003). Misery loves companies: Rethinking social initiatives by business. *Administrative Science Quarterly, 48,* 268–305.

McShane, L., & Cunningham, P. (2012). To thine own self be true? Employees' judgments of the authenticity of their organization's corporate social responsibility program. *Journal of Business Ethics, 108,* 81–100.

Merriman, K. K., Sen, S., Felo, A. J., & Litzky, B. E. (2016). Employees and sustainability: The role of incentives. *Journal of Managerial Psychology, 31,* 820–836.

Ones, D. S., & Dilchert, S. (2012). Environmental sustainability at work: A call to action. *Industrial and Organizational Psychology: Perspectives on Science and Practice, 5,* 444–466.

Opoku-Dakwa, A., Chen, C. C., & Rupp, D. E. (In press). CSR initiative characteristics and employee engagement: An impact-based perspective. *Journal of Organizational Behavior.* Retrieved from https://doi-org.eur.idm.oclc.org/10.1002/job.2281.

Paillé, P., & Mejía-Morelos, J. H. (2014). Antecedents of pro-environmental behaviors at work: The moderating influence of psychological contract breach. *Journal of Environmental Psychology, 38,* 124–131.

Pratt, M. G., & Ashforth, B. E. (2003). Fostering meaningfulness in working and meaningfulness at work: An identity perspective. In K. S. Cameron, J. E. Dutton, & R. E. Quinn (Eds.), *Positive organizational scholarship: Foundations of a new discipline* (pp. 309–327). San Francisco, CA: Berrett-Koehler.

Ramus, C. A., & Steger, U. (2000). The roles of supervisory support behaviors and environmental policy in employee 'ecoinitiatives' at leading-edge European companies. *Academy of Management Journal, 43,* 605–626.

Rich, B. L., LePine, J. A., & Crawford, E. R. (2010). Job engagement: Antecedents and effects on job performance. *Academy of Management, 53,* 617–635.

Robertson, J. L., & Barling, J. (2013). Greening organizations through leaders' influence on employees' pro-environmental behaviors. *Journal of Organizational Behavior, 34,* 176–194.

Rodrigo, P., & Arenas, D. (2008). Do employees care about CSR programs? A typology of employees according to their attitudes. *Journal of Business Ethics, 83,* 265–283.

Rokeach, M. (1973). *The nature of human values.* New York: Free Press.

Rupp, D. E. (2011). An employee-centered model of organizational justice and social responsibility. *Organizational Psychology Review, 1,* 72–94.

Rupp, D. E., & Bell, C. M. (2010). Extending the deontic model of justice: Moral self-regulation in third-party responses to injustice. *Business Ethics Quarterly, 20,* 89–106.

Rupp, D. E., & Mallory, D. B. (2015). Corporate social responsibility: Psychological, person-centric, and progressing. *Annual Review of Organizational Psychology and Organizational Behavior, 2,* 211–236.

Rupp, D. E., Shao, R., Skarlicki, D. P., Paddock, E. L., Kim, T. Y., & Nadisic, T. (2018). Corporate social responsibility and employee engagement: The moderating role of CSR-specific relative autonomy and individualism. *Journal of Organizational Behavior, 39,* 559–579.

Rupp, D. E., Shao, R., Thornton, M. A., & Skarlicki, D. P. (2013). Applicants and employees' reactions to corporate social responsibility: The moderating effects of first party justice perceptions and moral identity. *Personnel Psychology*, *66*, 895–933.

Scheidler, S., Edinger-Schons, L. M., Spanjol, J., & Wieseke, J. (2019). Scrooge posing as Mother Teresa: How hypocritical social responsibility strategies hurt employees and firms. *Journal of Business Ethics*, *157*, 339–358.

Schwartz, S. H. (1992). Universals in the content and structure of values: Theoretical advances and empirical tests in 20 countries. *Advances in Experimental Social Psychology*, *25*, 1–65.

Shen, J., & Benson, J. (2016). When CSR is a social normal: How socially responsible human resource management affects employee work behavior. *Journal of Management*, *42*, 1723–1746.

Slack, R. E., Corlett, S., & Morris, R. (2015). Exploring employee engagement with (corporate) social responsibility: A social exchange perspective on organisational participation. *Journal of Business Ethics*, *127*, 537–548.

Sonenshein, S., DeCelles, K. A., & Dutton, J. E. (2014). It's not easy being green: The role of self-evaluations in explaining support of environmental issues. *Academy of Management Journal*, *57*, 7–37.

Stevens, J. M., Steensma, H. K., Harrison, D. A., & Cochran, P. L. (2005). Symbolic or substantive document? The influence of ethics codes on financial executives' decisions. *Strategic Management Journal*, *26*, 181–195.

Vlachos, P. A., Panagopoulos, N. G., & Rapp, A. A. (2013). Feeling good by doing good: Employee CSR-induced attributions, job satisfaction, and the role of charismatic leadership. *Journal of Business Ethics*, *118*, 577–588.

Vlachos, P. A., Theotokis, A., & Panagopoulos, N. G. (2010). Sales force reactions to corporate social responsibility: Attributions, outcomes, and the mediating role of trust. *Industrial Marketing Management*, *39*, 1207–1218.

Weaver, G. R., Treviño, L. K., & Cochran, P. L. (1999a). Corporate ethics programs as control systems: Influences of executive commitment and environmental factors. *Academy of Management Journal*, *42*, 41–57.

Weaver, G. R., Treviño, L. K., & Cochran, P. L. (1999b). Integrated and decoupled corporate social performance: Management commitments, external pressures, and corporate ethics practices. *Academy of Management Journal*, *42*, 539–552.

West, B., Hillenbrand, C., & Money, K. (2015). Building employee relationships through corporate social responsibility: The moderating role of social cynicism and reward for application. *Group & Organization Management*, *40*, 295–322.

Wickert, C., & De Bakker, F. G. A. (2018). Pitching for social change: Toward a relational approach to selling and buying social issues. *Academy of Management Discoveries*, *4*, 50–73.

Wiernik, B. M., Ones, D. S., & Dilchert, S. (2013). Age and environmental sustainability: A meta-analysis. *Journal of Managerial Psychology*, *28*, 826–856.

Willness, C. R. (2019). When CSR backfires: Understanding stakeholders' negative responses to corporate social responsibility. In A. McWilliams, D. E. Rupp, D. S. Siegel, G. Stahl, & D. A. Waldman (Eds.), *The Oxford handbook of corporate social responsibility: Psychological and organizational perspectives* (pp. 207–240). New York: Oxford University Press.

Wrzesniewski, A., & Dutton, J. E. (2001). Crafting a job: Revisioning employees as active crafters of their work. *Academy of Management Review*, *26*, 179–201.

3 Development of Employee Engagement through CSR

Andy Kidd, Thomas Maak, Nicola Pless, and Howard Harris

Overview

Employee engagement is important as it can affect productivity, commitment and personal satisfaction, however many employees are not engaged or disengaged with their work. Corporate social responsibility (CSR) is used by organisations to engage their workforce and retain talent. This chapter explores the relationship between employee engagement and CSR. It outlines related concepts and the history of research in employee engagement. It explores the role of employees as implementers of CSR, not only as volunteers but also as part of a programme of employee-led CSR. It shows that a strong and positive link can be established between employee engagement and CSR, and considers the ways in which employee engagement may be used to enhance the achievement of both corporate and individual goals, although this will not be achieved where CSR is not well integrated in the organisation and employees view CSR as window-dressing. The chapter concludes by outlining some opportunities for further research.

Learning objectives

By the end of this chapter, readers should be able to:

- describe employee engagement theory development, operation and refinement
- describe ways in which employee engagement may benefit individuals and organisations
- show how ideas of CSR have changed over time
- describe CSR and employee engagement through 'employee as implementer and job crafter'
- demonstrate how CSR can lead employee engagement.

Introduction

In this chapter, we explore the relationship between employee engagement and corporate social responsibility (CSR). According to a recent Gallup poll (Harter, 2018), almost 70% of employees in the USA are not engaged at work. At the same time, companies are seeking to attract the best talent – and have trouble doing so. This is partly because choices have grown exponentially, and partly because talented potential employees are more selective: they look for meaning and fulfilment at work (Aguinis & Glavas, 2019; Rosso, Dekas & Wrzesniewski, 2010, 2011), for an organisation with a purpose and thus values they share.

Employees engage at work when they experience the work as meaningful. There are different psychological mechanisms discussed in the literature that facilitate the relationship between meaningful work and engagement, namely 'authenticity, self-efficacy, self-esteem, purpose, belongingness, transcendence, and cultural and interpersonal sensemaking' (Rosso et al., 2010, p. 108). According to Aguinis and Glavas (2019), the inclusion of CSR activities at work has the potential to activate these mechanisms and enable employees to seek and find meaningfulness through work. Employees, through CSR engagement, are enabled to employ more of their whole selves at work through extra-role involvement and perceptions of organisational support (Glavas, 2016).

Against this background, it comes as no surprise that companies have started to use CSR to engage their workforce (Glavas, 2016). A growing number of companies are specifically looking for employees who care about the state of the world and believe that their employer must play an active role in addressing the so-called grand challenges (George, Howard-Grenville, Joshi, & Tihanyi, 2016), such as climate change, poverty and social cohesion.

However, data on what companies do to attract, retain and develop employees through CSR (Mirvis, 2012) is very limited, in part, we argue, because the link between CSR and employee engagement is insufficiently explored and conceptualised. It is therefore both worthy and necessary to establish a clearer link between employee engagement and CSR. To do so, we will review research on employee engagement, CSR and the combination of both. We then establish how CSR relates to employee engagement and subsequently what role employees may take in contemporary CSR activities. We conclude our chapter with observations pertaining to future research and CSR practice.

Employee engagement

Engagement theorised

Early work on engagement theory arose from motivation (Alderfer, 1972; Maslow, 1970) and job design theories (Hackman & Oldham, 1980). Most prominently, Maslow presented a whole and dynamic person theory, introducing a hierarchy of needs that drive individuals to an ever-increasing higher purpose within a given cultural context. Alderfer categorised these into the existence, relatedness and growth needs of individuals. Kahn's (1990) seminal grounded ethnographic research integrated the motivational propositions of Maslow and Alderfer, with the research on job design of Hackman and Oldham.

Kahn's definition of personal engagement relates to task behaviours, connections to work, and to colleagues. Personal engagement is the result of a work situation with components of work elements, social systems and individual distractions. These situations or conditions are mediated by the psychological conditions of meaningfulness, safety and availability. Individual differences also mediate the outcomes of psychological presence, in the moment, that result in personal engagement. The outcome of personal engagement can be described as performance quality, the individual experience, systemic personal growth and improved productivity. Thus, for Kahn, the self, the preferred self, and the work task role, exist in a dynamic and negotiable relationship. Kahn's seminal research provides an important starting point that suggests the relevance of flexible forms of employee engagement, for example through modern-day CSR activities, enabling identity work, skill building and access to a deeper sense of meaning at work.

Development and justification of the concept

May, Gilson, and Harter (2004) further clarified the concept of employee engagement by differentiating and building on the concepts of job

involvement and flow, and by incorporating these into a framework supported by quantitative research. Brown and Leigh, building on Kahn's
research, described job involvement as 'a cognitive belief state of psychological identification with one's job' (Brown & Leigh, 1996, p. 361). Similarly, job involvement is described as a measure of the degree to which the
person's job is central to their identity (May et al., 2004). May and others
clarified engagement as being concerned more with the active use of emo-
tions and behaviours than with the cognitive matching of jobs, needs and
self-image as described by job involvement.

Flow at work is a mental experience where people are intensely involved
in an activity and nothing else seems to matter (Csikszentmihalyi, 1988).
The activity gives pleasure and energy, and there is an intrinsic interest to
continue. There is immersion in an activity which is the very essence of the
flow experience (Salanova, Bakker, & Llorens, 2006). Flow is a short-term
peak experience that is characterised by total absorption, enjoyment and
motivation. It is a state of total concentration, total immersion, where time
seems to fly and everything is forgotten in the moment. May and colleagues
describe 'flow' as being different to psychological engagement. Psychological engagement is not a 'peak' phenomenon, but one which varies, over
time, for any individual. Psychological engagement involves all aspects of a
person – cognitive, emotional and physical – whereas flow is described primarily as cognitive involvement with a task (May et al., 2004). These authors
used the concepts of job involvement and flow as a basis for the further
development of job engagement theory. They differentiated engagement
from 'job involvement' and 'flow', to construct a framework that validated
each of the psychological conditions of engagement as described by Kahn,
namely those of meaningfulness, availability and safety. Job enrichment
and work-role fit were both found to positively influence meaningfulness.
Supervisor relations had the most positive significant influence on psychological safety, and resources were a strong determinant of psychological
availability for the job.

Engagement operationalised

Prior to Kahn's (1990) research on engagement, burnout had been recognised in the health care sector, measured by the Maslach Burnout Inventory (MBI) and defined as a syndrome of emotional exhaustion (Maslach
& Jackson, 1981). From this and more generalised developments of burnout (Schutte, Toppinen, Kalimo, & Schaufeli, 2000), three key dimensions
were identified: exhaustion, cynicism and inefficacy (Maslach, Schaufeli, &
Leiter, 2001). Research to identify the causes and effects of burnout opened
a line of enquiry concerning positive psychology (Seligman & Csikszentmihalyi, 2000). It was then perhaps not coincidental that the research on
burnout expanded to include research on the positive opposite of burnout,

called engagement (Schaufeli, Salanova, González-Romá, & Bakker, 2002). Research in this field suggested that engagement, as the opposite of burn-out, equated to workloads that were sustainable, enabled thoughts of choice and control, involved a work community that was supportive, encouraged feelings of fairness and justice in the workplace, and involved work that was meaningful and valued (Maslach et al., 2001). From this approach, engagement was defined as a state of mind, a lasting cognitive state characterised by 'vigor, dedication, and absorption' (Bakker & Schaufeli, 2008, p. 151). These states relate to work activation (from vigour to exhaustion), work identification (from dedication to cynicism) and two other distinct constructs of absorption with work if engaged, or reduced efficacy if burnt out (Demerouti, Mostert, & Bakker, 2010).

Engagement refined

The next advance in theory development came from Macey and Schneider, concerned about the lack of precision in both academic and practitioner research and conceptualisation of the term 'engagement' (Macey & Schneider, 2008). Engagement was clarified to include trait engagement, relating to individual disposition; state engagement, relating to changeable feelings of energy and absorption in one's work; and behavioural engagement, relating to individual outcomes of extra-role behaviour. Macey and Schneider (2008) added a framework that considered a person's personality, feelings of engagement and resultant behavioural engagement in the form of organisational citizenship behaviour (OCB), proactive initiatives and the expansion of one's role. The framework constructed by Macey and Schneider was intended to clarify the confusion in the term and definition of 'engagement' that exists in the academic and practitioner literature. The organisational environment has direct and indirect effects on state and behavioural engagement, including the nature of the work (Oldham & Hackman, 2010; Roberts, Roberts, O'Neill, & Blake-Beard, 2008) and the nature of leadership (Breevaart, Bakker, Demerouti, & Derks, 2016; Hawkes, Biggs, & Hegerty, 2017; Waldman et al., 2013). The framework developed by Macey and Schneider (2008) describes employee traits that are mediated by the nature of the work and the leadership experienced, leading to feelings of state engagement. State engagement in turn leads to engaged behaviours as a result again of the leadership experienced by the individual. Leadership in the form of supervisory support gives employees the perception of organisational support, and engagement is positively impacted (Breevaart et al., 2016; Jin & McDonald, 2017).

The multiple roles faced by individuals in the workplace were further explored by Saks (2006). Saks differentiated between engagement with work and engagement with the organisation and used social exchange theory (SET) to more fully explain why individuals respond to the antecedents of engagement in varying degrees. SET contends that interactions between interdependent parties impose obligations (Slack, Corlett, & Morris, 2015), and that rules of exchange establish relationships between the parties that can develop into trusting, loyal and mutual commitments. Individuals who receive economic and socio-emotional resources from their organisation feel obliged to respond and to repay the organisation in kind. One way to do this is through varying degrees of engagement. Thus, SET gives the foundation for individuals to vary the degree of engagement depending on their perception of resources and benefits provided by their organisation.

Value congruence and meaningfulness at work

Moreover, the consequences and antecedents of job engagement were investigated and validated by Rich, LePine, and Crawford (2010). Engagement was seen to have strong associations with three antecedents: value congruence, perceived organisational support and core self-evaluation. Completing the link back to Kahn's (1990, 1992) seminal research, meaningfulness of work tasks encouraged individuals to feel valued and able to give more to their roles and to others. Meaningfulness also implicitly connects the values of the organisation, and the self-image of the individual, and the congruence of values positively relates to job engagement.

Hence, it is fair to say not only that employee engagement depends on several cognitive, emotional and behavioural dispositions, but also that value congruence and meaningfulness at work play an important role. One would expect an extended job role also to depend on the meaningfulness of the activity and the congruence of the individual's values with the role. Perceived organisational support in the form of supportive management and 'supportive and trusting interpersonal relationships with others' (Rich et al., 2010, p. 621) encourages an experience of psychological safety and the consequent ability to engage with the job. If the job is extended to include a more holistic approach to CSR, with the perceived support of management and others, then there would be an expectation that the conditions are in place for engagement with those CSR job tasks. Those who feel strongly about CSR could be expected to engage in CSR activities. The authors of a recent study showed that leadership plays an important role in this process. Transformational leaders help boost engagement 'by helping employees find the meaning and significance of their work, making them feel supported by the organisation and strengthening their sense of worth and competence' (Vila-Vazquez, Castro-Casal, Alvarez-Perez, & del Rio-Araujo, 2018; Wang & Xu, 2019).

Certain employees, whilst engaged in their work, look beyond self-actualisation to a higher level of motivation and growth. These employees 'come to identify with something greater than the purely individual self, often engaging in service to others' (Koltko-Rivera, 2006, p. 306). At this level of motivation, Koltko-Rivera continues, 'the individual's own needs are put aside, to a great extent, in favour of service to others'. Whilst some employees have needs that fit into the conventional workplace understanding of motivation and become engaged with work and CSR initiatives, there are others who engage with CSR outside of work as a service to others and to society at large (for example, see Bakker, 2015; Caniels, Semeijn, & Renders, 2018; Grant, 2007; Hu, Jiang, Mo, Chen, & Shi, 2016).

Corporate Social Responsibility (CSR)

Since CSR activities play a role in the relationship between meaning of work and employee engagement, we will introduce the concept in the following section before looking into the link between CSR and employee engagement, and the engagement of employees through CSR. As corporate misconduct grew in the 1970s and 1980s, and high-level cases such as Bhopal and Exxon Valdez made headlines, the stakeholder view of CSR began to dominate the discourse. Stakeholder theory provided a useful framework to understand the core constituencies of an organisation (Freeman, 2010), including employees, the environment and future generations, and the responsibilities towards these stakeholders. Consequently, 'we now see CSR initiatives in virtually all the developed nations, and initial thinking and developing taking place in emerging nations as well' (Carroll & Shabana, 2010, p. 86). The prominent justification was the business case for CSR, which has continued to be explored, justified and criticised (Crane, Palazzo, Spence, & Matten, 2014). The broad justification for CSR is that such initiatives provide direct and indirect benefits to the organisation. Such a broad view allows organisations to take advantage of opportunities and to 'create win–win relationships with its stakeholders' (Carroll & Shabana, 2010, p. 101), beyond risk management and mere compliance.

Perhaps the most influential framework for CSR was established by Carroll in 1991, and this became a baseline for further research. Carroll's framework referenced a pyramid of corporate social responsibility designed to understand the evolving nature of the organisation's economic, legal, ethical and philanthropic responsibilities (Carroll, 1991). From this and subsequent development, there has been an understanding of the evolving nature of the organisation, the context in which it finds itself, and the stakeholders who interact with each other in understanding CSR (Osagie, Wesselink, Blok, & Mulder, 2019).

Based on Carroll's 1991 framework and subsequent development, decision-makers in organisations where CSR is practised would reasonably be expected to respond to and call on moral and ethical considerations based on the social mores in which they operate (Sheehy, 2015).

Organisations operate in complex societies. Organisations themselves are complex systems, and interactions of the two make for a diversity of issues that would be addressed under the banner of CSR. At the same time, at the micro-level, the stakeholders (including employees) reveal themselves as complex individuals working within complex groups, in dynamic environments. CSR is not the same concept in the minds of all, such that sensemaking and framing of what CSR means within and for an organisation become important. Concomitantly, Basu and Palazzo defined CSR as 'the process by which managers within an organisation think about and discuss relationships with stakeholders as well as their roles in relation to the common good, along with their behavioural disposition with respect to the fulfilment and achievement of these roles and relationships' (Basu & Palazzo, 2008, p. 124). This definition places the responsibility for CSR firmly in the hands of the managers of the organisation (Christensen, Mackey, & Whetten, 2014; Hemingway & Maclagan, 2004; McWilliams, 2001; Pless & Maak, 2012).

But, whilst responsibility sits in the hands of managers, it is also the behaviour of other stakeholders that determines CSR outcomes for the organisation. In line with our topic, we now focus on the stakeholder group of employees, their CSR involvement and employee engagement.

CSR and employee engagement

Employees as implementers of CSR

As explained by Ferreira and Real de Oliveira (2014), CSR research has tended to focus on external stakeholders such as suppliers and shareholders, but the internal dimension of CSR relates to employees. Internal CSR is expressed as concern for employee well-being and training, but also with their participation in the business (Brammer, Millington, & Rayton, 2007). Whilst senior management usually creates and enables CSR initiatives, ultimately it is the employees of the firm, be they low-ranking employees or high-level executives, who actualise CSR with respect to various stakeholder beneficiaries (Maak, Pless, & Voegtlin, 2016). The context-specific nature of CSR forms the background as to how employees are motivated to care about their organisation's contribution to stakeholders and society at large. The source of motivation for such an outcome could come from the disposition of the employee. However, Grant (2007) suggested that the work context itself is a resource that employees draw upon. Grant argued that the relationships of employees with the beneficiaries of their efforts and the contact they have with benefitting stakeholders (e.g., customers), lead to the motivation to make a difference. Furthermore, employees commit to organisations with high levels of strategic CSR (Rodrigo, Aqueveque, & Duran, 2019) – that is, organisations that have coordinated, coherent and relevant CSR activities in alignment with their strategy and financial goals, where business decision-makers consider CSR outcomes, and CSR is considered critical for organisational survival (Rodrigo et al., 2019). Haski-Leventhal, Roza and Meijs (2017) suggest that such positive outcomes as commitment (also turnover, attraction, satisfaction and citizenship behaviour) are a result of the congruence between high levels of socially responsible behaviour and high levels of socially responsible identity – for both the employee and the organisation.

Employee-generated CSR programmes are a sign of engagement. Such programmes (also known as employee-led CSR) within organisations are bottom-up initiatives and are conceived, planned and implemented by employees rather than those at supervisory or management levels. Examples of such employee-led CSR are collecting blankets for pets after a bush fire and holding a coffee morning to collect for a charity. Grant (2012) contends that inadequacies in job design may trigger the motivation of employees to donate their time and skills. Inadequacies in job design relate not only to task characteristics, but also to the social and knowledge characteristics of a job. Inadequacies in task characteristics motivate certain employees to seek meaning in their job roles outside the nominal transactional task roles of employment, through employee-led CSR. Such inadequacies may also be revealed through a lack of 'identity, autonomy, and feedback', and this 'may activate the self-enhancement motive' (Grant, 2012, p. 598).

Rodell (2013) found that employees' desire for meaningful experiences 'grows from their positive work experiences' (p. 1287). Employees craft their job, and plan and implement programmes that contribute to their aspiration for a positive, meaningful outcome. Understanding the aspirations of employees to achieve a meaningful outcome through employee social responsibility (ESR) activities, and of the organisation to which they owe their employment, in order to achieve a CSR outcome, requires an appreciation of the congruence of the two (Haski-Leventhal et al., 2017).

Organisations range from those which have not yet started on the road to CSR, to those which exhibit high levels of both CSR identity and behaviour. Individual employees are the same, ranging from those with no CSR identity or behaviour, to those with high levels of both. The interplay between organisational CSR identity/behaviour and employee CSR identity/behaviour is revealed as entwined, behaviour based, identity based, or both low behaviour and low identity based (i.e., showing low social responsibility) (Haski-Leventhal et al., 2017, p. 38). These links are important for understanding employee engagement in CSR but are still understudied. It may be assumed that those employees who engage with CSR demonstrate both high levels of CSR identity and CSR engagement (showing CSR behaviour). They are self-motivated and craft their job through their management of time, resources and tasks, with or without the support of management.

Job crafting

Inadequacies in the social characteristics of jobs, those that lack social enrichment such as friendship and support, encourage employees to seek social connections outside their job role. The motivation to seek to overcome a lack of social enrichment is thus activated in such socially depleted job roles, in a depletion of belongingness and of self-protection. Volunteering initiatives are discussed as a means to create a sense of meaning and belonging (Pless, 2007). As described by Grant, employee volunteering is the giving of one's time, knowledge or skills, as part of a social responsibility activity during working hours, with or without pay or other compensation (Bussell & Forbes, 2008; Grant, 2012; Van der Voort, Glac, & Meijs, 2009). By crafting volunteering initiatives that satisfy the employee's aspiration for a positive moral outcome outside of their nominal job role, employees, to varying degrees, satisfy the belongingness and self-protection aspects of social relationships (Grant, 2012).

Inadequacies in knowledge characteristics of their job also encourage employees to seek remedies outside their nominal job role through job crafting. The lack of knowledge enrichment creates feelings of dissatisfaction and a search for more meaningful tasks that utilise the employee's skill variety, specialised knowledge, ability to problem-solve and other abilities. Such inadequacy of the job motivates the employee to seek improvement in the development of utilisation of skills or look for career enhancement (Grant, 2012). Once again, Grant proposed that, by engaging in volunteering initiatives that satisfy the employee's aspiration for a positive moral outcome outside of their job role, employees, to varying degrees, satisfy their need to more fully utilise their knowledge and skills by crafting their nominal job role. The discretionary behaviour of job crafting requires the employee to have a sense of autonomy, and the social skill to relate and gain the support of others such as co-workers, higher levels of management and significant others (Sekiguchi, Li, & Hosomi, 2017).

By empowering employees to seek resources, organisations may trigger the motivation of individuals to undertake challenges, with mutually beneficial results (Rodell, Booth, Lynch, & Zipay, 2017). For example, German software and cloud giant SAP runs several successful employee-engagement initiatives pertaining to CSR, including the top-talent-focused SAP.iO Venture Studio and the 'One Billion Lives' programme, which aims at implementation ideas in regard to the Sustainable Development Goals (SDGs) and saw more than 2000 employees participating in 2018 ('SAP Integrated Report 2018', n.d.). As Demerouti, Bakker, and Halbesleben (2015) contend, on days when employees sought such challenges and crafted their work, they were more engaged and less exhausted. The drivers are multifaceted and cover instrumental reasons such as ego, career and power; relational reasons encompassing external networks and internal groups; moral reasons for a meaningful existence; and individual reasons of personality traits and socio-demographics. The implication, suggested by Demerouti et al. (2015), is that organisations should encourage employee job crafting daily, particularly of resource seeking as this has the benefit of improved task performance through increased effective behaviour.

Linking these insights back to CSR, it becomes apparent that empowering employees to participate in CSR may have the potential to unleash employee engagement in ways other initiatives cannot – it connects the inherent needs of individuals for belonging, meaning and purpose to organisational objectives (Rupp, Shao, Skarlicki, Paddock, Kim, & Nadisic, 2018). More specifically, CSR can provide the platform for employees to *engage within* the organisation and within the realm of organisational interests to the benefit of the organisation and its stakeholders and the employee, by enabling them to engage in job crafting and socio-relational activities *on the job* and not as an unrelated add-on activity.

Employee perceptions of CSR

Employees perceive an organisation's CSR programme by assessing if the organisation is 'true to itself', compare the organisation to a 'referent standard', and do this by relying on 'cues' that allow a judgement to be made (McShane & Cunningham, 2012, p. 84). Employees assess the CSR programme considering the perceived identity of the organisation, look for congruence and concurrently check the currency of such programmes compared to the 'ever-changing standard of what should be' (McShane & Cunningham, 2012, p. 86). When perceived as congruent with the organisation, CSR programmes can provide employees with an enriched working life. Such enrichment, through CSR participation, may lead to increased pride for self, satisfaction with work, loyalty to the organisation and connectedness with others – an effect that Pless and Maak (2010) reported in their study of PricewaterhouseCooper's responsible leadership development programme, Ulysses (see also Pless, Maak, & Stahl, 2012).

Engaging employees through CSR

Our review suggests that there is a potential strong and positive link between CSR and employee engagement. More specifically, and extending Mirvis (2012), we can conclude that a holistic approach to CSR engages employees in several distinct ways: it *attracts* employees to an organisation; it helps employees to shape their *identity* at work; it provides opportunities to engage in *relational work* with stakeholders; it offers significant opportunities for *training and development*; and it provides new pathways for *job crafting and social intrapreneurship*.

Attraction

At a time when talent is embattled and sought after, and prospective employees care about the state of the world and the role of organisations in contributing to sustainable futures, employers need to take a stand on CSR. If done well, CSR may enhance the attractiveness of the organisation as an employer of choice. The boundary conditions to be met are that CSR is in line with the core values of the organisation, consistent and credible such that it is perceived as authentic, and not as simply paying lip-service to changing conditions on the 'market for virtue' (Vogel, 2005); that it provides opportunities for actual engagement; and that there is a sustainable commitment to CSR.

Employee identity

When most of the workforce are disenchanted with their jobs and/or employer, CSR helps to overcome the value gap and re-instil meaning, and possibly even purpose, into the work environment. In other words, CSR can lead to meaningfulness at work. Meaningfulness is a characteristic of work that facilitates both personal growth and motivation, and meaningfulness is the value that employees place on such work goals or purpose (May et al., 2004). Anita Roddick, the founder of The Body Shop, engaged employees in running sustainability campaigns in her shops to raise customer awareness for social and sustainability issues, thereby enriching their work experience and identity through contributing to something of 'greater significance than selling a pot of skin cream' (Roddick, cited in Pless, 2007, p. 446). Such CSR involvement displayed not only meaningfulness, but also the support of managers and co-workers and the willingness of employees to be available both physically and psychologically.

CSR may lead to the simultaneous expression of emotional, cognitive and behavioural engagement – personal engagement as described by Kahn. This form of engagement is dependent on the psychological conditions of meaningfulness, psychological safety through support from co-workers and managers, and psychological availability to be present in the moment (Kahn, 1990, 1992). If, and when, it happens, such engagement will lead to mutually beneficial results, such as engaged and motivated employees who are willing to go the extra mile and identify with their employer; and commitment to the organisation (Rodrigo et al., 2019), which in turn helps shape the identity of the employee as a 'whole person'. The latter can lead to more pronounced forms of self-expression and employee satisfaction. Indeed, as the SAP.iO Venture initiative shows, CSR programmes can be designed such that the best talent is not only attracted to engage in innovative CSR initiatives, but also that CSR becomes central to business innovation as such ('SAP Integrated Report 2018', n.d.).

Relational work

The autonomy and freedom of employees also draw upon relationships and communities, both within and outside the workplace. CSR may result in active role engagement with diverse stakeholders outside regular job boundaries. Such engagement will likely lead to added purpose and meaning at work, but, more importantly, also strengthen the relational abilities of staff and ties to stakeholders, resulting in both development opportunities for, and stronger relational ties to, stakeholders. Moreover, it will further result in an enhanced impact on society, contributing to a virtuous circle of CSR commitment, strengthened employee identity, social capital and a positive social impact within society (Maak, 2007).

Training and development

Some companies have started to incorporate a social service element (e.g., projects with communities locally or internationally) into their management and leadership development programmes, applying a service-learning methodology. Pless and Borecká (2014) provide an overview of different programmes, including Ernst & Young's Americas Corporate Responsibility Fellows Program, IBM's Corporate Service Corps and Intel's Education Service Corps Program. Research shows that the benefits of such CSR initiatives are multifold and lead to benefits not only for the involved community partners (e.g., by receiving pro bono support for addressing societal problems), but also for the companies through, for example, the competence development of participating staff, increased trust in the company culture and enhanced staff engagement and performance (Gitsham, 2012; Guarnieri & Kao, 2008; Pless & Borecká, 2014).

Job crafting and social intrapreneurship

Lastly, employee engagement with CSR follows from the employee's motivation and an ability to craft the job design to meet the demands of work and gain resources for extra activities. Employee autonomy and freedom to act enable a crafting of the job to allow extra activities over and above the regular requirements within the organisation. PricewaterhouseCoopers' award-winning Ulysses programme is an example of a CSR initiative that was initiated by staff at the local level and then developed, over time, from a grassroots CSR programme into a flagship global talent development programme for responsible leadership, by gaining support first from HR and then from top management (Pless et al., 2012).

CSR provides employees with unique job crafting opportunities, but it can also lead to employee-driven social intrapreneurship (Austin & Reficco,

2009), unleashing creative opportunities for social intrapreneurship and business innovation by staff within an organisation, as the previously mentioned SAP programme demonstrates ('SAP Integrated Report 2018', n.d.).

Conclusion

We believe that there are significant research opportunities along these core dimensions of CSR and employee engagement, and, given the scarcity of data, we suggest that it would be beneficial to address them. For example, we have argued that, by and large, CSR should have positive effects on employee engagement. However, not every employee may feel equally inspired or motivated. In fact, depending on how well CSR is integrated in an organisation, employees, like other stakeholders, may view CSR as window-dressing and adopt a cynical or outright critical view, with counterproductive effects among the workforce. Thus, we need more evidence to demonstrate the motivational effects of CSR and the contextual boundary conditions.

In many organisations, staff work at their limit. Hence, if CSR is to be successful and to unleash engagement, integrative measures need to be taken to make sure that CSR is not considered an additional workload, but an integral, enriching part of one's job. Again, we currently lack clear evidence as to CSR integration, job crafting and employee engagement, and encourage research at this important intersection.

Lastly, and building on earlier research on employee engagement, while the links between CSR and engagement are obvious and supported, we lack conceptual insight and empirical evidence on how CSR motivates employees, how it enhances perceived meaningfulness at work and, as a result, a stronger sense of purpose. We encourage future researchers to unpack this relationship and to shed light on the motivational complexity of an ever-changing work environment.

Questions for students

1. Give an example from your own experience of engagement (or disengagement) in a task you undertook in an organisation.
2. How does engagement at work enhance personal satisfaction?
3. How does engagement at work enhance corporate performance?
4. Discuss the likely public reaction to CSR which is principally seen as philanthropy, and CSR which engages with employees and stakeholders.
5. Should employees craft their job, or should the job incorporate CSR as standard practice?

References

Aguinis, H., & Glavas, A. (2019). On corporate social responsibility, sensemaking, and the search for meaningfulness through work. *Journal of Management*, *45*(3), 1057–1086.

Alderfer, C. P. (1972). *Existence, relatedness, and growth: Human needs in organizational settings*. New York: Free Press.

Austin, J. E., & Reficco, E. A. (2009). *Corporate social entrepreneurship*. Retrieved from https://papers.ssrn.com/abstract=1490345.

Bakker, A. B. (2015). A job demands–resources approach to public service motivation. *Public Administration Review*, *75*(5), 723–732.

Bakker, A. B., & Schaufeli, W. B. (2008). Positive organizational behavior: Engaged employees in flourishing organizations. *Journal of Organizational Behavior*, *29*(2), 147–154.

Basu, K., & Palazzo, G. (2008). Corporate social responsibility: A process model of sensemaking. *The Academy of Management Review*, *33*(1), 122–136.

Brammer, S., Millington, A., & Rayton, B. (2007). The contribution of corporate social responsibility to organizational commitment. *International Journal of Human Resource Management*, *18*(10), 1701–1719.

Breevaart, K., Bakker, A. B., Demerouti, E., & Derks, D. (2016). Who takes the lead? A multi-source diary study on leadership, work engagement, and job performance. *Journal of Organizational Behavior*, *37*(3), 309–325.

Brown, S. P., & Leigh, T. W. (1996). A new look at psychological climate and its relationship to job involvement, effort, and performance. *Journal of Applied Psychology*, *81*(4), 358–368.

Bussell, H., & Forbes, D. (2008). How UK universities engage with their local communities: A study of employer supported volunteering. *International Journal of Nonprofit and Voluntary Sector Marketing*, *13*(4), 363–378.

Caniels, M. C. J., Semeijn, J. H., & Renders, I. H. M. (2018). Mind the mindset! The interaction of proactive personality, transformational leadership and growth mindset for engagement at work. *Career Development International*, *23*(1), 48–66.

Carroll, A. B. (1991). The pyramid of corporate social responsibility: Toward the moral management of organizational stakeholders. *Business Horizons*, *34*(4), 39–48.

Carroll, A. B., & Shabana, K. M. (2010). The business case for corporate social responsibility: A review of concepts, research and practice. *International Journal of Management Reviews*, *12*(1), 85–105.

Christensen, L. J., Mackey, A., & Whetten, D. (2014). Taking responsibility for corporate social responsibility: The role of leaders in creating, implementing, sustaining, or avoiding socially responsible firm behaviors. *Academy of Management Perspectives*, *28*(2), 164–178.

Crane, A., Pallazzo, G., Spence, L. J., & Matten, D. (2014). Contesting the value 'creating shared value' concept. *California Management Review*, *56*(2), 130–154.

Csikszentmihalyi, M. (1988). The future of flow. In M. Csikszentmihalyi & I. S. Csikszentmihalyi (Eds.), *Optimal experience: Psychological studies of flow in consciousness*. (pp. 364–383). Retrieved from https://doi.org/10.1017/CBO9780511621956.022.

Demerouti, E., Bakker, A. B., & Halbesleben, J. R. B. (2015). Productive and counterproductive job crafting: A daily diary study. *Journal of Occupational Health Psychology*, *20*(4), 457–469.

Demerouti, E., Mostert, K., & Bakker, A. B. (2010). Burnout and work engagement: A thorough investigation of the independency of both constructs. *Journal of Occupational Health Psychology, 15*(3), 209–222.

Ferreira, P., & Real de Oliveira, E. (2014). Does corporate social responsibility impact on employee engagement? *Journal of Workplace Learning, 26*(3/4), 232–247.

Freeman, R. (2010). *Strategic management: A stakeholder approach.* Retrieved from doi:10.1017/CBO9781139192675.

George, G., Howard-Grenville, J., Joshi, A., & Tihanyi, L. (2016). Understanding and tackling societal grand challenges through management research. *Academy of Management Journal, 59*(6), 1880–1895.

Gitsham, M. (2012). Experiential learning for leadership and sustainability at IBM and HSBC. *Journal of Management Development, 31*(3), 298–307.

Glavas, A. (2016). Corporate social responsibility and employee engagement: Enabling employees to employ more of their whole selves at work. *Frontiers in Psychology, 7*, 1–10.

Grant, A. M. (2007). Relational job design and the motivation to make a prosocial difference. *Academy of Management Review, 32*(2), 393–417.

Grant, A. M. (2012). Giving time, time after time: Work design and sustained employee participation in corporate volunteering. *Academy of Management Review, 37*(4), 589–615.

Guarnieri, R., & Kao, T. (2008). Leadership and CSR – a perfect match: How top companies for leaders utilize CSR as a competitive advantage. *People and Strategy, 31*(3), 34–41.

Hackman, J. R., & Oldham, G. R. (1980). *Work redesign.* Reading, MA: Addison-Wesley.

Harter, J. K. (2018). *Employee engagement on the rise in the US.* August. Retrieved from https://news.gallup.com/poll/241649/employee-engagement-rise.aspx.

Haski-Leventhal, D., Roza, L., & Meijs, L. (2017). Congruence in corporate social responsibility: Connecting the identity and behavior of employers and employees. *Journal of Business Ethics, 143*(1), 35–51.

Hawkes, A. J., Biggs, A., & Hegerty, E. (2017). Work engagement: Investigating the role of transformational leadership, job resources, and recovery. *Journal of Psychology, 151*(6), 509–531.

Hemingway, C. A., & Maclagan, P. W. (2004). Managers' personal values as drivers of corporate social responsibility. *Journal of Business Ethics, 50*(1), 33–44.

Hu, J., Jiang, K., Mo, S., Chen, H., & Shi, J. (2016). The motivational antecedents and performance consequences of corporate volunteering: When do employees volunteer and when does volunteering help versus harm work performance? *Organizational Behavior and Human Decision Processes, 137*, 99–111.

Jin, M. H., & McDonald, B. (2017). Understanding employee engagement in the public sector: The role of immediate supervisor, perceived organizational support, and learning opportunities. *American Review of Public Administration, 47*(8), 881–897.

Kahn, W. A. (1990). Psychological conditions of personal engagement and disengagement at work. *Academy of Management Journal, 33*(4), 692–724.

Kahn, W. A. (1992). To be fully there: Psychological presence at work. *Human Relations, 45*(4), 321–349.

Koltko-Rivera, M. E. (2006). Rediscovering the later version of Maslow's hierarchy of needs: Self-transcendence and opportunities for theory, research, and unification. *Review of General Psychology, 10*(4), 302–317.

Maak, T. (2007). Responsible leadership, stakeholder engagement, and the emergence of social capital. *Journal of Business Ethics, 74*(4), 329–343.

Maak, T., Pless, N. M., & Voegtlin, C. (2016). Business statesman or shareholder advocate? CEO responsible leadership styles and the micro-foundations of political CSR. *Journal of Management Studies, 53*(3), 463–493.

Macey, W. H., & Schneider, B. (2008). The meaning of employee engagement. *Industrial & Organizational Psychology, 1*(1), 3–30.

Maslach, C., & Jackson, S. E. (1981). The measurement of experienced burnout. *Journal of Organizational Behavior, 2*(2), 99–113.

Maslach, C., Schaufeli, W. B., & Leiter, M. P. (2001). Job burnout. *Annual Review of Psychology, 52*(1), 397–422.

Maslow, A. H. (1970). *Motivation and personality* (2nd edition). New York: Harper & Row.

May, D. R., Gilson, R. L., & Harter, L. M. (2004). The psychological conditions of meaningfulness, safety and availability and the engagement of the human spirit at work. *Journal of Occupational & Organizational Psychology, 77*(1), 11–37.

McShane, L., & Cunningham, P. (2012). To thine own self be true? Employees' judgments of the authenticity of their organization's corporate social responsibility program. *Journal of Business Ethics, 108*(1), 81–100.

McWilliams, A. (2001). Corporate social responsibility: A theory of the firm perspective. *Academy of Management Review, 26*(1), 117–127.

Mirvis, P. (2012). Employee engagement and CSR: Transactional, relational, and developmental approaches. *California Management Review, 54*(4), 93–117.

Oldham, G. R., & Hackman, J. R. (2010). Not what it was and not what it will be: The future of job design research. *Journal of Organizational Behavior, 31*(2/3), 463–479.

Osagie, E. R., Wesselink, R., Blok, V., & Mulder, M. (2019). Contextualizing individual competencies for managing the corporate social responsibility adaptation process: The apparent influence of the business case logic. *Business & Society, 58*(2), 369–403.

Pless, N. M. (2007). Understanding responsible leadership: Role identity and motivational drivers. *Journal of Business Ethics, 74*(4), 437–456.

Pless, N. M., & Borecká, M. (2014). Comparative analysis of international service learning programs. *The Journal of Management Development, 33*(6), 526–550.

Pless, N. M., & Maak, T. (2010). Desarrollando líderes globales responsables [Developing responsible global leaders]. *UCJC Business and Society Review (formerly known as Universia Business Review), 27.* Retrieved from https://journals.ucjc.edu/ubr/article/view/751.

Pless, N. M., & Maak, T. (2012). Different approaches toward doing the right thing: Mapping the responsibility orientations of leaders. *Academy of Management Perspectives, 26*(4), 51–65.

Pless, N. M., Maak, T., & Stahl, G. K. (2012). Promoting corporate social responsibility and sustainable development through management development: What can be learned from international service learning programs? *Human Resource Management, 51*(6), 873–903.

Rich, B. L., LePine, J. A., & Crawford, E. R. (2010). Job engagement: Antecedents and effects on job performance. *Academy of Management Journal, 53*(3), 617–635.

Roberts, D. D., Roberts, L. M., O'Neill, R. M., & Blake-Beard, S. D. (2008). The invisible work of managing visibility for social change. *Business & Society, 47*(4), 425–456.

Rodell, J. B. (2013). Finding meaning through volunteering: Why do employees volunteer and what does it mean for their jobs? *Academy of Management Journal, 56*(5), 1274–1294.

Rodell, J. B., Booth, J. E., Lynch, J. W., & Zipay, K. P. (2017). Corporate volunteering climate: Mobilizing employee passion for societal causes and inspiring future charitable action. *Academy of Management Journal, 60*(5), 1662–1681.

Rodrigo, P., Aqueveque, C., & Duran, I. J. (2019). Do employees value strategic CSR? A tale of affective organizational commitment and its underlying mechanisms. *Business Ethics: A European Review, 28*(4), 459–475.

Rosso, B. D., Dekas, K. H., & Wrzesniewski, A. (2010). On the meaning of work: A theoretical integration and review. *Research in Organizational Behavior, 30,* 91–127.

Rosso, B. D., Dekas, K. H., & Wrzesniewski, A. (2011). Corrigendum to 'On the meaning of work: A theoretical integration and review'. *Research in Organizational Behavior, 31,* 277.

Rupp, D. E., Shao, R., Skarlicki, D. P., Paddock, E. L., Kim, T.-Y., & Nadisic, T. (2018). Corporate social responsibility and employee engagement: The moderating role of CSR-specific relative autonomy and individualism. *Journal of Organizational Behavior, 39*(5), 559–579.

Saks, A. M. (2006). Antecedents and consequences of employee engagement. *Journal of Managerial Psychology, 21*(7), 600–619.

Salanova, M., Bakker, A., & Llorens, S. (2006). Flow at work: Evidence for an upward spiral of personal and organizational resources. *Journal of Happiness Studies, 7*(1), 1–22.

SAP Integrated Report 2018. (n.d.). Retrieved from www.sap.com/integrated-reports/2018/en.html.

Schaufeli, W. B., Salanova, M., González-Romá, V., & Bakker, A. B. (2002). The measurement of engagement and burnout: A two sample confirmatory factor analytic approach. *Journal of Happiness Studies, 3*(1), 71–92.

Schutte, N., Toppinen, S., Kalimo, R., & Schaufeli, W. (2000). The factorial validity of the Maslach Burnout Inventory-General Survey (MBI-GS) across occupational groups and nations. *Journal of Occupational & Organizational Psychology, 73*(1), 53–66.

Sekiguchi, T., Li, J., & Hosomi, M. (2017). Predicting job crafting from the socially embedded perspective: The interactive effect of job autonomy, social skill, and employee status. *Journal of Applied Behavioral Science, 53*(4), 470–497.

Seligman, M. E. P., & Csikszentmihalyi, M. (2000). Positive psychology: An introduction. *American Psychologist, 55*(1), 5–14.

Sheehy, B. (2015). Defining CSR: Problems and solutions. *Journal of Business Ethics, 131*(3), 625–648.

Slack, R. E., Corlett, S., & Morris, R. (2015). Exploring employee engagement with (corporate) social responsibility: A social exchange perspective on organisational participation. *Journal of Business Ethics, 127*(3), 537–548.

Van der Voort, J. M., Glac, K., & Meijs, L. C. P. M. (2009). 'Managing' corporate community involvement. *Journal of Business Ethics, 90*(3), 311–329.

Vila-Vazquez, G., Castro-Casal, C., Alvarez-Perez, D., & del Rio-Araujo, L. (2018). Promoting the sustainability of organizations: Contribution of transformational leadership to job engagement. *Sustainability, 10*(11), 4109–4126.

Vogel, D. J. (2005). Is there a market for virtue? The business case for corporate social responsibility. *California Management Review, 47*(4), 19–45.

Waldman, D. A., Wang, D., Stikic, M., Berka, C., Balthazard, P. A., Richardson, T., Pless, N. M. & Maak, T. (2013). Emergent leadership and team engagement: An application of neuroscience technology and methods. *Academy of Management Annual Meeting Proceedings*, 632–637.

Wang, Z., & Xu, H. (2019). When and for whom ethical leadership is more effective in eliciting work meaningfulness and positive attitudes: The moderating roles of core self-evaluation and perceived organizational support. *Journal of Business Ethics, 156*(4), 919–940.

Corporate Social Responsibility and Gender

4

Nicole Strah, Cassondra Batz-Barbarich, and Deborah E. Rupp

Overview

This chapter examines corporate social responsibility (CSR) through the lens of gender. To accomplish this goal, we delineate the overlap between gender and CSR at both the organisational and individual levels of analysis. Specifically, we summarise the existing research on the role of gender as a consideration in the type of CSR policies that organisations implement, the effect of the gender of key decision-makers on organisations' CSR initiatives, and individual female employees' (and other female stakeholders') perceptions of and responses to CSR efforts. We draw the conclusion that this nascent area of research includes interesting findings, though continued theoretical and empirical work is needed to assert substantive claims on the complex relationships between CSR and gender at multiple levels of analysis.

Learning objectives

By the end of this chapter, readers should be able to:

- identify the key ways in which gender overlaps with CSR
- understand the connection between gender and CSR as a multilevel concept (gender in organisational CSR initiatives)
- detail the influence of gender on CSR initiatives, and men's and women's perceptions of and reactions to CSR initiatives
- describe the areas in which an established relationship between gender and CSR exists and where future research is necessary.

Introduction: CSR and gender

Corporate social responsibility (CSR) is defined as the economic, legal, ethical and discretionary societal responsibilities of organisations (Carroll, 1979; Carroll & Buchholtz, 2014); and as organisations' responsibilities to all stakeholders involved in their operations (e.g., employees, customers, the environment; see Aguinis, 2011). The importance of CSR is evidenced through its effects on firm-level performance as well as employee-related outcomes such as engagement, commitment and satisfaction (Aguinis & Glavas, 2012; Jones & Rupp, 2018). Despite an increased focus on individual stakeholders in CSR research, Rupp and Mallory (2015) note that our understanding of differential (demographic) group experiences of CSR is limited. However, a demographic that *has* begun to receive attention within the CSR literature is gender. This emerging research suggests that gender considerations have played an important role not only in how CSR practices have been developed within companies, but also in how stakeholders value, enact and respond to companies' CSR initiatives. Indeed, this literature has important implications for how group identities such as gender may influence individuals' value of CSR, engagement with an organisation as a result of its CSR, and participation in CSR activities.

Within this review, we summarise how CSR research has considered gender at both the organisational and individual levels of analysis – considering organisations as enactors of CSR and individuals both as enactors of and reactors to CSR (see Figure 4.1). To do this, we first review the model of CSR motives applied throughout our review. Next, we examine inherently gendered CSR initiatives, such as gender mainstreaming (where organisational policies are aimed at achieving gender equality). We then explore the impact of gender on key decision-makers' enactment of CSR. Finally, we examine the impact of stakeholders' gender on their perceptions of and reactions to CSR initiatives. We explore gendered motivations in each of these sections. We note that most of this research focuses on gender as differences and similarities between women and men. As such, this review is limited to a binary perspective on gender, though we briefly touch on work considering the perspectives of LGBTQ communities.

Corporate social responsibility

Aguilera, Rupp, Williams, and Ganapathi (2007) outlined a model, grounded in multiple needs theory, of the various actors that encourage the development of an organisation's CSR, as well as these actors' motivations for doing so (see also Graso, Camps, Strah, & Brebels' 2019 discussion of leaders' motives for enacting justice; as well as corresponding perspectives

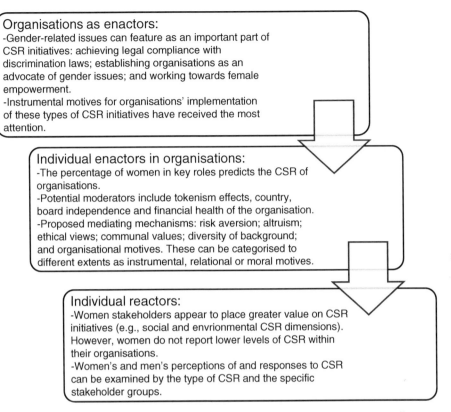

Organisations as enactors:
-Gender-related issues can feature as an important part of CSR initiatives: achieving legal compliance with discrimination laws; establishing organisations as an advocate of gender issues; and working towards female empowerment.
-Instrumental motives for organisations' implementation of these types of CSR initiatives have received the most attention.

Individual enactors in organisations:
-The percentage of women in key roles predicts the CSR of organisations.
-Potential moderators include tokenism effects, country, board independence and financial health of the organisation.
-Proposed mediating mechanisms: risk aversion; altruism; ethical views; communal values; diversity of background; and organisational motives. These can be categorised to different extents as instrumental, relational or moral motives.

Individual reactors:
-Women stakeholders appear to place greater value on CSR initiatives (e.g., social and envrionmental CSR dimensions). However, women do not report lower levels of CSR within their organisations.
-Women's and men's perceptions of and responses to CSR can be examined by the type of CSR and the specific stakeholder groups.

Figure 4.1.   Relationships between gender and CSR explored in this review

within the gender literature on employee responses to justice, in Strah, Rupp, Shao, & Skarlicki, 2019). Within this model, actors at each level of analysis (organisational, individual) value CSR initiatives due to three underlying categories of motivation: instrumental, relational and moral (deontic). Instrumental motives reflect self-interest-driven motives (parties care about CSR because it allows for personal gain). Relational motives revolve around the social exchange and social identity that CSR engenders (CSR allows for relationship development with important others), and moral motives refer to ethical principles (CSR is viewed as an inherent moral responsibility).

We focus on three (relatively micro) sets of CSR actors that have been examined through the lens of gender: organisations themselves, leaders in key organisational positions, and individual stakeholders (e.g., employees, consumers). In the following sections, we summarise the existing research on the connection between CSR and gender at each level, and then, within the context of this research, examine gendered motives (instrumental, relational and deontic) for CSR.

Organisations as enactors: gender initiatives as CSR

While organisations historically have not focused on gender as a part of their CSR frameworks (Larson & Freeman, 1997; Vilkė, 2011), this has changed more recently, with greater prioritisation for gender equality in the workplace and beyond (Thompson, 2008). Catalyst, a gender equity research and advisory group with over 300 members, found that many of their members – including Fortune 500 companies – took on CSR initiatives aimed at supporting women (Catalyst, 2003). In fact, over half of these organisations reported that gender equality was their most commonly targeted initiative related to diversity. This focus on gender-related CSR is important because it has become apparent that organisations contribute substantially to gender imbalance in society via the policies and practices that they support – both directly and tangentially (Le Bruyns, 2009). Therefore, gender equality is intricately tied to organisations' CSR initiatives as 'women's participation in the labour market is an ethical requirement to build the relationship between business and society' (Grosser, 2011, p. 74).

There are several types of gender-related initiatives employed by organisations discussed within the CSR literature. First, some initiatives focus on developing company policies to align with broader government legislation related to gender equality (Adams & Harte, 1999; Begum, 2018; Grosser & Moon, 2005). Some examples of these types of policies are those revolving around maternity leave or sexual harassment. Organisations' willingness to be transparent with gender-related CSR information promotes accountability for striving towards the gender equality goals set forth by governing bodies (Oliveira et al., 2018). Second, some organisations have sought to establish themselves as a source and promoter of knowledge related to issues of gender inequality globally, often involving glossy publicity materials and catchy viral videos, such as the publicity produced by Nike for the 'Girl Effect' campaign to advocate for women and girls across the world (Calkin, 2016) – though actions such as these can receive a backlash when they are identified as 'pink-washing' (i.e., organisations promoting themselves as leaders and advocates on social issues such as breast cancer, gender equality or LGBTQ rights, while engaging in practices that directly counteract or contradict their public stance on these issues; see Lubitow & Davis, 2011). Finally, other gender equality CSR initiatives focus on improving women's empowerment. One example of this is providing skill development and business and management education that enable women to fulfil their economic potential and independence (Thompson, 2008). General Electric's Women's Network (GE's WN) is a prominent and award-winning example of this type of effort. GE's WN has supported the career and educational advancement of women, providing over one million dollars in scholarships for young women to pursue STEM educational opportunities across 160 countries (General Electric, 2019).

Some have argued that organisations should be accountable for their internal processes and policies related to gender equality and not just philanthropy – placing importance on both the actual and perceived consequences of these organisations' actions towards obtaining gender equality (Le Bruyns, 2009; Stropnik, 2010). The various consequences of these gendered CSR initiatives speak to organisations' motives for their implementation.

Organisations' motivations

There are various perspectives regarding the motivations of organisations to invest in gender equality as a part of their CSR initiatives. First, organisations' motivation can derive from a morally driven desire to behave in a socially responsible manner (Begum, 2018; Lantos, 2001; Swanson, 1999). In this case, these initiatives are evaluated and designed (at least partially) around ethical standards (Bule & Tebar Less, 2016; Fortin & Jolly, 2015; Porter & Kramer, 2006). Here, organisations are motivated by social norms and values rather than financial gain (Begum, 2018; Garriga & Melé, 2004), aligning with Aguilera et al.'s (2007) descriptions of moral (i.e., ethical) motivations for CSR.

The economic (i.e., instrumental) perspective has received the most attention. Here, organisations' motives derive *solely* from the business case with an eye on the economic gains to be made by empowering women (Aguilera et al., 2007; Garriga & Melé, 2004; Swanson, 1995). The links between business success and equality of opportunity for women have been discussed at length, leading gender equality CSR to be viewed as 'big win' for business *and* society (Dex, 2004; Kingsmill, 2001; Singh & Vinnicombe, 2003; Vilkė, Raišienė, & Simanavičienė, 2014; Vinnicombe, 2004). The focus on the business case explicitly shifts the argument from moral-based motivations to profitability motives – 'doing good is good for business' (Shamir, 2008, p. 13).

The business case for CSR is not made solely on the basis of direct bottom-line profitability, but on the potential to indirectly impact the brand image in the marketplace and tap into previously untapped resources of women both as sources of labour and as consumers. For example, gender equality CSR initiatives are often sold as part of a 'brand identity', with McKinsey & Co. arguing that 'investing in making life better for women in developing countries can be an effective way to enhance a company's reputation and brand' (McKinsey & Co., 2010, p. 14), allowing organisations to 'capitalise on emerging business opportunities associated with doing, and being seen to do, good' (Newell & Frynas, 2007, p. 670). Similarly, others have stated that organisations caring about gender equality is a desirable quality for both consumers and investors, particularly women, who are choosing from a variety of businesses they can support or with whom they can conduct business (World Bank, 2011). Second, those promoting investment in CSR gender initiatives make the claim that women are an 'untapped' group of customers, employees and entrepreneurs and that 'unlocking the economic potential of half the world's population is nothing short of sound [business] strategy' (McKinsey & Co, 2010, p. 31; see also Calkin, 2016). Interestingly, a criticism of the business case is that it limits the extent to which all types of gender equality issues are addressed – as only gender-equality issues that are *profitable* are focused on rather than those that may not lead to financial gains by organisations (e.g., fair and equal wages for women; see Begum, 2018; Grosser, 2011).

Relational-based organisational motives for gender equality in CSR are closely connected to instrumental motives. Specifically, organisations may use initiatives related to gender equality to gain social legitimacy and greater social respect (Begum, 2018; Garriga & Melé, 2004). These are relational motives as they represent an organisation's drive to be a contributing member included in a larger group (e.g., their industry; see Aguilera et al., 2007). Importantly, these relational motives for inclusion and legitimacy depend on the norms of the industry in which the organisation operates.

This work suggests that organisations are increasingly paying attention to gender when developing CSR initiatives due to various motives. However, these organisational motives are inherently tied to the decisions of *individuals* within (and surrounding) the organisation, particularly women – who have their own motives for initiating, supporting and reacting to both gender-based CSR initiatives and broadly conceptualised CSR initiatives.

Individual enactors: gender of decision-makers and corporate social performance

Women have been increasingly gaining powerful roles in the workplace. For example, the percentage of women board directors in the USA increased from 12% in 2010 to 22% in 2017 (Catalyst, 2018). Consequently, research has examined the effect of having women in key organisational positions on social corporate performance.

Ibrahim and Angelidis (1994) found that women in key positions demonstrate a stronger preference for CSR compared to men. In a sample of corporate directors that rated the comparative importance of CSR dimensions (economic, legal, ethical and discretionary),[1] women rated discretionary initiatives as more important than men did, while men rated an organisation's economic responsibilities as more important. As the discretionary (in addition to ethical) dimensions most closely align with the most popularly used definitions of CSR (Rupp & Mallory, 2015), this work suggests the presence of female decision-makers will increase the value an organisation places on social responsibility (as it is popularly defined). Indeed, in their 2016 review, Rao and Tilt found that 12 of 13 studies reported a significant, positive relationship between female board members/directors and corporate social responsibility. Similarly, four out of six studies from their review found a significant positive relationship between women on boards and corporate social responsibility reporting. Further, Larrieta-Rubín de Celis et al. (2015) report that organisations with higher (as opposed to lower) percentages of women in several levels of management are more likely to engage in gender-related CSR activities. A few examples of the gender-related CSR initiatives companies could have engaged in were recruitment related (e.g., 'equal opportunities training for the team responsible for the selection process'), work–life balance related (e.g., 'flexible working hours') and community-related (e.g., supporting community initiatives around female entrepreneurship) (pp. 102–105).

Gender diversity within the corporate boards of 1,489 USA-based firms predicted the presence of CSR activities (broadly defined as including community, corporate governance, employee relations, environment, human rights, and product quality) (Harjoto, Laksmana, & Lee, 2015). The significant effect of boards' gender representation on CSR has been replicated by Setó-Pamies (2015) for broadly conceptualised CSR; by Post, Rahman, and Rubow (2011) for CSR strengths related to the environment (though the presence of three or more female directors only significantly predicted one out of several ECSR measures); and by Williams (2003) for philanthropic donations. Various other studies have also found that the gender diversity of boards and executives predicts CSR disclosure (Aslam, Makki, Mahmood, & Amin, 2018; Fernandez-Feijoo, Romero, & Ruiz, 2012; Harjoto & Rossi, 2019). Further, Zhang, Zhu, and Ding (2013) found that, in a sample of 516 companies, the percentage of women directors positively predicted the reputational-based CSR rankings of organisations within their own industries. Demonstrating the overall importance of these gender effects on CSR, Bear, Rahman, and Post (2010) reported that the gender composition of boards positively predicted firm reputation, and that CSR (broadly defined) mediated this relationship. Gender diversity within boards has also been shown to positively predict firm performance via the mediator of CSR reporting (Sial et al., 2018).[2] Collectively, these studies demonstrate a consistent relationship between women in leadership positions and an organisation's CSR.

That being said, boundary conditions on these effects have also been identified. The presence of a 'token' female board member does not necessarily affect CSR, as this positive effect may only emerge for boards that have more than two women (e.g., Harjoto & Rossi, 2019). Another moderator might be cultural context. While positive relationships between gender diversity within powerful positions and CSR or CSR reporting have been found in US, Spanish, Italian, Chinese, Australian and international samples (cited above), negative or null relationships have been reported among Indonesian (Margaretha & Isnaini, 2014) and Malaysian companies (Ahmad, Rashid, & Gow, 2018). Similarly, Issa and Fang (2019) reported that the number of women directors in a company was related to company CSR reporting in Bahrain and Kuwait, but not in four other Middle Eastern countries (Oman, Qatar, Saudi Arabia and the UAE). The extent to which these differences reflect sampling error versus meaningful variance across cultures requires careful future study. Indeed, Yasser, Al Mamun, and Ahmed (2017) report that the gender composition of company boards in Malaysia, Pakistan and Thailand positively predicts CSR, but only amongst boards with high independence, suggesting board independence may also play a critical role in the relationships among the gender composition of boards, CSR and culture. Finally, in a sample of Chinese companies, Zhang, Han, and Yin (2018) report a positive relationship between the percentage of women directors and charitable donations, but only among lower-performing firms. High-performing firms tend to give donations of a greater value, but this relationship significantly decreases as the proportion of women directors increases. Taken together, preliminary evidence suggests the presence of important moderators such as token status, culture, board independence and firm performance on the relationship between gender in leadership and CSR.

Women's motives for enactment

Instrumental, relational and moral motives have each been referenced within research considering gender effects on CSR. Zou, Wu, Zhu, and Yang (2018) suggest women may be motivated to enact CSR as board members as they tend to be more risk-averse than men (Byrnes, Miller, & Schafer, 1999). CSR is thought to reduce risk for firm leaders by promoting goodwill (Zou et al., 2018). Because this risk-driven motivation preserves perceptions of the board's leadership, it falls into instrumental CSR enactment motives (and relational motives, to a lesser extent, by increasing legitimacy perceptions). Another instrumental motive for women to initiate CSR revolves specifically around gender/diversity CSR initiatives. These social change-based initiatives allow greater opportunities for women to enter and advance within an organisation, which minimises a female director's chance of being a token and potentially expands her own opportunities (Derks, Van Laar, & Ellemers, 2016).

One of the most well-established findings within the gender literature is that women endorse higher communal traits and values (i.e., traits and values that revolve around connecting with and helping or supporting others or the larger community) compared to men (Diekman, Clark, Johnston, Brown, & Steinberg, 2011; Donnelly & Twenge, 2017). These traits and goals are relational in nature as they allow for the formation of relationships with others. However, traits that are rated as communal also tend to be rated as moral (Abele & Wojciszke, 2007), suggesting that women will prioritise enacting CSR for both relational and moral motives. These traits overlap with Zou et al.'s (2018) proposal that women prioritise CSR enactment as they are prone to altruism. Also, in line with moral motives, women rate a wider range of organisational behaviours as being unethical (Franke, Crown, & Spake, 1997), as compared to men. Viewing a wider range of behaviours as unethical likely encourages women to mitigate any potentially harmful or unethical behaviours on the part of the firm through CSR in order to 'do the right thing'.

It is important to acknowledge that the relationship between gender composition and CSR could also be due to factors outside of the specific motives of women. First, women may naturally bring a different perspective to boards. Specifically, researchers have theorised that women are thought to have different educational and experience-related backgrounds than their male counterparts (Bear et al., 2010; Larrieta-Rubín de Celis et al., 2015). This could allow for a wider range of perspectives that may help address the needs of various stakeholders, and lend sensitivity to CSR issues. Second, the apparent effect of women leaders on CSR could also be a function of organisational motives rather than individual enactor motives (in line with our earlier discussion; see Rao & Tilt, 2016). For example, Newman and Trump (2019) report that consumers are more sceptical of an environmental CSR pledge delivered by a male versus a female spokesperson (or a person with communal characteristics), speaking to an organisation's ability to increase the *perception* of their CSR amongst consumers based on gendered characteristics. Indeed, organisations may use the presence of women in key positions as a signal that they are socially responsible (Bear et al., 2010). Additionally, companies that value corporate social change (particularly on dimensions related to diversity) may be more likely to attract and promote women. These possibilities demonstrate that the direction of causality between the presence of women in key organisational roles and organisations' CSR should be critically examined in this context.

Overall, having women in key positions within an organisation is positively related to CSR activities. However, more work is needed to confirm the moderators, mediating mechanisms (i.e., motives) and causal direction of this relationship. We now turn to the role of gender in stakeholders' perceptions of and reactions (both attitudinal and behavioural) to CSR.

Individuals as reactors: gender differences in reactions to CSR

Previous research has found that women stakeholders value or expect CSR to a greater extent than men and are more in favour of using an organisation's resources to benefit the larger society (Arlow, 1991; Calabrese,

Costa, & Rosati, 2016; Del Mar Alonso-Almeida, Fernández de Navarrete, & Rodriguez-Pomeda, 2015; Droms Hatch & Stephen, 2015). However, this gender difference seems to revolve around the *expectations* of ethical and just behaviour, rather than differences in the *perceptions* of behaviour. Specifically, while women have higher expectations that organisations should engage in CSR, men and women tend to equally report on their organisation's CSR level (Calabrese et al., 2016). Women are also more likely to report that organisations should prioritise ethics, when compared to men, but are not necessarily more likely to perceive ethics as being tied to positive business outcomes (Luthar, DiBattista, & Gautschi, 1997). However, researchers have noted that existing research findings vary on whether, or the extent to which, gender influences CSR values, CSR perceptions and CSR effects on organisational attitudes (and similar outcomes; see Calabrese et al., 2016). Two apparent moderators that might explain this variance are the CSR dimension types and the stakeholder groups considered.

Variability across dimensions

While some research suggests that women prioritise many types of CSR more strongly than men (Calabrese et al., 2016; Del Mar Alonso-Almeida et al., 2015; Lämsä, Vehkapera, Puttonen, & Pesonen, 2008), other research has suggested gender differences emerge based on the type of CSR being studied.[3] For example, some work suggests men prioritise economic-driven priorities more strongly than women (Burton & Hegarty, 1999; Ibrahim & Angelidis, 1994). While some work suggests women prioritise legal and ethical CSR dimensions more strongly than men (Del Mar Alonso-Almeida et al., 2015; Lämsä et al., 2008), Ibrahim and Angelidis (1994) report that gender differences do not emerge for these dimensions. In contrast, Burton and Hegarty (1999) found that women rated the importance of the ethical dimension more highly than men, while there was no gender difference in the importance of the legal dimension. Other CSR priorities such as social, philanthropic (discretionary) and environmental are often rated as more important by women than men (Aspen Institute, 2008; Del Mar Alonso-Almeida et al., 2015; Ibrahim & Angelidis, 1994; Prasad, Marlow, & Hattwick, 1998). Research has also indicated that female job-seekers more strongly prioritise diversity-related CSR as compared to men when searching for a job (Backhaus, Stone, & Heiner, 2002).

Variability across stakeholders

Earlier, we discussed how women in management value CSR compared to men. Evidence suggests that perceptions of and responses to CSR differ across gender for other stakeholder groups as well. Much of the evidence in the previous section was conducted on undergraduate and graduate students, implying the perspective of either consumers or potential employees. Research on various, specific stakeholder groups is more limited.

Employees: while there are often no gender differences found in women's and men's perceptions of CSR, McDaniel, Shoeps, and Lincourt (2001) found, in a survey of over 1,500 employees of one organisation, that female employees rated the organisation's environment as less ethical compared to male employees. This finding contrasts with the research we review above that suggested men and women do not report differences in their perceptions of CSR. This discrepancy between the perceptions of employees and the broader population in perceptions of CSR could be due to the greater insight into the inner workings of organisations held by employees. That is, perhaps women's greater expectation for CSR leads to lower perceptions of CSR, but only when women have enough information about the company (through exposure as an employee). Another possibility is that internal discrepancies in the treatment of men and women may lead to differences in their access to information and communications regarding CSR initiatives, or in the decision-making power to influence CSR programmes.

CSR perceptions may also act as a stronger predictor of organisational commitment for women employees as compared to men (Peterson, 2004; though see Brammer, Millington, & Rayton, 2007 for results where CSR appears to serve as a similarly strong predictor of organisational commitment across gender). Greening and Turban (2000) found that women are also significantly more likely than men to indicate that they would pursue a job at, and accept a job offer from, companies demonstrating diversity-related CSR.

Consumers: researchers have also highlighted the importance of gender as a key factor in understanding consumer perceptions of organisations' CSR initiatives (Patino, Kaltcheva, Pitta, Sriram, & Winsor, 2014). Calabrese et al. (2016) suggest that female consumers have higher expectations for CSR, but this does not translate into lower perceptions of actual CSR (as we discuss above). Additionally, Roberts (1993) reports that women score higher on a scale of socially responsible consumer behaviour, as compared to men (e.g., buying environmentally friendly products, or not supporting companies that discriminate against minorities). However, we note that the results on gender differences in ethical perceptions of, or reactions to, ethical business practices can be mixed (Calabrese et al., 2016; Collins, 2000). For example, some researchers have found that while women endorsed stronger attitudes towards CSR, men reported a higher likelihood of modifying consumer behaviour and attitudes based on CSR (Hur, Kim, & Jang, 2016; Jones et al., 2017). Kim, Kwak, and Babiak (2015) also found that when the organisation in question was a sports team, CSR initiatives drove positive attitudes towards the team more so for men than women. This highlights that the extent to which gender influences the responses to CSR may tie into the stereotypical gendered nature of the initiative (Hyllegard, Yan, Ogle, & Attmann, 2010; Patino et al., 2014). Research studies in this area are still limited in number, so future research is needed to further explore these issues.

Investors: while less research has considered the gender of investors as a stakeholder (shareholder) group in perceptions of, or reactions to, CSR, the research that has been carried out is largely consistent with that which has been reviewed thus far. For example, Nath, Holder-Webb, and Cohen (2013) reported on data from 750 US-based retail investors, showing that women reported a greater use of CSR information previously and greater anticipated need for CSR information in the future to make investment decisions. However, it is important to note that the effect sizes reported in this research were small and that tests of statistical significance had a high cut-off (significance was calculated for a one-tailed test and the significance of previously used CSR information was listed as $p < .10$). Further work to understand the relationship for this stakeholder group is certainly required.

Multiple stakeholders' motives

Just as female leaders may enact CSR for relational (to develop relationships) and moral (to do the right thing) reasons, women from various stakeholder groups may value, respond to and wish to engage in organisations' CSR initiatives for the same reasons. Indeed, there is some additional work in support of the moral perspective. Droms Hatch and Stephen (2015) reported that ratings of moral identity predicted beliefs about the extent to which organisations should engage in CSR for women but not men.

It is important to note that instrumental motives would differ from our section on the motives of women leaders as enactors of CSR. Specifically, women employees, consumers and investors may see organisations' CSR information as a signal that an organisation is trustworthy and will treat them well (Aguilera et al., 2007). As a historically marginalised and relatively risk-averse group, women may value these signals more than men.

Overall, these results suggest that women from various stakeholder groups place greater value on CSR compared to men. Additionally, it appears that gender plays a role in how individual stakeholders respond to CSR initiatives within a company, in terms of work-related attitudes and behaviours. However, the literature on gendered perceptions of and reactions to CSR policies on the part of various stakeholders is extremely small and somewhat inconsistent, demonstrating the importance of future research. Important considerations within these results are the type of CSR being studied and the stakeholder group being examined.

Implications for practice

Our summary of gender and CSR research reveals practical implications for organisations. First, organisations should think carefully about whether their CSR policies specifically include issues related to gender or gender equality. Certain instrumental, relational or moral organisational goals could be met through introducing new or more expansive gender-related CSR initiatives. Second, organisations should also consider the scientific evidence that suggests various female stakeholders prioritise CSR to a greater extent than men. Further, organisations should consider that having more female leaders is associated with greater CSR on their part. Though the direction of causality is unclear, gender equality goals (met through gender representation in leadership roles) and CSR goals appear to be intertwined. Further, preliminary evidence suggests that various female stakeholders may be more likely to engage with an organisation based on that organisation's CSR policies and transparency compared to male stakeholders. While evidence on gendered CSR priorities has not consistently translated into stakeholders' perceptions of or reactions to CSR, future work may reveal that organisations can engage greater numbers of female stakeholders (e.g., job-seekers, current employees, consumers, investors) through their CSR policies.

Conclusion

This review has demonstrated the important role of exploring gender as a variable in CSR research. We first discussed how organisations are increasingly acknowledging their responsibility to include gender equality within their CSR initiatives. Research focuses on various gender-focused CSR initiatives commonly employed, and theorises on the organisational motivations for these initiatives. Second, we examined the empirical findings linking women in decision-making roles (e.g., corporate boards) to the corporate social performance of firms. Further, we summarised the conditions under which these effects might change (e.g., the cultural context or the financial performance of the firm), necessitating careful future work. Finally, we reviewed empirical work examining the extent to which gender influences perceptions of and reactions to CSR amongst various stakeholders, finding that women tend to prioritise CSR more strongly than men. However, gendered attitudinal and behavioural responses to CSR may be more complicated than that.

Our review highlights some important areas for future research. The current literature has demonstrated that there is an association between gender and CSR, both when examining the gender composition of boards in predicting a firm's CSR and the extent to which gender influences individual stakeholders' reactions to CSR. However, while numerous theories are offered for these findings, very few mediation tests have been conducted, leaving the actual cause of these relationships unclear. Further, this literature would benefit from examining the causal direction of the relationship between gender board composition and CSR. Additionally, systematic research should directly test moderators of the effects reviewed herein. Finally, future research should examine the role of gender in CSR from a broader perspective. For example, some work has specifically considered LGBTQ-relevant issues within CSR policies (e.g., organisations' policies regarding domestic partner benefits; see Gupta, Briscoe, & Hambrick, 2017) and has found that LGBTQ consumers may have a stronger response to CSR (especially diversity-related CSR) compared to individuals who do not identify as being a part of these communities (Canas & Sondak, 2014). Overall, the importance of the unique implications of CSR for this specific group of stakeholders – women – highlights the necessity of exploring CSR through the lens of additional groups.

Questions for students

1. What are the three levels of analysis at which research has examined the overlap between CSR and gender?
2. What are some of the reasons why women may value CSR more than men?
3. Why can we not necessarily conclude that an increase in the gender composition of corporate boards has caused organisations to focus more on CSR?

Notes

1. The economic dimension refers to earning a profit and fulfilling consumers' needs; the legal dimension refers to an organisation following the law (e.g., following equal employment opportunity laws); the ethical dimension refers to meeting and supporting the values or norms of society; while discretionary refers to making social/philanthropic contributions to society that have not been required by the previously listed dimensions (Burton & Hegarty, 1999; Ibrahim & Angelidis, 1994).
2. See Eagly (2016) for a review on the broader findings on the relationship between gender diversity in leadership and firm-level outcomes.
3. See note 1 for a description of the 'types' of CSR.

References

Abele, A. E., & Wojciszke, B. (2007). Agency and communion from the perspective of self versus others. *Journal of Personality and Social Psychology, 93*(5), 751–763.

Adams, C. A., & Harte, G. (1999). *Towards corporate accountability for equal opportunities performance.* London: Certified Accountants Educational Trust.

Aguilera, R. V., Rupp, D. E., Williams, C. A., & Ganapathi, J. (2007). Putting the S back in corporate social responsibility: A multilevel theory of social change in organizations. *Academy of Management Review, 32*(3), 836–863.

Aguinis, H. (2011). Organizational responsibility: Doing good and doing well. In S. Zedeck (Ed.), *APA handbook of industrial and organizational psychology, 3: Maintaining, expanding, and contracting the organization* (pp. 855–879). New York: American Psychological Association.

Aguinis, H., & Glavas, A. (2012). What we know and don't know about corporate social responsibility: A review and research agenda. *Journal of Management, 38*(4), 932–968.

Ahmad, N. B. J., Rashid, A., & Gow, J. (2018). Corporate board gender diversity and corporate social responsibility reporting in Malaysia. *Gender, Technology and Development, 22*(2), 87–108.

Arlow, P. (1991). Personal characteristics in college students' evaluations of business ethics and corporate social responsibility. *Journal of Business Ethics, 10*(1), 63–69.

Aslam, S., Makki, M. A. M., Mahmood, S., & Amin, S. (2018). Gender diversity and managerial ownership response to corporate social responsibility initiatives: Empirical evidence from Australia. *Journal of Managerial Sciences, 12*(2), 131–151.

Aspen Institute (2008). *Where will they lead? MBA students' attitudes about business and society.* New York: Center for Business Education.

Backhaus, K. B., Stone, B. A., & Heiner, K. (2002). Exploring the relationship between corporate social performance and employer attractiveness. *Business & Society, 41*(3), 292–318.

Bear, S., Rahman, N., & Post, C. (2010). The impact of board diversity and gender composition on corporate social responsibility and firm reputation. *Journal of Business Ethics, 97*(2), 207–221.

Begum, M. I. A. (2018). Corporate social responsibility and gender commitments of commercial banks in Bangladesh. *Journal of International Women's Studies, 19*(6), 87–105.

Brammer, S., Millington, A., & Rayton, B. (2007). The contribution of corporate social responsibility to organizational commitment. *The International Journal of Human Resource Management, 18*(10), 1701–1719.

Bule, T., & Tebar Less, C. (2016). *Promoting sustainable development through responsible business conduct, in Development Co-operation Report 2016: The sustainable development goals as business opportunities.* Paris: OECD Publishing.

Burton, B. K., & Hegarty, W. H. (1999). Some determinants of student corporate social responsibility orientation. *Business & Society, 38*(2), 188–205.

Byrnes, J. P., Miller, D. C., & Schafer, W. D. (1999). Gender differences in risk taking: A meta-analysis. *Psychological Bulletin, 125*(3), 367–383.

Calabrese, A., Costa, R., & Rosati, F. (2016). Gender differences in customer expectations and perceptions of corporate social responsibility. *Journal of Cleaner Production, 116*, 135–149.

Calkin, S. (2016). Globalizing 'girl power': Corporate social responsibility and transnational business initiatives for gender equality. *Globalizations, 13*(2), 158–172.

Canas, K., & Sondak, H. (2014). *Opportunities and challenges of workplace diversity*. Upper Saddle River, NJ: Pearson Education.

Carroll, A. B. (1979). A three-dimensional conceptual model of corporate performance. *Academy of Management Review, 4*(4), 497–505.

Carroll, A. B., & Buchholtz, A. K. (2014). *Business and society: Ethics, sustainability, and stakeholder management*. Stamford, CT: Nelson Education.

Catalyst. (2003). *2002 Catalyst member benchmarking survey*. New York: Catalyst Publications.

Catalyst. (2018). *Quick take: Women on corporate boards*. New York: Catalyst Publications.

Collins, D. (2000). The quest to improve the human condition: The first 1,500 articles published in Journal of Business Ethics. *Journal of Business Ethics, 26*(1), 1–73.

Del Mar Alonso-Almeida, M. D. M., Fernández de Navarrete, F. C., & Rodriguez-Pomeda, J. (2015). Corporate social responsibility perception in business students as future managers: A multifactorial analysis. *Business Ethics: A European Review, 24*(1), 1–17.

Derks, B., Van Laar, C., & Ellemers, N. (2016). The queen bee phenomenon: Why women leaders distance themselves from junior women. *The Leadership Quarterly, 27*(3), 456–469.

Dex, S. (2004). The business case for family friendly policies. In *ESRC Gender Mainstreaming Seminar*. London: DTI.

Diekman, A. B., Clark, E. K., Johnston, A. M., Brown, E. R., & Steinberg, M. (2011). Malleability in communal goals and beliefs influences attraction to stem careers: Evidence for a goal congruity perspective. *Journal of Personality and Social Psychology, 101*(5), 902–918.

Donnelly, K., & Twenge, J. M. (2017). Masculine and feminine traits on the Bem Sex-Role Inventory, 1993–2012: A cross-temporal meta-analysis. *Sex Roles, 76*(9–10), 556–565.

Droms Hatch, C., & Stephen, S. A. (2015). Gender effects on perceptions of individual and corporate social responsibility. *Journal of Applied Business and Economics, 17*(3), 63–71.

Eagly, A. H. (2016). When passionate advocates meet research on diversity, does the honest broker stand a chance? *Journal of Social Issues, 72*(1), 199–222.

Fernandez-Feijoo, B., Romero, S., & Ruiz, S. (2012). Does board gender composition affect corporate social responsibility reporting? *International Journal of Business and Social Science, 3*(1), 31–38.

Fortin, C., & Jolly, R. (2015). The United Nations and business: Towards new modes of global governance? *IDS Bulletin, 46*(3), 45–58.

Franke, G. R., Crown, D. F., & Spake, D. F. (1997). Gender differences in ethical perceptions of business practices: A social role theory perspective. *Journal of Applied Psychology, 82*(6), 920–934.

Garriga, E., & Melé, D. (2004). Corporate social responsibility theories: Mapping the territory. *Journal of Business Ethics, 53*(1–2), 51–71.

General Electric. (2019). *Women's network*. Retrieved from https://jobs.gecareers. com/global/en/womens-network.

Graso, M., Camps, J., Strah, N., & Brebels, L. (2019). Organizational justice enactment: An agent-focused review and path forward. *Journal of Vocational Behavior, 116*, 103296.

Greening, D. W., & Turban, D. B. (2000). Corporate social performance as a competitive advantage in attracting a quality workforce. *Business & Society, 39*(3), 254–280.

Grosser, K. (2011). *Corporate social responsibility, gender equality and organizational change: A feminist perspective* (Doctoral dissertation, University of Nottingham).

Grosser, K., & Moon, J. (2005). Gender mainstreaming and corporate social responsibility: Reporting workplace issues. *Journal of Business Ethics, 62*(4), 327–340.

Gupta, A., Briscoe, F., & Hambrick, D. C. (2017). Red, blue, and purple firms: Organizational political ideology and corporate social responsibility. *Strategic Management Journal, 38*(5), 1018–1040.

Harjoto, M., Laksmana, I., & Lee, R. (2015). Board diversity and corporate social responsibility. *Journal of Business Ethics, 132*(4), 641–660.

Harjoto, M. A., & Rossi, F. (2019). Religiosity, female directors, and corporate social responsibility for Italian listed companies. *Journal of Business Research, 95*, 338–346.

Hur, W. M., Kim, H., & Jang, J. H. (2016). The role of gender differences in the impact of CSR perceptions on corporate marketing outcomes. *Corporate Social Responsibility and Environmental Management, 23*(6), 345–357.

Hyllegard, K. H., Yan, R. N., Ogle, J. P., & Attmann, J. (2010). The influence of gender, social cause, charitable support, and message appeal on Gen Y's responses to cause-related marketing. *Journal of Marketing Management, 27*(1–2), 100–123.

Ibrahim, N. A., & Angelidis, J. P. (1994). Effect of board members' gender on corporate social responsiveness orientation. *Journal of Applied Business Research, 10*, 35–40.

Issa, A., & Fang, H. X. (2019). The impact of board gender diversity on corporate social responsibility in the Arab Gulf states. *Gender in Management: An International Journal, 34*(7), 577–605.

Jones III, R. J., Reilly, T. M., Cox, M. Z., & Cole, B. M. (2017). Gender makes a difference: Investigating consumer purchasing behavior and attitudes toward corporate social responsibility policies. *Corporate Social Responsibility and Environmental Management, 24*(2), 133–144.

Jones, D. A., & Rupp, D. E. (2018). Social responsibility IN and OF organizations: The psychology of corporate social responsibility among organizational members. In D. S. Ones, N. Anderson, C. Viswesvaran, & H. K. Sinangil (Eds.), *The handbook of industrial, work and organizational psychology* (pp. 333–350). London: Sage.

Kim, K. T., Kwak, D. H., & Babiak, K. (2015). Gender differences on the effect of CSR engagement on team attitude and loyalty: A case study of a professional soccer club in Korea. *International Journal of Sport Management and Marketing, 16*(1–2), 92–111.

Kingsmill, D. (2001). *A review of women's employment and pay*. London: Women and Equality Unit.

Lämsä, A., Vehkapera, M., Puttonen, T., & Pesonen, H. L. (2008). Effect of business education on women and men students' attitudes on corporate responsibility in society. *Journal of Business Ethics, 82*(1), 45–58.

Lantos, G. P. (2001). The boundaries of strategic corporate social responsibility. *Journal of Consumer Marketing, 18*(7), 595–632.

Larrieta-Rubín de Celis, I., Velasco-Balmaseda, E., Fernández de Bobadilla, S., Alonso-Almeida, M. D. M., & Intxaurburu-Clemente, G. (2015). Does having women managers lead to increased gender equality practices in corporate social responsibility? *Business Ethics: A European Review, 24*(1), 91–110.

Larson, A., & Freeman, R.E. (1997) Introduction. In A. Larson & R. E. Freeman (Eds.), *Women's studies and business ethics: Towards a new conversation* (pp. 3–8). New York: Oxford University Press.

Le Bruyns, C. (2009). Corporate social responsibility and gender justice in South Africa. *International Journal of Public Theology, 3*(2), 222–237.

Lubitow, A., & Davis, M. (2011). Pastel injustice: The corporate use of pinkwashing for profit. *Environmental Justice, 4*(2), 139–144.

Luthar, H. K., DiBattista, R. A., & Gautschi, T. (1997). Perception of what the ethical climate is and what it should be: The role of gender, academic status, and ethical education. *Journal of Business Ethics, 16*(2), 205–217.

Margaretha, F., & Isnaini, R. (2014). Board diversity and gender composition on corporate social responsibility and firm reputation in Indonesia. *Jurnal Manajemen dan Kewirausahaan* [*Journal of Management and Entrepreneurship*], *16*(1), 1–8.

McDaniel, C., Shoeps, N., & Lincourt, J. (2001). Organizational ethics: Perceptions of employees by gender. *Journal of Business Ethics, 33*(3), 245–256.

McKinsey & Company (2010). *The business of empowering women*. London: McKinsey & Company.

Nath, L., Holder-Webb, L., & Cohen, J. (2013). Will women lead the way? Differences in demand for corporate social responsibility information for investment decisions. *Journal of Business Ethics, 118*(1), 85–102.

Newell, P., & Frynas, J. G. (2007). Beyond CSR? Business, poverty and social justice: An introduction. *Third World Quarterly, 28*(4), 669–681.

Newman, K. P., & Trump, R. K. (2019). Reducing skepticism about corporate social responsibility: Roles of gender and agentic-communal orientations. *Journal of Consumer Marketing, 36*(1), 189–196.

Oliveira, M., Júnior, M., de Oliveira Lima, S., & de Freitas, G. (2018). The influence of the characteristics of the national business system in the disclosure of gender-related corporate social responsibility practices. *Administrative Sciences, 8*(14), 1–17.

Patino, A., Kaltcheva, V. D., Pitta, D., Sriram, V., & Winsor, R. D. (2014) How important are different socially responsible marketing practices? An exploratory study of gender, race, and income differences. *Journal of Consumer Markets, 31*(1), 2–12.

Peterson, D. K. (2004). The relationship between perceptions of corporate citizenship and organizational commitment. *Business & Society, 43*(3), 296–319.

Porter, M. E., & Kramer, M. R. (2006). The link between competitive advantage and corporate social responsibility. *Harvard Business Review, 84*(12), 78–92.

Post, C., Rahman, N., & Rubow, E. (2011). Green governance: Boards of directors' composition and environmental corporate social responsibility. *Business & Society, 50*(1), 189–223.

Prasad, J. N., Marlow, N., & Hattwick, R. E. (1998). Gender-based differences in perception of a just society. *Journal of Business Ethics, 17*(3), 219–228.

Rao, K., & Tilt, C. (2016). Board composition and corporate social responsibility: The role of diversity, gender, strategy and decision making. *Journal of Business Ethics, 138*(2), 327–347.

Roberts, J. A. (1993). Sex differences in socially responsible consumers' behavior. *Psychological Reports, 73*, 139–148.

Rupp, D. E., & Mallory, D. B. (2015). Corporate social responsibility: Psychological, person-centric, and progressing. *Annual Review of Organizational Psychology and Organizational Behavior, 2*(1), 211–236.

Setó-Pamies, D. (2015). The relationship between women directors and corporate social responsibility. *Corporate Social Responsibility and Environmental Management, 22*(6), 334–345.

Shamir, R. (2008). The age of responsibilization: On market-embedded morality. *Economy and Society, 37*(1), 1–19.

Sial, M., Zheng, C., Cherian, J., Gulzar, M. A., Thu, P., Khan, T., & Khuong, N. (2018). Does corporate social responsibility mediate the relation between boardroom gender diversity and firm performance of Chinese listed companies? *Sustainability, 10*(10), 3591.

Singh, V., & Vinnicombe, S. (2003). The 2002 female FTSE index and women directors. *Women in Management Review, 18*(7), 349–358.

Strah, N., Rupp, D.E., Shao, R., & Skarlicki, D. (2019). *Gendered reactions to organizational justice: A meta-analysis*. 79th annual meeting of the Academy of Management, Boston, MA, July.

Stropnik, N. (2010). How can corporate social responsibility contribute to gender equality and work–life balance: Example of the 'Family-Friendly Enterprise' certificate in Slovenia. *Our Economy, 56*(5–6), 11–20.

Swanson, D. L. (1995). Addressing a theoretical problem by reorienting the corporate social performance model. *Academy of Management Review, 20*(1), 43–64.

Swanson, D. L. (1999). Toward an integrative theory of business and society: A research strategy for corporate social performance. *Academy of Management Review, 24*(3), 506–521.

Thompson, L. J. (2008). Gender equity and corporate social responsibility in a post-feminist era. *Business Ethics: A European Review, 17*(1), 87–106.

Vilkė, R. (2011). Corporate social responsibility implementation effectiveness improvement in Lithuania: Model of local government involvement. Vilnius: Mykolas Romeris University.

Vilkė, R., Raišienė, A. G., & Simanavičienė, Ž. (2014). Gender and corporate social responsibility: 'Big wins' for business and society? *Procedia-Social and Behavioral Sciences, 156*, 198–202.

Vinnicombe, S. (2004). *The business case for women directors*. Paper presented at ESRC Gender Mainstreaming Seminar. London: DTI.

Williams, R. J. (2003). Women on corporate boards of directors and their influence on corporate philanthropy. *Journal of Business Ethics, 42*(1), 1–10.

World Bank. (2011). *World development report 2012: Gender equality and development*. Washington, DC: World Bank.

Yasser, Q. R., Al Mamun, A., & Ahmed, I. (2017). Corporate social responsibility and gender diversity: Insights from Asia Pacific. *Corporate Social Responsibility and Environmental Management, 24*(3), 210–221.

Zhang, J., Han, J., & Yin, M. (2018). A female style in corporate social responsibility? Evidence from charitable donations. *International Journal of Disclosure and Governance, 15*(3), 185–196.

Zhang, J. Q., Zhu, H., & Ding, H. B. (2013). Board composition and corporate social responsibility: An empirical investigation in the post Sarbanes-Oxley era. *Journal of Business Ethics, 114*(3), 381–392.

Zou, Z., Wu, Y., Zhu, Q., & Yang, S. (2018). Do female executives prioritize corporate social responsibility? *Emerging Markets Finance and Trade, 54*(13), 2965–2981.

Part 3
Processes

5 Understanding the Long-Term CSR Engagement Strategies of Organisational Change Agents

Angela van der Heijden and Jacqueline M. Cramer

Overview

This chapter shows how organisations can achieve long-term involvement and ownership of their corporate social responsibility (CSR) initiatives. It highlights how central actors, called change agents, engage people throughout the organisation in sustainability efforts. Longitudinal research in 18 pioneering companies examines what the change agents took into account, how they behaved and interacted, and the changing contexts in which they acted. It also distinguishes four engagement strategies that the change agents developed and used over time. The strategies incorporate top-down CSR ambitions, while allowing for local interpretations and bottom-up room for manoeuvre. They can be used as exemplary management tools to translate and align CSR in local contexts.

Introduction

The need to advance the management of sustainability issues in organisations has never been so great. Companies are increasingly dependent on both the natural and socio-economic environments, and the embedding of sustainability has become a challenge that encompasses management strategies at all organisational levels (Starik & Kanashiro, 2013). Therefore, it is becoming increasingly evident that not only the company's board but also its employees need to be engaged to achieve sustainability objectives (De Bakker, Den Hond, King, & Weber, 2013; Taneja, Taneja, & Gupta, 2011). This organisation-wide involvement in the management of corporate sustainability is hereafter referred to as corporate social responsibility (CSR).

Recently, several studies have called for more research on understanding the internal engagement processes that are necessary to manage and embed CSR at all levels of the organisation (Zollo, Cennamo, & Neumann, 2013). The call for research on organisational engagement stems from the notion that the concept of CSR only gains meaning when it is strongly embedded in the organisation and understood by its staff (Basu & Palazzo, 2008; Crane & Glozer, 2016).

The challenge to engage others involves gaining the support of the whole organisation, which requires practitioners to interact in an understandable language and reach a local consensus (Benn, Edwards, & Angus-Leppan, 2013). Embedding CSR issues in corporate practices concerns not only expanding the scope of their responsibility, but also improving collaboration as well (Den Hond, De Bakker, & Neergaard, 2007). It requires the integration of ecological and socio-economic ideas at operational, strategic and normative organisational levels (Baumgartner & Rauter, 2017). Organisation members need to make collective sense of CSR processes that are often internally complex and require balancing economic, ethical, legal and social responsibilities across the organisation (Zollo et al., 2013).

This idea of engagement emphasises the relevance of research on intangible and processual interactions that comprise sensemaking, and that are part of managing CSR engagement. Examples of these engagement processes are creating collective commitment, identifying paths of action and sharing values in organisations (Crane, Pallazzo, Spence, & Matten, 2014). Such engagement processes unfold, to a large extent, through key organisational practitioners, also referred to as 'change agents' (Dunphy, Griffiths, & Benn, 2007; Visser & Crane, 2010), who work to pull people together, gain support and involve the whole organisation, and who face the struggles and tensions associated with transitioning to CSR practice (Cramer & Van der Heijden, 2006; Sonenshein, 2016).

This chapter examines how change agents interact and collaborate to help CSR become adopted and understood throughout the organisation. The agents' ways of doing so are studied in two stages: first during the start-up and then during the spread of CSR engagement within companies. Drawing on a two-stage, longitudinal, multiple-case study of CSR management in Dutch companies, we answer the following research question: What are change agents' engagement strategies during the start-up and spread phase of CSR and how does their involvement change over time?

Organisational sensemaking as a theoretical lens

In this chapter, the perspective of organisational sensemaking is used as a theoretical lens to better understand organisational engagement for CSR. The sensemaking perspective was introduced by the psychologist Weick (e.g. 1979, 1995, 2001) into management research in the 1970s as a new line of thought. The sensemaking perspective is useful for the analysis in this chapter, because it focuses on the social-behavioural aspect of engagement processes in organisations (Douglas & Wykowski, 2017).

From the sensemaking perspective, an organisation is a social reality that is constructed interactively by organisation members. People interactively make meaning of new or unexplored organisational issues and come to see their environment in a similar way (Balogun, Jacobs, Jarzabkowski, Mantere, & Vaara, 2014). They find common ground on the goals, ambitions, interests and values of CSR. It is important to realise that common ground is not a stable state of everyone sharing the same definition and meaning of CSR, but refers to 'a dynamic state, a process of communicating, updating, tailoring, and repairing mutual understandings' (Edelenbos & van Meerkerk, 2018, p. 2095).

Guiding concepts

While important in the field, sensemaking is a theoretical construct that is difficult to operationalise (Sandberg & Tsoukas, 2015). Therefore, in this chapter the sensemaking literature is operationalised by focusing on the main types of social interaction: *communicating, acting* and *building relationships* by change agents. These three guiding concepts function as a lens that helps to focus data analysis (Boeije, 2010).

First, the change agents must *communicate* in an understandable, tailor-made language throughout the whole organisation. When organisation members talk or interact among themselves and with outsiders, they use language, vocabularies, conversations and dialogue that capture the character of their organisation (Weick, Sutcliffe, & Obstfeld, 2005). Once a general idea is translated for the local context, it gains ground. Second, *acting* is a tool to engage others. People think through acting (Gioia, 2006). Change agents focus on emergent and often small actions that can have a large effect on spreading ideas on CSR. Third, the interactions involved in *building relationships* show how change agents create ongoing working relationships with other organisational actors (Langley & Tsoukas, 2010).

Methods

Drawing on a longitudinal, multiple-case study of 18 Dutch companies, this chapter presents qualitative research on the level of social interactions between individuals. The research design is based on purposeful and nesting sampling to select the company cases and key informants (Patton, 2015). The original sample consisted of 18 pioneering companies, which were either Dutch or operating in the Netherlands:

- AVR Holding (waste management)
- PAP Egg Group (boiled and peeled eggs)
- Coca-Cola Enterprises Netherlands (soft drinks and beverages)
- Peeze Coffee (coffee roasting and machinery)
- DSM (chemicals)
- Perfetti Van Melle (confectionery)
- Dumeco (a meat specialist)
- Pinkroccade (ICT)
- Interface (a carpet manufacturer)
- Rabobank Group (financial services)

- KLM (an airline company)
- Sodexho, Netherlands (catering)
- Nuon (a multi-utility company distributing water and energy)
- StoraEnso Fine Paper Berghuizer Mill (a paper mill)
- Ordina (ICT)
- Uniqema (oil and chemicals)
- Ouwehands Zoo Rhenen (a zoo)
- Ytong (a supplier of autoclaved, aerated concrete bricks).

As summarised in Figure 5.1, the 18 companies were brought together as a maximum variation selection: a purposefully picked group of pioneers in corporate social responsibility. The study analysed what was required to start up the engagement processes. Next, a follow-up study of six companies (a nested sample) focused on the engagement processes needed to spread CSR (Onwuegbuzie & Leech, 2007).

Data were collected using a mix of document analysis and individual and group interviews, the latter of which were taped and transcribed verbatim. The consistency of the data was tested by a triangulation of methods and sources (Boeije, 2010; Yin, 2003). The data and the interpretations were verified through account and member checks of the reconstructions with all participating change agents to establish credibility (Lincoln & Guba, 1985).

The analysis of the data followed an inductive route that began with a thick description in the form of case histories, pulling together the interview accounts and the documentary data (Lincoln & Guba, 1985; Pettigrew, 1990). The key examples of social engagement interactions were clustered for each case, using the three guiding concepts of communicating, acting and building relationships (Van der Heijden & Cramer, 2012, 2017).

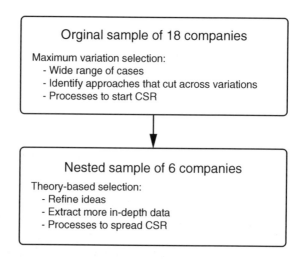

Figure 5.1.   Qualitative research design

Findings

Engagement strategies carried out by change agents

The empirical study showed how change agents in organisations play a catalysing and indispensable role in CSR engagement. The change agents were directors, senior managers or employees specifically charged with managing CSR. They first helped get new issues off the ground. Most of them were also able to help the new issues become embedded in their organisations. The change agents used various social interactions to articulate and interpret the issues and engage people throughout the organisation in CSR efforts. The findings revealed distinct ways of interacting developed by the change agents during the start-up and the spreading of CSR within the organisations.

Start-up of CSR engagement: an exploration strategy

In the 18 companies studied, engagement started with a diffuse sensitivity to CSR. A particular reason or set of reasons formed the starting point to take up an issue or to become interested in the concept of CSR. These triggers varied from criticism by an NGO about a company's packaging policy to an assessment of future market opportunities or the personal conviction of the director or CEO. Change agents also linked their efforts to the societal discussion about corporate responsibility.

Most of the change agents reported that they experienced uncertainty about what CSR is and isn't. In order to get started with engagement, they wanted to get a better picture of the general CSR concept and of the issues at hand. This uncertainty marked the occasion of their beginning to search for a meaning of corporate responsibility and the issues involved. The change agents appeared to create almost identical strategies of exploration.

As part of their exploration strategies, the three issues the change agents struggled most with were gathering information, transferring new ideas to other people and departments in the organisation and, conversely, obtaining support from management. They described this process of dealing with uncertainty as the emergence of a general awareness that motivated them to explore the importance of CSR issues for the organisation.

At first, the change agents were looking for more information about where to start and what to do. They were unsure of determining the environmental or social issues within the broad CSR concept that could relate to their organisation. When they gained some experience with implementing CSR, they expressed uncertainty about choosing new priorities or expanding the scope of their activities. The change agents explained that they discovered the response options that were open to them by taking part in formal and informal discussions and meetings, executing a baseline measurement

Table 5.1.   Change agent interactions in exploration strategy

Communicating	Acting	Building relationships
Formal internal discussions and meetings	Execute a baseline measurement	Emphasise client wishes on CS, corporate image-building and personal enthusiasm
Informal internal discussions and (lunch)meetings	Select relevant issues in meetings between managers and coordinators	Gain visibility and management support
Consult external information sources	Make CS activities comprehensible for employees	
Exchange information and experiences in round tables	Focus on direct benefit targets, e.g., lower costs and company reputation	

in the organisation, obtaining information from external information sources and/or exchanging information and experiences with each other (Table 5.1).

Then, when starting to transfer the information they had gathered about the general concept to the context of their own organisation, the change agents were confused about the diversity of expectations and possibilities in managing CSR. They reported that the ideas were too complex or roles and responsibilities were not clearly defined. Their efforts were increasingly focused on the comprehensibility of CSR actions, gaining visibility and visualising direct benefits.

Spreading of CSR engagement: pragmatic and systematic strategies

The start-up of interactions was followed by the spreading stage, involving interactions to adapt the general concept of CSR to the company or to specific departments or subsidiaries of the company. The findings showed how change agents translated their interactions into the ways of working in their organisation in various manners of communicating, acting and building relationships. Their choices were dependent on the regular way of working of their organisation.

While each change agent approach was different, two types of overarching engagement strategies were revealed, which were based on whether the change agents characterised their company's way of working as pragmatic or systematic (see Table 5.2).

In companies that were more pragmatically oriented, the practical elements, such as short-term strategies, a quick plan of action, and internal and external communication, were taken up first. In line with their organisation's forthright way of working, the change agents concentrated on selecting elements that they could translate into clear and tangible, local goals. The change agents focused on implementation through action, while formalisation followed at a later stage. The change agents quickly set priorities at the

Table 5.2. Change agent interactions in pragmatic and systematic strategies

Pragmatic strategy	Systematic strategy
Discuss CS implementation in short management meetings	Discuss CS implementation in regular and long management meetings
Set priorities on management level with focus on executing activities	Set priorities on management level with focus on documenting themes
Establish CS activities by starting with small pilot projects	Establish CS activities by starting to set up an organisational structure
Follow up with broader project activities; sometimes a framework for projects	Follow up with formalisation by registering CS implementation in reports and systems

management level, with a focus on executing concrete activities. They set up a plan of action with small and visible pilot projects.

Internal communication about CSR was managed in informal settings, often in the hallway or during lunch meetings. Change agents informed organisation members and simultaneously solicited their ideas about social responsibility. Often, a special term or programme was created as a framework for communication about the CSR projects.

In companies with a systematic way of working, on the other hand, change agents experienced the implementation of CSR as an orderly sequence of events. They gave prominence to the systematic, structure-related elements of formulating vision and policy, anchoring CSR aspects in policy and quality and management systems, and annual reporting. The quality and management systems were often already present in the company and were complemented by additional audits and manuals. Change agents focused on documenting their choices before taking action. Baseline measurements were used as measuring tools and became part of the CSR policy. Annual CSR reports were devised according to the then newly established guidelines of the Global Reporting Initiative. Notably, instead of setting pragmatic short-term priorities, the systematically working change agents established long-term CSR goals.

Similar to the pragmatic approach, systematic change agents consulted people across the organisation about their ideas on CSR. However, while in pragmatic strategies the internal communication and consultation often took place informally, in systematic companies these discussions were more formal, controlled and top-down.

The discovery of the connection between change agent interactions and the company's perceived way of working (work culture) enabled the categorisation of two strategies. In addition, it was found that the interactions often overlapped and demonstrated a cyclical pattern of communicating, acting and building relationships. The cycle was set in motion when new CSR ideas were introduced at different times, followed by translation of the interactions, which in turn often occasioned new information needs and the corresponding explorative interactions. Thus, the organisational engagement was encouraged when change agents continued to initiate and follow up on their efforts, and let the process develop into an ongoing cycle of social interactions.

The follow-up findings revealed that, over time, the strategies of change agents gradually converged, because they increasingly incorporated both pragmatic and systematic CSR elements. While the pragmatic and systematic strategies had created leeway for CSR ideas to spread the engagement to departments and subsidiaries, over time the strategies of change agents gradually aimed to involve more people throughout the organisation. They customised their interactions to fit their company's organisational procedures and processes. The different types of social interactions that helped the change agents achieve these farther-reaching local customisations are summarised in Table 5.3.

The study also revealed that the freedom to make decisions at a local level in the organisation is crucial for effective engagement in CSR. In fact, the broader and more adaptable scope of social engagement processes increasingly defined the roles of change agents in the long-term embedding of CSR.

In accordance with the previous stage, the longitudinal study showed that the continuation of different ways of interacting by internal change agents is key in the operationalisation of this process. What may seem contradictory is that continuous cycles are set in motion through reflective pauses. Reflection proved to be an essential link that became apparent when change agents started to define their expected ambitions and outcomes. They took time to reflect on their processes and transfer their expectations to other people. The findings showed that expressing expectations can motivate others and result in different courses of action in order to achieve CSR goals.

Table 5.3. Change agent interactions in commitment strategies

Communicating (to promote and exchange CSR ideas)	Acting (to spread actions and improve performance)	Building relationships (to collaborate from within the organisation with external network)
Distribute overviews of policy, programs, projects and results	Promote CSR framework (in the form of program, department, policy, label/criteria)	Mobilise others in organisation, utilising local voice in policy and decisions – i.e. authority to make CSR decisions is spread throughout the organisation
Organise knowledge exchange meetings to develop local CSR language	Awareness and use of freedom of decision-making (authority to act independently)	Build two-way relationships with chain partners, through dialogues on improving mutual performance
Set up projects that encourage internal communication	Organise and promote small, visible joint actions with chain partners	Extend relationship building to collaborative network of stakeholders on technology, societal issues; towards joint innovation
Utilise local performance targets or project demands		Build external network with societal and knowledge stakeholders (NGOs, governments, universities)

Discussion and conclusion

This chapter examines how organisational change agents interact and collaborate to help CSR issues become embedded in their organisation. The findings demonstrate how their engagement interactions contribute, over time, to a more thorough integration of CSR within the organisation. The identification of active strategies developed by internal change agents to engage organisation members in shaping ideas, has made the less tangible and collaborative side of CSR embedding more explicit and tangible.

In essence, the longitudinal analysis reveals how, on the one hand, the different change agents tend to converge in their ways of acting. In most companies, a socially shared reality of CSR is established, over time, that involves both pragmatic and systematic elements. On the other hand, each company's change agents have helped shape different localised interpretations of that reality.

In this friction between general process development and locally defined interpretations of CSR lie essential properties of the adaptivity of organisational engagement. Therefore, this study makes several contributions to the CSR management literature about ways to understand and manage adaptive engagement.

First, this chapter illustrates the importance of *time* for the adaptivity of CSR engagement. The sense-making perspective has allowed for examining engagement interventions that are ongoing instead of momentary. The results show that, in the long term, the adaptivity is revealed through the ongoing development of interventions that gradually change organisational routines. Change agents engage organisation members in ongoing dialogue and build shared mental frameworks for new ideas, in cycles of starting and spreading, through formal and informal interactions.

Second, this chapter contributes empirical knowledge on engagement strategies to the CSR management literature. The application of the sense-making lens over a long time period offers new insights into the different types of interventions carried out by change agents, and their perceived effectiveness. The interventions combine into engagement strategies to communicate, mobilise action and build collaboration.

The results also draw attention to the debate on different modes of strategy-making in the CSR management literature. In line with Neugebauer, Figge, and Hahn (2016) and Hahn and Aragón-Correa (2015), we argue that planned strategy-making should be complemented by strategy-making on CSR embedding that is less tangible, cannot be planned and emerges from practice. The sense-making perspective has helped us to understand how, over time, diverse interpretations of issues become tangible when the general concept of CSR is translated by change agents into words, actions and work relationships that fit the local way of working, even at the level of subsidiaries or departments. These localised shared meanings shape the identity of each firm's CSR strategy. Importantly, the evolution of engagement strategies adapting to local contexts appears to be essential for the progress of CSR processes.

Third, this chapter provides new insights into the ideas of adaptive capacity and values practice (Zollo et al., 2013). It shows how the (re)organisation of routines, local collaboration and personal capabilities are closely intertwined in adaptive engagement processes. Change agents play an entrepreneurial role in the translation of corporate CSR values and beliefs into goals, policies, programmes, projects, targets, meetings and conversations that meet the already available values at the collective and individual levels. Notably, change agents try to change existing values but also aim to align their ideas to existing organisational and personal interests and values. This suggests that understanding values helps them in adapting the organisational routines (Feldman, 2000).

Fourth, it is important to realise that the cycle of ongoing engagement interactions is maintained by reflection. Observations on the cyclical process have demonstrated that change agents are generally positioned in the organisation to coordinate between the top-management rationale behind decision-making and the implementation in practice. As they understand both logics, the key role of change agents is to adopt a reflective stance and to envisage and refine alternative courses of action to achieve the CSR ambitions. This capacity to understand both logics and be aware of resources, opportunities and constraints, also termed 'reflexivity' (Sharma & Good, 2013), is key for change agents.

Fifth, the findings contribute to Weick's recent exploration into the understanding of organisational behaviour as a process of ongoing modifications in 'breadth, substance and credibility as the person doing the explaining is modified by ongoing experience' (Weick, 2017, p. 1). Change agents built trust and took advantage of the credibility they acquired through previously obtained results. They always tried to find opportunities and searched for leeway for change. The agents adhere to the role that Wilson and Barbat (2015) identified as the political entrepreneur, who continuously searches for ways to enhance engagement in CSR issues. Not knowing in advance which approach would be most effective, the change agents learned through trial and error. Over time, their accumulated experience and expertise led to better personal networking skills and an increased competence to assess and predict opportunities, which all strengthened the credibility of their proposals.

Taken together, organisational engagement has proven to be a process of translating understanding of the broadly defined CSR concept into diverse organisational settings, practices and routines. This chapter's new insights on change agents' adaptive engagement strategies are meant to be indicative of the kinds of practices involved in organising corporate CSR processes. They enable a better understanding of the navigation of social interactions that help to start and spread embedding in organisations.

Implications for practice

This chapter highlights how change agents convince others to collaborate on CSR issues. It has become clear that their focus is on determining a joint direction that incorporates top-down CSR ambitions, while allowing for local interpretations and bottom-up room for manoeuvre. The findings make practical contributions, both for top management and for organisational change agents.

In organising the implementation of CSR, top management may consider new insights about the importance of encouraging emergent processes and supporting the change agent role. To achieve this, management can allow room for trial and error and for the long-term perspective. It also helps to stimulate the decentralisation of decision-making and CSR structures, and to assess the entrepreneurial qualities of endorsed change agents.

Change agents may use the provided understanding of the four engagement strategies to narrow and shorten their search for ways to align CSR ambitions in local contexts. Although the strategies can be helpful management tools, change agents will always have to make interpretations and adjust them to organisational perceptions and work areas, the embedding stage, public opinion and their envisaged CSR challenges. Therefore, finding common ground will never be a plannable endeavour from start to finish.

Questions for students

1. What can companies do to engage employees as change agents and why is this important?
2. Why would a better understanding of employee engagement processes contribute to the organisational embedding of CSR?
3. What are the main engagement strategies carried out by organisational change agents to stimulate the adoption of CSR in the local organisational context?
4. How does CSR help employees to make sense of their environment?

References

Balogun, J., Jacobs, C., Jarzabkowski, P., Mantere, S., & Vaara, E. (2014). Placing strategy discourse in context: Sociomateriality, sensemaking, and power. *Journal of Management Studies*, *51*(2), 175–201.

Basu, K., & Palazzo, G. (2008). Corporate social responsibility: A process model of sensemaking. *Academy of Management Review*, *33*(1), 122–136.

Baumgartner, R. J., & Rauter, R. (2017). Strategic perspectives of corporate sustainability management to develop a sustainable organisation. *Journal of Cleaner Production, 140*, 81–92.

Benn, S., Edwards, M., & Angus-Leppan, T. (2013). Organisational learning and the sustainability community of practice: The role of boundary objects. *Organisation and Environment, 26*(2), 184–202.

Boeije, H. (2010). *Analysis in qualitative research*. London: Sage.

Cramer, J., & Van der Heijden, A. (2006). Corporate social responsibility as a tailor-made search process. In J. Jonker & M. De Witte (Eds.), *The challenge of organising and implementing corporate social responsibility* (pp. 211–222). Basingstoke: Palgrave.

Crane, A., & Glozer, S. (2016). Researching corporate social responsibility communication: Themes, opportunities and challenges. *Journal of Management Studies, 53*(7), 1223–1252.

Crane, A., Pallazzo, G., Spence, L. J., & Matten, D. (2014). Contesting the value 'creating shared value' concept. *California Management Review, 56*(2), 130–154.

De Bakker, F. G., Den Hond, F., King, B., & Weber, K. (2013). Social movements, civil society and corporations: Taking stock and looking ahead. *Organisation Studies, 34*(5–6), 573–593.

Den Hond, F., De Bakker, F. G. A., & Neergaard, P. (Eds.). (2007). *Managing corporate social responsibility in action: Talking, doing and measuring*. Aldershot, Hants: Ashgate Publishing.

Douglas, N., & Wykowski, T. (2017). *Rethinking management: Confronting the roots and consequences of current theory and practice*. London: Palgrave Macmillan.

Dunphy, D., Griffiths, A., & Benn, S. (2007). *Organisational change for corporate sustainability: A guide for leaders and change agents of the future*. New York: Routledge.

Edelenbos, J., & van Meerkerk, I. (2018). Finding common ground in urban governance networks: What are its facilitating factors? *Journal of Environmental Planning and Management, 61*(12), 2094–2110.

Feldman, M. S. (2000). Organisational routines as a source of continuous change. *Organisation Science, 11*(6), 611–629.

Gioia, D. A. (2006). On Weick: An appreciation. *Organisation Studies, 27*(11), 1709–1721.

Hahn, T., & Aragón-Correa, J. A. (2015). Toward cognitive plurality on corporate sustainability in organisations: The role of organisational factors. *Organisation and Environment, 28*(3), 255–263.

Langley, A., & Tsoukas, H. (2010). Introducing perspectives on process organisation studies. In T. Hernes & S. Maitlis (Eds.), *Process, sensemaking and organising: Perspectives on process organisation studies*. Oxford: Oxford University Press.

Lincoln, Y. S., & Guba, E. G. (1985). *Naturalistic inquiry*. London: Sage.

Neugebauer, F., Figge, F., & Hahn, T. (2016). Planned or emergent strategy making? Exploring the formation of corporate sustainability strategies. *Business Strategy and the Environment, 25*(5), 323–336.

Onwuegbuzie, A. J., & Leech, N. L. (2007). Sampling designs in qualitative research: Making the sampling process more public. *The Qualitative Report, 12*(2), 19–20.

Patton, M. Q. (2015). *Qualitative research and evaluation methods: Integrating theory and practice*. London: Sage.

Pettigrew, A. M. (1990). Longitudinal field research on change: Theory and practice. *Organisational Science, 3*, 267–292.

Sandberg, J., & Tsoukas, H. (2015). Making sense of the sensemaking perspective: Its constituents, limitations, and opportunities for further development. *Journal of Organisational Behavior, 36*, 6–32.

Sharma, G., & Good, D. (2013). The work of middle managers: Sensemaking and sensegiving for creating positive social change. *Journal of Applied Behavioral Science, 49*(1), 95–122.

Sonenshein, S. (2016). How corporations overcome issue illegitimacy and issue equivocality to address social welfare: The role of the social change agent. *Academy of Management Review, 41*(2), 349–366.

Starik, M., & Kanashiro, P. (2013). Toward a theory of sustainability management: Uncovering and integrating the nearly obvious. *Organization & Environment, 26*(1), 7–30.

Taneja, S. S., Taneja, P. K., & Gupta, R. K. (2011). Researches in corporate social responsibility: A review of shifting focus, paradigms, and methodologies. *Journal of Business Ethics, 101*(3), 343–364.

Van der Heijden, A., & Cramer, J. (2012). Change agent sensemaking for sustainability in a multinational subsidiary. *Journal of Organisational Change Management, 25*(4), 535–559.

Van der Heijden, A., & Cramer, J. (2017). Change agents and sustainable supply chain collaboration: A longitudinal study in the Dutch pig farming sector from a sensemaking perspective. *Journal of Cleaner Production, 166*, 967–987.

Visser, W., & Crane, A. (2010). *Corporate sustainability and the individual: Understanding what drives sustainability professionals as change agents* (SSRN Paper Series No. 1, 25 February). Retrieved from https://papers.ssrn.com/sol3/papers.cfm?abstract_id=1559087.

Weick, K. E. (1979). *The social psychology of organising*. New York: Random House.

Weick, K. E. (1995). *Sensemaking in organisations*. Thousand Oaks, CA: Sage.

Weick, K. E. (Ed.). (2001). *Making sense of the organisation*. Malden, CA: Blackwell Publishing.

Weick, K. E. (2017). Perspective construction in organisational behavior. *Annual Review of Organisational Psychology and Organisational Behavior, 4*, 1–17.

Weick, K. E., Sutcliffe, K. M., & Obstfeld, D. (2005). Organisation science and the process of sensemaking. *Organisation Science, 16*(4), 409–421.

Wilson, K., & Barbat, V. (2015). The supply chain manager as political-entrepreneur? *Industrial Marketing Management, 49*, 67–79.

Yin, R. K. (2003). *Case study research*. Thousand Oaks, CA: Sage.

Zollo, M., Cennamo, C., & Neumann, K. (2013). Beyond what and why: Understanding organisational evolution towards sustainable enterprise models. *Organisation & Environment, 26*(3), 241–259.

6 The Role of Internal Communication in Encouraging Employee Engagement in CSR: A Sense-Making Approach

Riccardo Wagner, Lonneke Roza, and Debbie Haski-Leventhal

Overview

Internal communication is often seen as a tool to convince employees of the importance of corporate social responsibility (CSR) and to engage them in CSR activities. However, such a rather instrumental view does not do justice to the complexity and constitutive significance of the internal communication and discourse among employees on CSR. Indeed, this chapter shows that establishing CSR within an organisation is a complex narrative process. Even an above-average CSR performance and a wide range of mainstream CSR communication efforts are no guarantee for stimulating employee engagement in CSR. Based on a comprehensive qualitative case study, this chapter shows that employees tend to actively withdraw from engaging in CSR if the internal communication suppresses individual and collective sense-making. Hence, an integrative and individualistic communication approach is required for providing employees with connective narrative resources, and empowers them to tell stories actively. Ultimately, this provides them with a deeper meaning behind the CSR concept and lets them internalise the discourse. Only then can managers build a more coherent CSR management and communication practice.

Learning objectives

By the end of this chapter, readers should be able to:

- detail the role of (internal) communications in engaging employees in CSR
- demonstrate that building a discourse through internal communications is key to engaging employees in CSR
- explain how integrative and individualistic communication approaches can lead to higher employee engagement in CSR.

Introduction

The role of internal communication in the development and implementation of corporate social responsibility (CSR) is treated ambiguously in the literature. Foremost, the existing literature emphasises *why* companies should engage in CSR and shows that employee motivation and retention are essential factors in CSR strategies (Schmitt & Röttger, 2011). In addition, contributions from practitioners and empirical research have highlighted positive relationships between CSR practices and employee motivation (Mory, 2014). More broadly, the CSR management literature aims to anticipate social demands, to obtain a social licence to operate and to achieve a concrete competitive advantage (Beckmann, Morsing, & Reisch, 2006; Breitbarth, 2011; May, 2011). When scholars do focus on corporate stakeholders, they tend to focus mainly on external stakeholder groups (Frynas & Yamahaki, 2016) as targets for CSR messages (Bhattacharya, Sen, & Korschun, 2008; Waddock & Googins, 2011). Even when the role of employees in externally communicating CSR is emphasised, employees are mostly seen as messengers of CSR activities (Morsing, Schultz, & Nielsen, 2008).

Furthermore, the models underlying these approaches tend to follow a rather simple view of communication: top-down to employees or inside-out to external stakeholders (Heinrich, 2013). However, establishing CSR within is a complex and dynamic process between the organisation and its employees, both as a group and as individuals. Hence, this requires a similarly complex analytical approach if practical management techniques are to be generated from it.

Indeed, research has shown that employees can contribute significantly to the positive perception of CSR policies and practices of both customers and business partners (Coombs & Holladay, 2012). Hence, explicitly considering, addressing and analysing employees as a stakeholder group in CSR communication research so far are very much required (Crane & Glozer, 2016; Frynas & Yamahaki, 2016). It is important to note that these gaps relate to the micro-level of employee perception of CSR initiatives and communication; the meso-level, of internal organisational processes and internal communication; and the macro-level, of the community which is impacted by all of the above (Wehmeier & Schultz, 2011).

Therefore, this chapter responds to the need for communication-centric work that helps to understand CSR as a continuous activity through which individuals and organisations 'fathom, construct, negotiate and adapt what it means to be a socially responsible organisation' (Christensen & Cheney, 2011, p. 491) – in other words, the dynamics between corporate communications, internal (informal) communications and the engagement of employees in CSR.

CSR internal communication

While, in simple terms, communication is an exchange of information, the concept is actually more complex and includes multiple domains (Kalla, 2005). For instance, internal communication incorporates: (1) business communication, which is about the development of verbal and non-verbal communication within an organisation for operational purposes (Reinsch, 1996); (2) management communication, which is essentially the communication of managers of an organisation with the ultimate purpose of achieving effectiveness (Smeltzer, 1996); and (3) corporate communication, described as images received by the audiences of an organisation – here employees (Argenti & Forman, 2002).

Communication can have multiple functions (Cornelissen, 2017). First, it can be informative by being merely an exchange of information to raise awareness about a certain topic (Losee, 1999), such as CSR. Second, communication can be persuasive as it has the potential to lead to actions, behavioural changes or decision-making (Kalla, 2005). In the context of this chapter, persuasive communication would be used to engage employees in CSR initiatives or a CSR approach. Moreover, communication is an attempt to build a shared understanding and meaning between the organisation and its stakeholders through a dialogue (Johnson-Cramer, Cross, & Yan, 2003). Internal communications aim to involve employees in a conversation to give them a voice in the development and implementation of CSR. These are essential functions of internal communication if the company is to change employees' perceptions about their employer's sustainability and CSR commitment (Christensen & Cornelissen, 2013). The dialogue strategy, however, is considered to be the most effective way in engaging employees as it results in companies adjusting their behaviour based on employee feedback and involvement (Cornelissen, 2017).

Therefore, in recent years, management research has increasingly developed a view towards interactive relationship building and stakeholder dialogue as an integral part of CSR (Freeman, 1984; Haski-Leventhal, 2018). Accordingly, the aim is no longer to just inform stakeholders about CSR activities, but also to actively involve them in the process (Morsing & Schultz, 2006). Such stakeholder integration should ideally lead to a common understanding of which CSR activities are appropriate for the organisation (for more details, see Bartlett & Devin, 2011). This approach may lead to a shared narrative, joint sensemaking and deeper meaning.

To achieve this, we suggest implementing the dialogue strategy, which includes five key factors: (1) stakeholder integration and inclusion; (2) openness to all topics of discussion; (3) tolerance to critical views; (4) stakeholder empowerment; and (5) transparency or availability of information about the results (Pedersen, 2006). In addition, and regardless of the communication strategy, effective CSR communication must consider what to communicate and where (Du, Bhattacharya, & Sen, 2010).

What to communicate (content)

Content is key in any communication strategy, and there are three stages in the creation of content. First, it starts with strategic intent or the purpose of the message. This is followed by a determination of themes, from which the message will be drawn. Finally, the choice of the message style is made, depending on the purpose and content of the message (Cornelissen, 2017). This message can be crafted in a specific manner to convey the content more effectively, using rational reasoning, emotional appeal or symbols (Cornelissen, 2017).

There is an abundance of literature on message framing and its three basic choices. Risky framing assumes manipulation of the perception of risk by emphasising either a positive or negative outcome of an event. Goal framing is meant to nudge the target audience to act in a certain way by emphasising the loss coming from not behaving the way a message suggests, instead of the gain from behaving that way. Attribute framing promotes an item or an action by emphasising a positive or negative attribute of the item, thus making it out to be perceived as more salient (e.g. Levin, Schneider, & Gaeth, 1998).

The problem with CSR internal communication is the perception of CSR as an extra-role activity. Hence, communication about this topic may be considered less significant or inferior to the communication of in-role related matters, such as employee and financial performance, and, consequently, be ignored (Kim & Grunig, 2011; Ramus & Killmer, 2007). To avoid this issue, it is essential to ensure that CSR is recognised as being strategically important to the organisation (Haski-Leventhal, 2018). Therefore, internal

CSR communication should not only be about showcasing the achievements of the organisation, but also framed as information which is consistent with the CSR strategy (Bhattacharya et al., 2008). As such, it is necessary to clarify CSR motivation and the underlying goals, tactics and clear measurements of progress (Quinn & Dalton, 2009; Tench, Sun, & Jones, 2014).

Where and how to communicate (channels and processes)

In order to achieve communication effectiveness, the use of multiple communication channels is recommended (Tench et al., 2014). The effectiveness of a communication channel highly depends on the related objectives and strategy. For instance, if a company uses an informational strategy, a one-way communication channel, such as memos or mass emails, could be effective (Johnson-Cramer et al., 2003). On the other hand, if a persuasive or dialogue strategy is being applied, two-way communication channels, such as forum posts or meetings, are recommended (Cornelissen, 2017).

Communication channels vary by media richness. Media richness theory states that a rich communication channel is that which ensures the absence of equivocality in communication (Dennis & Kinney, 1998). This can be achieved through instant feedback, the ability to read body language, personalisation and variety of language use. Indeed, the 'richest' communication channel is the face-to-face conversation, where people can see each other's body language, hear the intonation of voice and quickly update an understanding about communicated content, thus avoiding equivocality. These highly rich communication channels are of essence for a successful implementation of dialogue strategy in CSR communication (Cornelissen, 2017). As such, companies simply sending widespread emails about CSR efforts may not be as effective as using face-to-face all-employee meetings or engaging videos.

Furthermore, social presence is imperative in persuasive and dialogue communication strategies. It is referred to as the acoustic, visual and physical contact that can be achieved (Short, Williams, & Christie, 1976). The more interpersonal and synchronous communication is, the greater the social presence it has. It may seem that highly rich channels must also have a significant social presence, however this may not be the case; for instance, public speakers have a strong social presence, but if, for example, an audience is not allowed to ask questions and clarify equivocal situations, the communication will not be very rich (Kaplan & Haenlein, 2010). Therefore, when it comes to CSR, it is important not only that employees are communicated to, but also that platforms and opportunities exist to enable employees to engage in a meaningful conversation about their employer's efforts in this area.

Credibility of communication

The effectiveness of communication is highly dependent on the credibility of the information. Information is considered more credible when it is perceived to be less controlled by an organisation such as word of mouth (Du et al., 2010). Indeed, informal communication, which is a source of information perceived to be independent of organisational attitudes and positions, is considered more credible (Cornelissen, 2017). Therefore, informal communication may be considered as more effective and, if passed on informally by keen employees, it may have a better effect.

However, CSR research also gives cues on the role of formal communication in engaging employees in CSR, but it seems to depend on whom the messenger is. Leadership support and active internal communication about this support are crucial in employee engagement in CSR (Roza, Haski-Leventhal, & Meijs, 2017). Indeed, executive support is one of the most influential factors affecting employee attitudes towards CSR (Collier & Esteban, 2007; Ramus & Steger, 2000). Hence, it is particularly powerful in shaping employee perceptions of CSR prominence. Communication about CSR initiatives from organisational leadership is expected to trickle down to the lower levels of the hierarchy, thus reaching all associates within an organisation (Antonakis & Atwater, 2002). Not only is what they say important, but also what type of behaviour they are showcasing. Indeed, leaders are role models who communicate not only with words but also with actions. If leaders signal negative attitudes, they do not demonstrate socially responsible behaviour, or, if employees feel a lack of support from their organisational leaders, these employees will be discouraged to engage in CSR (Ramus & Steger, 2000).

The role of employee sensemaking and sensegiving

People constantly construct their reality in light of their socialisation and their expectations of other individuals. Through sensemaking, people (including employees) interpret the actions of other actors to generate meaning (Weick, 1995). Sensemaking is a process which involves the retrospective development of plausible explanations to rationally justify a person's actions when contradictory cues interrupt a person's ongoing activities (Maitlis & Sonenshein, 2010). To do so, people use current cues with past frame reference (Weick, 1995).

This concept offers a rich starting point for an analysis of CSR institutionalisation (Wehmeier & Schultz, 2011) because the associated processes, structures and contents are viewed in full detail. Following this 'communication constitutes organisations' (CCO) approach (Ashcraft, Kuhn, & Cooren, 2009; Cooren, Taylor, & van Every, 2006) implies shifting CSR internal communication to the centre of consideration, since it acts as an active and constituent force in the construction of organisations (Christensen & Cornelissen, 2013).

Organisations are thus created, maintained and changed in a communicative process of co-orientation (Kuhn, 2008). As such, internal CSR communication is understood as a constitutive process, through which actors explore, construct, negotiate and modify what it means to be a responsible and rule-compliant organisation (Christensen & Cheney, 2011). Following this perspective, internal CSR communication is a circular sensemaking and sensegiving process, undertaken by individuals and the whole organisation. CSR itself is, in this view, a social narrative created within a public discourse: companies do not only create their own CSR stories (sensegiving); at the same time, they try to generate meaning from the CSR concept itself through narratives. CSR communication can, therefore, be seen as a sensemaking process (Wehmeier & Schultz, 2011).

This sensemaking process is embedded in a superordinate social-constructive process of organising through communication, in which the reality of the company is continuously recreated and defined (Czarniaswska, 2004). At the core of this process, narration and storytelling function as fundamental social processes, which provide meaning, orientation, norm-setting, complexity reduction and identity (Brown, Denning, Groh, & Prusak, 2005) for employees.

Based on the above, we define internal CSR communication as the processes of formal, informal and related instrumental communication that take place within the structures and networks of an organisational system for the translation (sensegiving), negotiation and interpretation (sensemaking) of the collective narratives associated with the institutionalisation of corporate responsibility.

Based on the above literature review, we focus our empirical research on the following questions: What are the internal communication processes for constructing and negotiating the meaning and significance of CSR among employees? Could CSR internal communication engage employees and transcend passivity?

Research design

The research on which this chapter is based was designed as a comprehensive qualitative case study and carried out over a period of over 18 months. The studied company is a medium-sized German insurance group organised as a mutual insurance association, which had over a decade of CSR work. CSR is firmly anchored in the company's mission statement. This company has been focusing on CSR communication – publishing a sustainability report for several years and operating its own specific sustainability website. The company has received several prestigious awards and accolades for this outstanding CSR work.

To collect the data for this study, two preliminary steps were taken. The first step consisted of 10 interviews with experts, mostly from large and well-known German companies, all of which had been active in CSR for over five years. The interview participants were all responsible either for CSR communication or for management of the entire CSR programme. The second explorative step consisted of a comprehensive analysis of CSR-relevant documents, i.e., reports on the internal and external CSR communication of the investigated case study company. By the end, over 120 documents had been subject to structured content analysis.

Based on this exploration, empirical data collection was followed, in the investigated case study company, by a methodological triangulation, by combining interviews, observations and document analysis. Semi-structured interviews were conducted with employees and managers of the company. These were complemented by partially structured interviews, which were conducted spontaneously and at random with employees of the company at events such as the company's annual sustainability day. A total of 29 interviews were conducted with 39 employees, including seven interviews with executive managers. In addition, three informal discussions with the company's sustainability officer and two speeches by the chairman of the management board and a member of the external sustainability advisory board were recorded, transcribed and analysed.

Furthermore, a total of eight participant observations of network events were made over a period of one year. These included meetings of the company's sustainability board, meetings with the management board, workshops with employees and the company's sustainability day. The observations were summarised in a protocol and then analysed in a structured way.

Findings: separate story worlds, formulaic language and employee passivity

This chapter aims to describe internal communication processes for constructing and negotiating the meaning and significance of CSR, through which narratives and stories become visible for sensegiving and sensemaking. The data analysis showed which stories and lines of argumentation were spread across the company in connection with CSR. The different themes and stories of the employees and managers also became visible.

In the studied company, CSR was an active part of the sensemaking process but it was rarely an issue for the employees. A visible sign of this was the lack of active interest among employees in the contents of internal CSR communication. Involvement with the topic was somewhat random and rarely went beyond a few, rather spontaneous statements of agreement or displeasure towards colleagues.

Therefore, the majority of sensegiving narratives were hardly taken up or were even completely ignored by employees. The most significant aspect is that the corporate vision ('We want to make life better') generally did not leave a lasting impression on employees. In all these encounters, no employee was able to establish the relatively obvious connection between this vision and the sustainability strategy, or to recall it when asked.

A look at the narrative also reveals that there are three quite central narrative motives in the sensegiving of the company's executives, of which only one finds its equivalent in the sensemaking of the employees. The two central CSR narratives of the 'CSR leader' ('first mover') and the 'CSR quality leader' (represented through awards and external praise) occupied a dominant position in corporate sensegiving, without finding an equivalent echo among employees. There was a significant gap in the mutual translation and negotiation of CSR and the company's strategy. Extensive use of the narrative 'external confirmation' was assessed by the employees with scepticism and restraint.

It is also interesting that the narrative of 'competitive advantage through CSR', which played an essential role in the official sensegiving argumentation, has not been actively used on the part of employees – quite the contrary. Central to the sensemaking of employees was the fact that there were no real stories or evidence of the actual economic relevance of CSR at the company – both among employees and among managers. This leads to relevant gaps in sensemaking and internal discourse.

Nevertheless, an interesting finding is the fundamental acceptance of CSR. Unsurprisingly, the narrative 'companies have social responsibility' was central to the official sensegiving. Equally, albeit usually only on request, the employees confirmed this narrative. At a fundamental level, it is therefore apparent to all those involved in the institutionalisation process that business plays a special social role and that sustainability is consequently on the company agenda. Employees were much more aware of narratives such as 'CSR as an add-on', i.e. as an additional, unremunerated effort. Another common narrative was 'CSR as an expert topic', for which others would be well paid and for which one cannot allow oneself an opinion due to the complexity of the topic. The highest agreement in the narratives was found in the general assessment of the working environment and corporate culture, which may be regarded as value-oriented and stable. However, the influence of the corporate culture, which was experienced as harmonious, also showed adverse effects, which were reflected in many discourse closings and in sensemaking suppressing formulations and processes.

One possible explanation for the above was the company's decision to communicate CSR to employees as an explicit request or instruction of the management. This mainly left questions of how, and not of whether or why. Not least because of the formerly somewhat authoritarian leadership culture, there were hardly any approaches and opportunities for individual decisions, i.e. sensemaking, at the micro-level, which were associated with the basic CSR strategy. Also, there was a very formulaic use of 'recurring sentence' building blocks that have described and justified CSR. This includes narratives such as 'CSR lies in our DNA', consequently leaving no room for sensemaking and discoursing.

The observed narratives thus showed a very different perception and storytelling of CSR among managers and employees. However, this did not lead to confrontation. On the contrary, as stated earlier, all parties agreed that CSR is essential. But, on the part of the employees, this did not lead to engagement or commitment. The narrative of the employees clearly showed a retreat into passivity and caution against too much criticism – and this despite the fact that there were some uncertainties (the economic effectiveness of CSR) and questions (the impact on the work situation) that would have justified more discourse. In general, the company had hardly any stories of (successful) change, and it lacked a common language or shared narrative that would support sensemaking and storytelling for change through CSR.

The company worked intensively with the topic of CSR in its official communication and practices on outstanding CSR management. Nevertheless, access to the discourse was severely restricted to a few executives on the company's CSR board. In the team meetings of employees, the topic was practically never addressed by the representatives of middle management, which shows a clear disconnect between top and middle management. Accordingly, CSR was also seen by employees as a topic that is only relevant for some colleagues in the company and which runs parallel to the 'actual' business. Furthermore, certain departments, such as sales, have largely eluded the topic, although they have a significant influence on the perception and status of CSR.

Our study shows that there is no simple mechanism to connect professional CSR and a high level of employee engagement with and commitment to CSR. Even in a company that has had professional CSR management for years, a comprehensive internal and external CSR communication and an explicit integration of CSR, employees and middle managers were only somewhat interested in CSR. The necessary level of CSR activities was dependent on the actions of only a few activists. Most employees showed a certain 'positive passivity', which is expressed in awarding their employer with an 'internal license to operate', while avoiding an active commitment or willingness to participate. This is highly relevant for business practice because such an environment makes it much more challenging to initiate comprehensive innovation processes in conjunction with CSR.

All in all, there were no other opportunities for exchange and knowledge transfer on CSR within the company so that only passive information on the subject remained. The ability to narrate, which allows for social exchange based on shared stories, was thus also severely limited and left little room for the necessary uncertainties and free spaces without which sensemaking cannot happen.

Discussion

The communicative view of the institutionalisation of CSR showed that there were considerable deficits in internal CSR communication within the studied company. These deficits made individual and collective sensemaking of employees as well as the necessary exchange of identity-creating stories more difficult (Weick, 1995). The narrative content analysis showed the deficiency of shared narratives, which justify CSR, fill it with meaning and establish a connection to the everyday life of the employees. The few dominant narratives also showed a clear division of the story worlds of managers and employees in the company and a language that tended to close the discourse. In interaction with a cultural pressure for harmony, which is initially a symbol of a positive corporate culture, negative processes of employee withdrawal developed. Despite CSR management efforts, internal CSR communication did not lead to the desired CSR commitment on the part of employees.

We found that most employees showed CSR passivity, mainly due to several factors. First, a stable economic environment, which in principle tends to inhibit change processes and commitment because it suppresses the sense of urgency which is necessary for any change, could also lead to passivity. Furthermore, robust corporate culture and identification may lead to some levels of harmony and conformity pressure, which inhibits critique and joint discourse. Passivity can also be nurtured by narrative gaps regarding the corporate strategy and CSR, for example if it remains unclear what economic relevance and impact the topic has. It is thus important to make CSR an explicit part of the corporate strategy and to incorporate it into employees' formal roles (Haski-Leventhal, 2018). Finally, if there are structural holes and cliques in corporate networks, passivity can be fostered – for example, when managers do not take an issue further to their employees or even actively boycott it, or if one department acts largely autonomously and is non-compliant with the overall CSR strategy.

On the sides of communication and sensemaking, discourse-closing and dominant sensegiving narratives with little communicative scope, which suppress sensemaking, as well as a lack of social sensemaking opportunities and meeting spaces (also due to intense workloads and information overload), promote passivity. Moreover, a more rational and micro-oriented 'CSR PR' (Wagner, 2019), that is mainly focused on communicating success and progress to the disadvantage of CSR communication to encourage discourse and storytelling, will further employee passivity and hinder sensemaking. Little attention was paid to including the dialogue strategy in CSR communication with employees (see Cornelissen, 2017), which could foster a deeper meaning of CSR for employees. Rather, it remained on the level of being informative as it merely created awareness about CSR (see Losee, 1999).

Implications for practice

The case presented in this chapter outlines the point that CSR communication is still understood primarily as information on success and progress and a persuasion to feel positive about the matter. A more integrative view is still the exception. To this end, firms should focus more intensively on taking a dialogue approach in communication – not only with external stakeholders, which is increasingly the case, but also in internal communications with employees. Here, the use of storytelling and the creation of meeting places for employees that promote collective and individual sensemaking, should be stimulated. This research also shows that a much more detailed view is needed and that simple demands – for example, 'more dialogue', 'more democracy' – are not enough, because employee passivity, as the easy way out, may be more widespread than the leadership believes it to be. In the long term, this passivity may prohibit the firm's transformation into a truly sustainable and inclusive company.

As laudable as the intention may be to promote identification, motivation and ultimately meaning, CSR as a topic as well as the working environment are to be understood as a complex system, and the abilities of employees, purely in terms of attention, economy and intellect, are limited. Companies who desire to make progress and decrease employee passivity must curb instrumental points of view and develop holistic, process-oriented approaches. CSR managers and corporate leaders are advised to take the sensemaking perspective seriously. To do so, they should continuously collect and analyse narrative patterns and then reinforce positive habits and restrain negative ones. It is always vital to think multicausal because it is never merely a trick which makes the institutionalisation of CSR successful – it still requires several coherent perspectives for CSR to 'make sense' and provide meaning that leads to action.

Limitations and future research

The study contributes, as a qualitative case study of a consciously chosen, holistically representative individual case, to the understanding of the institutionalisation of CSR by internal communication. As such, further research is needed to uncover a general regularity in the sense of statistical representation. The findings presented here do not claim to be transferable to other companies or generalised to other contexts. Rather, the results presented here are to be regarded as broadly applicable or transferable in the manner of analytical understanding.

Furthermore, this study focused on one company in Germany. We acknowledge that in other companies, nations and cultures, the results could be different, and the scope of such studies needs to be expanded to establish such differences. A large-scale study can compare various communication styles, channels and contents, to examine the impact of (or at least the relationship with) employee engagement and commitment, or the decrease in employee passivity. The concept of employee passivity in CSR is an interesting aspect of the discourse of CSR and employee engagement, and it was not sufficiently discussed or studied in the existing literature. Further studies of this specific construct would enrich our understanding of this phenomenon.

Conclusion

Internal CSR communication, which mainly targets the organisation's internal stakeholders (employees), is a complex, narrative-creating process. However, if done well, CSR communication can not only lead to higher levels of employee engagement but may also increase the company's CSR scopes and impacts. Our case study demonstrated how employees withdrew from engaging in CSR when internal communication suppressed individual and collective sensemaking. We, therefore, argue that an integrative and individualistic communication approach is required to provide employees with a shared narrative and a sense of affiliation, and to transform them into CSR storytellers. Ultimately, this will provide employees with CSR internalisation and meaningfulness, offering a more comprehensive way of connecting CSR and employee engagement.

Questions for students

1. Why is internal CSR communication so important to engaging employees in CSR and the company's culture?
2. What aspects of content could enrich internal CSR communication?
3. Why are some employees active in CSR while others remain passive?
4. What can companies do to increase the effectiveness of their internal CSR communication and engage employees?

References

Antonakis, J., & Atwater, L. (2002). Leader distance: A review and a proposed theory. *The Leadership Quarterly, 13*(6), 673–704.

Argenti, P. A., & Forman, J. (2002). *The power of corporate communication: Crafting the voice and image of your business.* New York: McGraw-Hill Professional.

Ashcraft, K. L., Kuhn, T. R., & Cooren, F. (2009). Constitutional amendments: 'Materializing' organizational communication. *Academy of Management Annals, 3*(1), 1–64.

Bartlett, J. L., & Devin, B. (2011). Management, communication, and corporate social responsibility. In Ø. Ihlen, J. L. Bartlett, & S. May (Eds.), *The handbook of communication and corporate social responsibility* (pp. 47–66). Malden, MA: Wiley-Blackwell.

Beckmann, S. C., Morsing, M., & Reisch, L. A. (2006). Strategic CSR communication: An emerging field. In M. Morsing & S. C. Beckmann (Eds.), *Strategic CSR communication* (pp. 11–36). Copenhagen: Jurist- og Økonomforbundets Forlag.

Bhattacharya, C. B., Sen, S., & Korschun, D. (2008). Using corporate social responsibility to win the war for talent. *MIT Sloan Management Review*, *49*(2), 37–44.

Bhattacharya, C. B., Sen, S., & Korschun, D. (2011). *Leveraging corporate responsibility: The stakeholder route to maximizing business and social value*. New York: Cambridge University Press.

Breitbarth, T. (2011). *The business case for corporate social responsibility: Evolution, construction and manifestation in Europe*. Munich: AVM-Verlag.

Brown, S. L., Denning, S., Groh, K., & Prusak, L. (2005). *Storytelling in organizations: Why storytelling is transforming 21st century organizations and management*. Burlington, MA: Butterworth-Heinemann.

Christensen, L. T., & Cheney, G. (2011). Interrogating the communicative dimensions of corporate social responsibility. In Ø. Ihlen, J. L. Bartlett, & S. May (Eds.), *The handbook of communication and corporate social responsibility* (pp. 491–504). Malden, MA: Wiley-Blackwell.

Christensen, L. T., & Cornelissen, J. (2013). Bridging corporate and organizational communication: Review, development and a look to the future. In A. Zerfaß, L. Rademacher, & S. Wehmeier (Eds.), *Organizational communication and public relations: Research paradigms and new perspectives* (pp. 43–72). Wiesbaden: Springer.

Collier, J., & Esteban, R. (2007). Corporate social responsibility and employee commitment. *Business Ethics: A European Review*, *16*(1), 19–33.

Coombs, W. T., & Holladay, S. J. (2012). *Managing corporate social responsibility: A communication approach*. Malden, MA: Wiley-Blackwell.

Cooren, F., Taylor, J. R., & van Every, E. J. (2006). *Communication as organizing*. Mahwah, NJ: Lawrence Erlbaum.

Cornelissen, J. (2017). *Corporate communication*. London: Sage.

Crane, A., & Glozer, S. (2016). Researching CSR communication: Themes, opportunities and challenges. *Journal of Management Studies*, *53*(7), 1223–1252.

Czarniaswska, B. (2004). *Narratives in social science research*. London: Sage.

Dennis, A. R., & Kinney, S. T. (1998). Testing media richness theory in the new media: The effects of cues, feedback, and task equivocality. *Information Systems Research*, *9*(3), 256–274.

Du, S., Bhattacharya, C. B., & Sen, S. (2010). Maximizing business returns to corporate social responsibility (CSR): The role of CSR communication. *International Journal of Management Reviews*, *12*(1), 8–19.

Freeman, R. E. (1984). *Strategic management: A stakeholder approach*. Boston, MA: Pitman.

Frynas, J. G., & Yamahaki, C. (2016). Corporate social responsibility: Review and roadmap of theoretical perspectives. *Business Ethics: A European Review*, *25*(3), 258–285.

Haski-Leventhal, D. (2018). *Strategic corporate social responsibility: Tools and theories for responsible management*. London: Sage.

Heinrich, P. (2013). *CSR and communication*. Wiesbaden: Springer Gabler.

Johnson-Cramer, M. E., Cross, R. L., & Yan, A. (2003). Sources of fidelity in purposive organizational change: Lessons from a re-engineering case. *Journal of Management Studies, 40*(7), 1837–1870.

Kalla, H. K. (2005). Integrated internal communication: A multidisciplinary perspective. *Corporate Communications, 10*(4), 302–314.

Kaplan, A. M., & Haenlein, M. (2010). Users of the world, unite! The challenges and opportunities of social media. *Business Horizons, 53*(1), 59–68.

Kim, J. N., & Grunig, J. E. (2011). Problem solving and communicative action: A situational theory of problem solving. *Journal of Communication, 61*(1), 120–149.

Kuhn, T. R. (2008). A communicative theory of the firm: Developing an alternative perspective on intra-organizational power and stakeholder relationships. *Organization Studies, 29*(8/9), 1227–1254.

Levin, I. P., Schneider, S. L., & Gaeth, G. J. (1998). All frames are not created equal: A typology and critical analysis of framing effects. *Organizational Behavior and Human Decision Processes, 76*(2), 149–188.

Losee, R. M. (1999). Communication defined as complementary informative processes. *Journal of Information, Communication and Library Science, 5*(3), 1–15.

Maitlis, S., & Sonenshein, S. (2010). Sensemaking in crisis and change: Inspiration and insights from Weick (1988). *Journal of Management Studies, 47*(3), 551–580.

May, S. (2011). Organizational communication and corporate social responsibility. In Ø. Ihlen, J. L. Bartlett, & S. May (Eds.), *The handbook of communication and corporate social responsibility* (pp. 87–109). Malden, MA: Wiley-Blackwell.

Morsing, M., & Schultz, M. (2006) Corporate social responsibility: Stakeholder information, response and involvement strategies. *Business Ethics: A European Review, 15*(4), 323–338.

Morsing, M., Schultz, M., & Nielsen, K. U. (2008). The 'Catch 22' of communicating CSR: Findings from a Danish study. *Journal of Marketing Communications, 14*(2), 97–111.

Mory, L. (2014). *Soziale Verantwortung nach innen: Dimensionen, Wirkungsbeziehungen und Erfolgsgrößen einer internen CSR* [Internal social responsibility: Dimensions, impact relationships and success factors of an internal CSR]. New York: Springer.

Pedersen, E. R. (2006). Making corporate social responsibility (CSR) operable: How companies translate stakeholder dialogue into practice. *Business and Society Review, 111*(2), 137–163.

Quinn, L., & Dalton, M. (2009). Leading for sustainability: Implementing the tasks of leadership. *Corporate Governance: International Journal of Business in Society, 9*(1), 21–38.

Ramus, C. A., & Killmer, A. B. (2007). Corporate greening through prosocial extra role behaviours: A conceptual framework for employee motivation. *Business Strategy and the Environment, 16*(8), 554–570.

Ramus, C. A., & Steger, U. (2000). The roles of supervisory support behaviors and environmental policy in employee 'ecoinitiatives' at leading-edge European companies. *Academy of Management Journal, 43*, 605–626.

Reinsch Jr, N. L. (1996). Business communication: Present, past, and future. *Management Communication Quarterly, 10*(1), 27–49.

Roza, L., Haski-Leventhal, D. & Meijs, L. C. P. M. (2017). *Engaging your workforce in corporate social responsibility programs: Five strategies to drive engagement.* Philadelphia, PA: Satell Institute.

Schmitt, J., & Röttger, U. (2011). Corporate responsibility. In J. Raupp, S. Jarolimek, & F. Schultz (Eds.), *CSR handbook* (pp. 173–187). Wiesbaden: VS Verlag.

Short, J., Williams, E., & Christie, B. (1976). *The social psychology of telecommunications*. New York: John Wiley & Sons.

Smeltzer, L. R. (1996). Communication within the manager's context. *Management Communication Quarterly*, *10*(1), 5–26.

Tench, R., Sun, W., & Jones, B. (2014). Introduction: CSR communication as an emerging field of study. In R. Tench, W. Sun, & B. Jones (Eds.), *Communicating corporate social responsibility: Perspectives and practice* (pp. 3–25). Bingley, UK: Emerald.

Waddock, S., & Googins, B. K. (2011). The paradoxes of communicating corporate social responsibility. In Ø. Ihlen, J. L. Bartlett, & S. May (Eds.), *The handbook of communication and corporate social responsibility* (pp. 23–43). Malden, MA: Wiley-Blackwell.

Wagner, R. (2019). *Effective internal CSR communication: Sense and motivation for corporate social responsibility* [in German]. Wiesbaden: Springer Gabler.

Wehmeier, S., & Schultz, F. (2011). Communication and corporate social responsibility: A storytelling perspective. In Ø. Ihlen, J. L. Bartlett, & S. May (Eds.), *The handbook of communication and corporate social responsibility* (pp. 467–488). Malden, MA: Wiley-Blackwell.

Weick, K. E. (1995). *Sensemaking in organizations*. Thousand Oaks, CA: Sage.

7 Social Intrapreneurship: A New Horizon for Employee Engagement in CSR

Debbie Haski-Leventhal, Ante Glavas, and Lonneke Roza

Overview

Social intrapreneurship is a voluntary and informal employee-led process of utilising entrepreneurial principles to address social or environmental challenges while contributing to the objectives of established organisations. It has emerged in the last decade as a new phenomenon which attracted the attention of scholars and practitioners alike. As a process that melanges social impact and business knowledge and tools, social intrapreneurship is a subset of social entrepreneurship and business intrapreneurship. Social intrapreneurship occurs when employees innovate solutions for social and environmental issues, and, as such, it can help to enhance the connection between CSR and employee engagement. Consequently, this novel concept offers outstanding opportunities for companies, employees and community organisations. However, it also presents several challenges due to multiple goals and stakeholders. This chapter, therefore, discusses the emerging trend of social intrapreneurship in the context of this book to offer some insights for research and implications for practice.

Learning objectives

By the end of this chapter, readers should be able to:

- show that social intrapreneurship is an emerging manifestation of employee engagement in CSR
- demonstrate how social intrapreneurship contributes to employee engagement through CSR
- explain how it enables companies and employees to use social innovation to address social and environmental issues
- discuss how social intrapreneurship is built on social entrepreneurship and business intrapreneurship
- debate the related valuable opportunities and ongoing challenges that companies and employees need to recognise.

Introduction

Social intrapreneurship occurs when employees engage in social innovation while being employed by an organisation, usually a business (Kistruck & Beamish, 2010; Mair & Martí, 2006). This new concept has been capturing the minds of corporate social responsibility (CSR) practitioners (Davis & White, 2015; Grayson, McLaren, & Spitzeck, 2014) and scholars (Alt & Craig, 2016; Carrington, Zwick, & Neville, 2018; Halme, Lindeman, & Linna, 2012) due to its innovative nature. Social intrapreneurship is an emerging movement, captured with an increasing number of examples, case studies, bodies and organisation, such as Aspen's First Movers programme and the League of Social Intrapreneurs. It is significant because social intrapreneurship enables business organisations to connect to social impact opportunities (Conger, McMullen, Bergman, & York, 2018; Wry & Haugh, 2018), with the related benefits including innovation, improved reputation, increased employee engagement and reduced turnover. As such, social intrapreneurship can present a new opportunity for business to be more sustainable and impactful, and to address the sustainable development goals (Jenkins, 2018).

Despite the fast-growing interest in social intrapreneurship, more studies are needed (Kuratko, McMullen, Hornsby, & Jackson, 2017). To address this gap, this chapter will examine the related concepts of business intrapreneurship and social entrepreneurship and the merged concept of social intrapreneurship. We will cover the emerging literature on this topic to define and explain social intrapreneurship, detail its benefits and shed light on what helps to promote it. More specifically, we will discuss social intrapreneurship and employee engagement while using three case studies. These aspects will enable us to discuss the related challenges and opportunities. The chapter concludes with a discussion and implications for practice, particularly for businesses and CSR managers.

Based on the existing literature and three case studies, this chapter aims to answer the following research questions: What is social intrapreneurship and how does it relate to other concepts such as business intrapreneurship and social entrepreneurship? What are the related opportunities and challenges? What can companies do to enhance social intrapreneurship?

Literature review

Social intrapreneurship is a hybrid concept, mainly based on two previously developed concepts (Alt & Geradts, 2019): social entrepreneurship (Choi & Majumdar, 2014; Dacin, Dacin, & Tracey, 2011) and intrapreneurship (Kacperczyk, 2012). As it is usually encouraged by a corporation to create social impact, it also falls under the scholarship of CSR (Alt & Geradts, 2019; Campbell, 2007; Carroll, 1999). Social intrapreneurs occupy an intersectional space within the large corporate form at the crossroads of innovation, profit and social good (Belinfanti, 2015). They usually possess knowledge about the organisation and its market environment, hold entrepreneurial and social skills, and are driven by societal values to achieve social impact (Brenneke & Spitzeck, 2010; Hemingway, 2005).

As Alt and Geradts (2019) put forward, 'social intrapreneurship is a unique amalgam of concepts that relate to each element of the term: the social, the internal, and the entrepreneurial' (p. 1). Moreover, the authors state that, first, social intrapreneurship is driven by social responsibility to address social or environmental challenges, beyond the interests of private individuals and organisations (Alt & Geradts, 2019; Jenkins, 2018). Second, social intrapreneurship is led by employees, of an established organisation, usually with the support and encouragement of this organisation (Belinfanti, 2015). It occurs when an entrepreneurial employee develops a new product, service or business model to create value for society that is also profitable for the organisation itself (Jenkins, 2018). Third, it develops through entrepreneurial principles, based on the identification of both business and social opportunities (Shane & Venkataraman, 2000). Notably, social intrapreneurship is led by employees, on a voluntary basis (Davis & White, 2015). It is similar to the concept of corporate social entrepreneurship, which was defined by Austin, Leonard, Reficco, and Wei-Skillern (2006) as a process of extending the firm's domain of competence through an innovative leveraging of resources, aimed at the simultaneous creation of economic and social value. Subsequently, social intrapreneurs are often described as 'disruptive' because they devise new ways to tackle social problems, in a manner that disrupts traditional operating models or long-standing assumptions (Belinfanti, 2015).

Consequently, we build on the definition put forward by Alt and Geradts (2019, p. 2): 'social intrapreneurship [is] a discretionary and informal employee-led process of identification and exploitation of entrepreneurial opportunities that address social or environmental challenges while contributing to the objectives of established organizations'. With this definition in mind, we examine the related literature on social entrepreneurship, business intrapreneurship and CSR. We will then present three case studies of social intrapreneurship to discuss the related opportunities and challenges.

Social intrapreneurship and entrepreneurship

As a process that melanges social impact and business knowledge and tools, social intrapreneurship is a subset of social entrepreneurship (Cornwall, 1998; Dees, 1998). Social entrepreneurship is a process through which social and environmental issues are tackled via entrepreneurial avenues (Mair & Martí, 2006). It is a practice in which an entrepreneur sets out to address social problems by integrating business management skills with social sector acumen to yield a sustainable enterprise that produces both financial and social returns (a double bottom line) (Germak & Robinson, 2014). Social entrepreneurs are those change agents in the social sector who 'adopt a mission to create and sustain social value, recognise and relentlessly pursue new opportunities to serve that mission (and) engage in a process of continuous innovation, adaption and learning' (Dees, 1998, p. 4).

A social enterprise is usually established in order to create social value and address societal issues which markets and governments are unable to resolve (Di Domenico, Haugh, & Tracey, 2010; Rosenzweig, 2004). Subsequently, a social enterprise often operates in the middle of the spectrum between traditional not-for-profit organisations and traditional for-profits (Dees & Anderson, 2006). Therefore, the success of a social enterprise is driven by the financial sustainability of the enterprise and by its ability to achieve a defined social mission and impact (Di Domenico et al., 2010; Kickul & Lyons, 2016).

The social impact (or mission-related impact) is a crucial aspect of both social entrepreneurship and social intrapreneurship. It is defined as changes to 'people's way of life, their culture, community, political systems, environment, health and wellbeing, personal property and rights and their fears and aspirations' (Vanclay, 2003, p. 2). Further, Auerswald (2009, p. 52) described social impact as 'the creation of benefits or reductions of costs for society – through efforts to address societal needs and problems – in ways that go beyond the private gains and general benefits of market activity'.

However, while there are many similarities between social entrepreneurship and social intrapreneurship, differences between them also exist. Social entrepreneurship is usually led by the individual social entrepreneur, independent of any existing organisation, whereas social intrapreneurship is led by an employee *within* an established organisation, and sometimes with the support and encouragement of the employer (Belinfanti, 2015). Social intrapreneurs are thus challenged to advocate for their ideas to the organisational management team who may or may not be interested in and committed to socially responsible activities (Alt & Craig, 2016). In addition to the challenges every social entrepreneur faces, social intrapreneurs need to work within the existing framework of a for-profit company and convince gatekeepers of the essence of this work for the company and society. On the other hand, the existing resources of the company and the social intrapreneur's job security could ease the process and encourage more people to address social issues through the power of business.

Social intrapreneurship and business intrapreneurship

In addition to social entrepreneurship, social intrapreneurship is a subset of more conventional business intrapreneurship. The term intrapreneurship refers to a system that allows an employee to act like a business entrepreneur within a company or other organisation, leading to new ventures and capital (Kacperczyk, 2012). According to Antoncic and Hisrich (2001), intrapreneurship has four distinct dimensions: (1) the new-business-venturing dimension (pursuing and entering new businesses related to the firm's current products or markets); (2) the innovativeness dimension (the creation of new products, services and technologies); (3) the self-renewal dimension (strategy reformulation, reorganisation and organisational change); and (4) the proactivity dimension (top-management orientation in pursuing enhanced competitiveness, initiative and risk-taking, and competitive aggressiveness). Thus, intrapreneurship is viewed as being beneficial for the revitalisation and performance of corporations.

Intrapreneurship may lead to innovative new products that a company can sell. This was the case, for example, with Sony's PlayStation, invented by Ken Kutaragi, a Sony employee, who tinkered with his daughter's Nintendo. Kutaragi spent much time on this idea, but initially he did not have the support of Sony's management, who were hesitant to join a gaming industry they considered to be a waste of time. However, with the support of one senior employee, the PlayStation became one of Sony's most successful products, and Kutaragi later became the chairman and CEO of Sony Computer Entertainment (Alvisi, Narduzzo, & Zamarian, 2003).

However, there are major differences between social intrapreneurship and business intrapreneurship. While business intrapreneurship focuses on the expansion and diversification of current business, social intrapreneurship concentrates on the pursuit of social and environmental objectives. Consequently, when social intrapreneurship occurs in profit-maximising organisations, the multiple objectives of social intrapreneurial initiatives create ambiguity regarding the employee's identity and intended impact. While business intrapreneurs need to convince the company of the value of their innovation, such as in the case of Sony, social intrapreneurs need to extract more effort to convince internal and external stakeholders of the business and social value of their innovation. Internally, social intrapreneurs may be confronted by colleagues and managers who perceive such initiatives as insignificant 'philanthropic activities', disconnected from the business objectives. At the same time, external stakeholders may see it as impression management or 'greenwashing' (Tracey & Stott, 2017). Thus, social intrapreneurs need to meet the dual, and sometimes contradictory, expectations of various stakeholders, and this may be more challenging than business intrapreneurship or social entrepreneurship.

Social intrapreneurship, CSR and employee engagement

As social intrapreneurship is aimed at creating social value and addressing social challenges through a for-business organisation, it is closely related to the concept of CSR (Alt & Geradts, 2019). As it is usually done by an innovative employee who desires to contribute to society and make a difference, it is also closely related to employee engagement.

Social intrapreneurship can be an innovative way for companies to offer solutions to pressing global issues, while also serving their instrumental, moral and relational motives to do so (Aguilera, Rupp, Williams, & Ganapathi, 2007). It may also help companies to become more strategic in their CSR, offering a holistic approach and utilising the company's resources, knowledge, talent, intellect and skills to create a positive social impact (Haski-Leventhal, 2018). Furthermore, social intrapreneurship is an effective way of engaging internal stakeholders in the company's CSR, to help it achieve its social mission, in addition to its profit mission (Girschik, 2020).

Social intrapreneurship can lead to a high level of employee engagement, which is a desirable condition, with an organisational purpose, indicating employee involvement, commitment, enthusiasm, focused effort and energy (Macey & Schneider, 2008). Employee engagement is often perceived as both a state of mind and a behaviour that link employees and employers beyond formalised role requirements (Saks, 2006). As per this book, CSR can help engage employees by showing them that their employer 'cares' (about them and about society) and through activities which provide social affiliation, pride and purposefulness, such as corporate volunteering (Haski-Leventhal, Roza, & Meijs, 2017).

Social intrapreneurship can be a particularly effective way of engaging employees in and through CSR (see Chapter 3 by Glavas and Willness). According to engagement theory (Kahn, 1990; Rich, LePine, & Crawford, 2010), the pathways for engagement include meaningfulness and purpose in work, psychological availability and psychological safety. Social intrapreneurship might foster meaningfulness and greater purpose in work for those employees who desire that their work contributes to addressing societal and environmental challenges (Aguinis & Glavas, 2019). In addition, companies high in CSR have been found to better support their employees, thus improving psychological safety (Ditlev-Simonsen, 2015; Glavas & Kelley, 2014; Shen & Benson, 2016). Finally, psychological availability has been found to be related to belief in one's self, which in turn influences those who try to advance social issues in a firm (Sonenshein, DeCelles, & Dutton, 2014).

Furthermore, social intrapreneurship is a form of job crafting (Wrzesniewski & Dutton, 2001). In job crafting, employees proactively expand or modify their work roles in order to include aspects that they deem to be important (Bakker, 2010). Similarly, employees might include CSR as part of their role in a company as a way to be more engaged in CSR (Godkin, 2015).

Based on self-determination theory (Ryan & Deci, 2000), social intrapreneurship can assist in meeting the three vital needs of employees: autonomy, competence and relatedness (Rupp, Shao, Skarlicki, Paddock, Kim, & Nadisic, 2018). Accordingly, humans thrive when they feel competent, autonomous and related to others around them (Deci & Ryan, 2000). The need for autonomy implies acting with a sense of volition, having the experience of choice and feeling like the initiator of one's own actions. Competence refers to feeling like one can master and accomplish tasks. The need for relatedness means feeling connected with others and having meaningful relationships (Ryan & Deci, 2000). Thus, social intrapreneurship can help meet employees' needs, as it is usually led by the employee on a voluntary basis (autonomy), using and increasing one's innovation, skills and talent (competence), in order to help others in the community (relatedness). This, in turn, can lead to high levels of job satisfaction, affective commitment and retention (Deci & Ryan, 2000).

Compared to other ways of engaging employees in CSR, including corporate volunteering (Rodell, Breitsohl, Schröder, & Keating, 2016), payroll giving (Haski-Leventhal, 2013) and even employee-led CSR (Haski-Leventhal et al., 2017), social intrapreneurship can be a powerful and impactful way of engaging employees in the company's social efforts. It can have a spillover effect when other employees are exposed to social innovation led by their peers, with the support of their employer (Wang, Tong, Takeuchi, & George, 2016). However, it may be a more challenging channel of involving employees in CSR as social intrapreneurship requires entrepreneurial action and innovation as driving forces (Shepherd & Patzelt, 2011), which is not achievable by all employees. That being said, companies may imple-ment the research on encouraging business intrapreneurship (e.g., Kacper-czyk, 2012) to learn how to encourage innovation and entrepreneurial spirit among employees, while also learning how to create a shared social purpose and impact of the organisation (Kuratko, Hornsby, & McMullen, 2011).

CSR can offer a strong platform for social innovation and intrapreneur-ship, as it provides employees with the security and safety net that some social entrepreneurs may lack (Dees, 1998; Germak & Robinson, 2014). Using the company's time and resources, with the support and encouragement of the company, may help social entrepreneurs to overcome their lack of resources. However, CSR programmes often remain reactive instead of proac-tively supporting social intrapreneurs and offering investment opportunities which could maximise their impact (York & Venkataraman, 2010).

Furthermore, social intrapreneurs are challenged to situate their novel ideas in relation to existing CSR programmes and goals, which may be con-fining rather than supportive of innovation (Bansal, Jiang, & Jung, 2015). Social intrapreneurs often need to convince CSR managers of the impor-tance of their ideas by using the required language and the company's values, mission and purpose. In some cases, this may be challenging, par-ticularly if CSR is narrowly defined within the company.

Some employees, therefore, begin to seek external support and resources to succeed in their endeavours, such as through impact investing. Impact investing refers to the provision of financial and other kinds of support to social enterprises and social impact organisations with the aim of gaining a social and financial return on investment (Agrawal & Hockerts, 2019). As impact investing is slowly becoming part of CSR (Höchstädter & Scheck, 2015), with an increasing number of companies adding impact investing to their CSR programmes and their socially responsible investment, there is a great opportunity for companies to invest in their own social intrapreneurs. Providing funding and grants for social impact which encourages social innovation can be a powerful way of aligning social intrapreneurship with CSR. Many companies, such as Accenture, Deloitte, NN Group and Book-ing.com, offer internal online platforms where employees are encouraged to contribute to the CSR goals of the company. Through these platforms, employees are stimulated to act upon their own personal values in line with the corporate values, have autonomy to choose to work on what they find important and are facilitated in seeking support by their colleagues in terms of time, expertise, funds or other resources needed for their project at hand. Another, more embedded, way to facilitate employees in developing social intrapreneurial ideas is to give employees resources (such as funding and other corporate resources) to develop ideas that are in line with their sus-tainability and/or social innovation ambitions. For instance, General Electric facilitates social intrapreneurs from within the existing structure rather than setting up new divisions or specific programmes. It is stimulated across divisions such as Energy, Technology, and Consumer & Industrial (Aguinis & Glavas, 2013).

Three social intrapreneurship examples

A first example comes from the USA dairy industry and highlights the point that social intrapreneurship can take different forms. Quite often, social intrapreneurs are portrayed as a lone wolf battling for CSR causes within a corporation. However, in the case of Erin Fitzgerald, this occurred within an industry association of complex stakeholders, encompassing $125 billion in annual revenue and ranging from production, processing and transport to retail. Erin Fitzgerald worked within the industry's central organisation, Dairy Management Inc., and convinced industry leadership to create an industry-wide plan for being socially and environmentally responsible. What started as an idea evolved over the next decade, during which she initiated 10 environmental initiatives across the value chain, valued at $250 million. In this case, an individual intrapreneur who was driven by the purpose and values of CSR, created CSR innovations within the existing system. Importantly, this initiative was rooted in business logic and was in line with the dominant economic logic of the institution. Notably, key stakeholders joined the effort and worked together, forming a sustainability council comprised of 125 representative organisations in the value chain. Thus, it took a combination of individual and contextual factors to succeed.

A second example comes from the Netherlands. In 2013, two members of staff at ABN AMRO, one of the largest financial services organisations in the country, led an initiative that later became known as Circle.[1] Dick Lussing, the then facility services manager, and Hans de Jong, a senior project manager, imagined a meeting place in the heart of the business centre of Amsterdam, in which sustainability was core. This was to serve the company, the business community in which it operated and the general community as well. It was meant to educate and inspire about conducting business in the most sustainable way, following the principles of circular economy. This project required convincing not only the company's leaders, but also the builders and architects with whom they worked. Working with key stakeholders, the group was determined in its decision to move forward with a sustainable mindset. The team was extended to four social intrapreneurs and took a radical decision, to bring the process to a halt and only work with people who were prepared to deliver on the sustainability goals. The principles were clear: minimal single use of raw materials, being as energy-neutral as possible and with everything designed to be disassembled later. Circle opened its doors in 2017 with its sole purpose to accelerate the transition to a circular economy. It has exhibition spaces to educate on circular economy (where even the chairs are made from recycled materials and fabric from old cloth), a restaurant with the ambition of reducing food waste, and coffee stalls which employ people with hearing impairment where customers learn to use sign language to order their coffee.

A third example occurred in Australia, taking place in Westpac, one of the four largest banks in Australia. As part of its CSR and employee engagement, Westpac allowed teams and departments to choose the targets of their corporate volunteering and giving. Through social intrapreneurship, one of their employees led a new social enterprise, 'I am a Boat Person Inc.'. Daniel Heycox, ER Consultant, Employee Relations and Policy at Westpac, wanted to address the issue of refugees in Australia, and particularly the negative perception of them as 'boat people'. While working at Westpac, Heycox innovated his idea and established a not-for-profit organisation, aimed at helping refugees. Initially, the organisation offered general help to refugees. However, through work and consultancy with his peers and employer, Heycox refined the idea, and the organisation evolved to offer financial literacy to refugees. Consequently, this social intrapreneurship is aligned with what Westpac does and can be seen as an example of strategic CSR (Haski-Leventhal, 2018). Heycox, who still works at Westpac while being the co-founder and managing director of the not-for-profit, managed to work with his entire Westpac team to support this organisation, through donations of time, skills, money and other resources. Westpac became a major sponsor of this organisation.

Opportunities and challenges

The unique nature of social intrapreneurship – as it integrates profits and income, employment and entrepreneurship, and internal and external work – presents several outstanding opportunities and challenges for companies, employees and the social sector.

Opportunities

For **employers**, there is an incredible opportunity to create innovative solutions to social issues while promoting the brand of the company, its innovation level, employee engagement and performance, and its stakeholder integration. For example, social intrapreneurship can enhance corporate social innovation, which is a strategy that combines a unique set of corporate assets (innovation capacities, marketing skills, managerial acumen, employee engagement, scale, etc.) to co-create breakthrough solutions to complex economic, social and environmental issues (Mirvis & Googins, 2017; Mirvis, Herrera, Googins, & Albareda, 2016). In doing so, it enables the firm to become more innovative and disruptive in general – both sought-after capacities in today's market. As such, Venn and Berg (2013) assert that social intrapreneurship can create a competitive advantage for companies.

Furthermore, social intrapreneurship can be a vital opportunity for **employees** to use their skills and passion and do something meaningful through their work. Mirvis and Googins (2018) argue that employees, particularly younger ones, are eager to engage in social innovation and meaningful work. According to Myler (2013), intrapreneurship is not just a way of engaging employees, but is also the next level of employee engagement. He claims that while the engaged employee is emotionally connected to the workplace, the intrapreneur is connected to the 'bigger picture' and uses existing assets to address market problems. Social intrapreneurship can be seen as the next level up, because it also helps to address a social or an environmental problem and engage employees through a sense of meaningfulness (Aguinis & Glavas, 2019). As such, social intrapreneurship can benefit interested employees through the opportunity to do creative and innovative work, engage with others, and apply organisational and personal assets to address an essential issue. This, in turn, can help to facilitate a sense of engagement, pride, affiliation, meaningfulness, purposefulness and well-being.

Finally, social intrapreneurship presents a remarkable opportunity for the **community** and the social sector to partner with corporations in a novel way. While the community has been working with the business sector for decades through philanthropy and CSR, social intrapreneurship can open up a new pathway for collaboration. Moving beyond money or even skill-based volunteering, community organisations can utilise corporate innovation and talent to find novel solutions to environmental and social problems. Social intrapreneurship can also be a form of collaboration between the firm and other organisations, both for-profits and not-for-profits (Mirvis & Googins, 2018). Another pathway to benefit the broader community from social intrapreneurship in the long run is by influencing the behaviour of partners within the company's value chain. The above Dutch example of Circle demonstrates that the intrapreneurs of ABN AMRO were able to stimulate and push for more sustainable decisions among their value chain. Indeed, the architect, the construction builder, the municipality, the facilities services organisation and the restaurant were pushed to think beyond their normal scope to truly adopt circular thinking in their contributions to Circle.

Challenges

One of the related challenges of social intrapreneurship is social value creation being **peripheral to organisational functioning** (Alt & Geradts, 2019). When social intrapreneurs operate within organisations that have profit maximisation as their primary goal (Alt & Geradts, 2019; Santos, 2013), it can be challenging to work on an initiative which is outside the realm of the organisation. While companies may lead activities that correspond to a social logic, these are usually less accepted than activities that correspond to the dominant commercial logic (Besharov & Smith, 2014; Margolis & Walsh, 2003). We need to further shed light on how social intrapreneurs depart from the 'business as usual' approach to navigate the path dependencies of profit-maximising organisations despite institutional pressures. The path to success may, therefore, require strategic skills, emotional intelligence and labour, risk taking and excellent networking capacity (Anderson & Bateman, 2000; Wickert & De Bakker, 2018). As Aguinis and Glavas (2013) explained, CSR can be embedded or peripheral and the challenge for social intrapreneurs is shifting their CSR initiatives from the periphery to them becoming embedded in their institutions.

A second challenge, as put forward by Alt and Geradts (2019), is based on social entrepreneurship and social intrapreneurship being **hybrid activities with multiple goals**. At the very least, such activities have financial sustainability and social impact as the two main goals, and these two may contradict each other (Dees, 1998; Kacperczyk, 2012). Specifically, social intrapreneurship usually has an organisational goal or needs to align with the general mission and goals of the organisation in which the social intrapreneur operates (Belinfanti, 2015). Social intrapreneurial initiatives are often considered ambiguous, as they do not fit the established templates for relationships between business and society. Consequently, the legitimacy of social intrapreneurship as a distinct category may come into question (Conger et al., 2018).

Third, by its nature, social intrapreneurship requires a **multi-stakeholder approach**, which can be challenging for some people and organisations. While social intrapreneurship may come across as individual employees working by themselves to create innovative solutions and social impact, it is rarely the case. Social intrapreneurship is usually done in teams and/or in collaboration with other organisations, such as the aforementioned community organisations (Mirvis & Googins, 2018). This can be both an asset and a challenge due to the advantages and disadvantages of working with others (Weller, Boyd, & Cumin, 2014). For example, research shows that some CSR programmes lack the required focus on the needs of community organisations (Lee, 2010). Furthermore, the amalgamation of multiple goals and stakeholders may challenge social intrapreneurs in gaining legitimacy. Social intrapreneurs must convince internal stakeholders that their initiatives are a legitimate way to contribute to their organisations, and external stakeholders that these initiatives create social value.

Another major challenge for social intrapreneurs is that often CSR is **extra-role** and may create additional demands on employees, their time, resources and focus. Consequently, their core role may suffer, and it may lead to burnout (Aguinis & Glavas, 2019). Glavas (2016) found that the more CSR is perceived as extra-role, the weaker the relationship is between CSR and employee engagement. The reason for this is that CSR is often peripheral and not embedded in a company's core strategy and daily activities (Aguinis & Glavas, 2013), resulting in employees having to devote time outside of their regular daily work in order to address CSR – employees might be motivated to do so initially, but after a while it can lead to resource and psychological drain on them (Aguinis & Glavas, 2019).

In addition to the above, Jenkins (2018) details another three challenges: (1) the 'corporate immune system', where systems and executives are focused mainly on defending and expanding existing businesses, rather than starting new ones; (2) the opportunity cost of investment: the results of innovation are never certain, and this uncertainty may increase in the context of social and environmental issues; and (3) capability: social intrapreneurs may work in various roles and not necessarily possess the required knowledge and skills to create a sustainable social enterprise.

Discussion

As an increasing number of companies aim nowadays to address social and environmental issues, create social impact and help to achieve the sustainable development goals, social intrapreneurship can become a useful force in attaining these ambitions. While it is not an entirely new phenomenon, it is only in the last decade or so that scholars and practitioners have begun to name it as such and draw significant attention to it (Jenkins, 2018).

It is a thought-provoking concept which integrates business intrapreneurship and social entrepreneurship (Belinfanti, 2015), two other concepts that have emerged in the last few decades. Both hold a promise of innovation and ground-breaking thinking, but the former aims at expanding an existing company and its profit, while the latter exists to create social impact. Both have similarities and differences to social intrapreneurship. Business intrapreneurship is also led by an employee within an existing company, but its goal is profit; while social entrepreneurship shares the same social goals as social intrapreneurship, but it is done outside an existing organisation. Figure 7.1 summarises the related concept and the positioning of social intrapreneurship.

Based on our cases and descriptions in this chapter, we distinguish between three social intrapreneurial strategies. First, social intrapreneurs may develop ideas that contribute directly to the value chain or the core business of the company. Here, the aim of the social intrapreneur is to make the company more sustainable and, by doing so, the social intrapreneur creates social impact. Innovative companies, such as DSM, encourage social intrapreneurship as part of their innovation strategy. Second, social intrapreneurs develop ideas that stimulate sustainable and inclusive practices among clients or business partners. Here, social intrapreneurs actively take up projects that involve clients. In the example of ABN AMRO and Circle, the social intrapreneurs did not only want to create a 'product' for

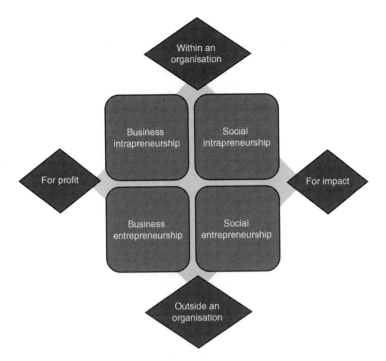

Figure 7.1. The social intrapreneurship model

ABN AMRO (i.e., Circle) that was fully based on sustainable principles, but also to motivate their business partners and the Amsterdam municipality in going beyond their current sustainability practices. Lastly, social intra-preneurs develop ideas that have business relevance, but are developed to directly contribute to the community without changing commercial activities in the market. This social intrapreneurial strategy includes mostly charitable or non-profit initiatives of employees.

As such, social intrapreneurship is particularly significant in the context of employee engagement in and through CSR. It offers a novel way to ena-ble employees to work with a sense of purpose and to utilise their talent, skills and innovation to address a social problem that matters to them. With the support of the firm, employees can work collaboratively and creatively on a project that is meaningful – to them, the company and society. This, in turn, can lead to higher levels of motivation, engagement, recruitment and retention. Using the self-determination theory (Ryan & Deci, 2000), we showed that social intrapreneurship can address the three primary needs of autonomy, competence and relatedness. In summary, social intrapreneur-ship can be a powerful and impactful tool to engage employees and impact the world.

However, based on the emerging literature on social intrapreneurship, it appears that this new approach to addressing societal issues through the power of business and entrepreneurship is a complex one. It is based on multiple goals, and the social intrapreneur usually needs to work with several stakeholders, each with a different mindset, language and goals. This position may be difficult and frustrating at times, and unique resources and support are required to advance social intrapreneurship. Consequently, while social intrapreneurship presents remarkable opportunities for companies, employees and the community, it is not without its challenges. Being peripheral to organisational functioning and including hybrid activities with multiple goals and stakeholders are two of its most crucial challenges.

Research has yet to capture this new phenomenon and all its aspects and consequences. We need empirical studies to capture the determinants, motivations, processes, underlying mechanisms, outcomes and impact of social intrapreneurship. This should be done on the three levels of analysis – micro (the social intrapreneur), meso (the organisation within which social intrapreneurs operate) and macro (society and the community). Quantitative and qualitative studies are needed to capture this process and the relationship between the aforementioned aspects (e.g., motivation and impact). Furthermore, longitudinal research and process models are needed as social intrapreneurship is a process that unfolds over time. Finally, to advance the field, what is needed is an understanding of the theoretical boundaries of social intrapreneurship, especially in terms of how similar to and different from extant theory it is (e.g., business intrapreneurship and social entrepreneurship, as we have put forward in this chapter).

Implications for practice

As social intrapreneurship gains momentum, an increasing number of companies become interested in cultivating it within their organisation. To do so effectively, the first important step is to demonstrate a holistic approach to social responsibility, with socially responsible identity and behaviour (Haski-Leventhal et al., 2017), which can encourage employees to become part of this approach. This will address the major challenge of social intrapreneurship being peripheral to organisational functioning.

Furthermore, companies should proactively encourage social intrapreneurship by presenting it, recognising it and promoting the existing work of social intrapreneurs. Companies can demonstrate how social intrapreneurship supports their overall efforts to create a positive impact and tie it to their CSR. For example, social intrapreneurship can become an essential part of the company's stakeholder integration and work towards the sustainable development goals. It can be an integral aspect of the firm's sustainability and assist it in finding innovative solutions for climate change and the environment.

Jenkins (2018) suggests several ways in which companies can support their employees who want to become social intrapreneurs. First, it is vital to offer financial support and access to funding. This helps intrapreneurs to overcome the opportunity cost of investment. Ideally, the goal is not to set up a new investment process, but to provide resources which intrapreneurs can use to develop their ideas to the point that they compete successfully in existing processes. Second, it is essential to offer capability building. Intrapreneurs value coaching to help them solve problems as they arise. Third, social intrapreneurship benefits from a strong network, and companies can aid social intrapreneurship by leveraging their existing network of partners and stakeholders to start up and maintain a social venture.

In addition to these valuable recommendations, we suggest three further ways of supporting social intrapreneurship. First, companies could set up an in-house incubator and accelerator for employees who want to start a social enterprise. Such an incubator would be more suitable than the general incubators people can join, as it would help the social intrapreneur to align with the company's goals and CSR. Second, companies could assist their social intrapreneurs in navigating through multiple goals and stakeholders. This is one of the major challenges of social intrapreneurship due to the requirement of addressing multiple goals and people. For example, companies could use their in-house training facilities to train employees in pitching their ideas to various parties. Finally, in addition to the holistic approach, companies need to show support for social intrapreneurship from the top. The emerging literature on the topic shows that often social intrapreneurs are not supported by their managers and/or by heads of the company. A CEO who believes in CSR and social impact, who leads by example and 'walks the talk', will encourage and support social intrapreneurship.

Conclusion

Social intrapreneurship is a fascinating new phenomenon that integrates exciting ideas, such as innovation, sustainable development, social impact and creativity. It offers a new pathway for those companies that want to be more responsible and impactful (i.e., for CSR). It offers an opportunity to engage employees in CSR like never before, with a genuine opportunity to solve and address society's most significant issues. It also presents an opportunity for community organisations and not-for-profits to find new ways to collaborate with business and enhance the social causes they promote. As it is an emerging concept, additional research and managerial practices are required for social intrapreneurship to increase its visibility and impact.

Questions for students

1. How and why should companies promote social intrapreneurship?
2. Why should employees get involved in social intrapreneurship, and how?
3. Why and how is social intrapreneurship connected to employee engagement through CSR?
4. What other opportunities and challenges arise from social intrapreneurship?
5. Find an example of social intrapreneurship from your country that is not mentioned in this chapter. What makes it an interesting example of social intrapreneurship? What are the related benefits and challenges in this example?

Note

1. This is a summary of the case description found at https://circl.nl/themakingof/en.

References

Agrawal, A., & Hockerts, K. (2019). Impact investing: Review and research agenda. *Journal of Small Business & Entrepreneurship, 3*, 1–29.

Aguilera, R. V., Rupp, D. E., Williams, C. A., & Ganapathi, J. (2007). Putting the S back in corporate social responsibility: A multilevel theory of social change in organizations. *Academy of Management Review, 32*(3), 836–863.

Aguinis, H., & Glavas, A. (2013). Embedded versus peripheral corporate social responsibility: Psychological foundations. *Industrial and Organizational Psychology: Perspectives on Science and Practice, 6*, 314–332.

Aguinis, H., & Glavas, A. (2019). On corporate social responsibility, sensemaking, and the search for meaningfulness through work. *Journal of Management, 45*, 1057–1086.

Alt, E., & Craig, J. B. (2016). Selling issues with solutions: Igniting social intrapreneurship in for-profit organizations. *Journal of Management Studies, 53*(5), 794–820.

Alt, E., & Geradts, T. (2019). *Social intrapreneurship: Unique challenges and opportunities for future research*. Paper presented at the 79th annual meeting of the Academy of Management, Boston, MA, July. Retrieved from https://journals.aom.org/doi/pdf/10.5465/AMBPP.2019.188.

Alvisi, A., Narduzzo, A., & Zamarian, M. (2003). PlayStation and the power of unexpected consequences. *Information Communication & Society, 6*(4), 608–627.

Anderson, L. M., & Bateman, T. S. (2000). Individual environmental initiative: Championing natural environmental issues in US business organizations. *Academy of Management Journal, 43*(4), 548–570.

Antoncic, B., & Hisrich, R. D. (2001). Intrapreneurship: Construct refinement and cross-cultural validation. *Journal of Business Venturing, 16*(5), 495–527.

Auerswald, P. (2009). Creating social value. *Stanford Social Innovation Review, 7*(2), 51–55.

Austin, J., Leonard, H., Reficco, E., & Wei-Skillern, J. (2006). Corporate social entrepreneurship: A new vision for CSR. In M. Epstein & K. Hanson (Eds.), *The accountable corporation* (pp. 237–248). Westport, CT: Praeger.

Bakker, A. B. (2010). Engagement and 'job crafting': Engaged employees create their own great place to work. In S. L. Albrecht (Ed.), *Handbook of employee engagement: Perspectives, issues, research and practice* (pp. 229–244). Northampton, MA: Edward Elgar.

Bansal, P., Jiang, G. F., & Jung, J. C. (2015). Managing responsibly in tough economic times: Strategic and tactical CSR during the 2008–2009 global recession. *Long Range Planning, 48*(2), 69–79.

Belinfanti, T. C. (2015). Contemplating the gap-filling role of social intrapreneurship. *Oregon Law Review, 94*, 67–107.

Besharov, M. L., & Smith, W. K. (2014). Multiple institutional logics in organizations: Explaining their varied nature and implications. *Academy of Management Review, 39*(3), 364–381.

Brenneke, M., & Spitzeck, H. (2010). Social intrapreneurs: Bottom-up social innovation. *International Review of Entrepreneurship, 8*(2), 157–176.

Campbell, J. L. (2007). Why would corporations behave in socially responsible ways? An institutional theory of corporate social responsibility. *Academy of Management Review, 32*(3), 946–967.

Carrington, M., Zwick, D., & Neville, B. (2018). Activism and abdication on the inside: The effect of everyday practice on corporate responsibility. *Journal of Business Ethics*, online first. Retrieved from https://link.springer.com/article/10.1007/s10551-018-3814-5.

Carroll, A. B. (1999). Corporate social responsibility: Evolution of a definitional construct. *Business & Society, 38*(3), 268–295.

Choi, N., & Majumdar, S. (2014). Social entrepreneurship as an essentially contested concept: Opening a new avenue for systematic future research. *Journal of Business Venturing, 29*(3), 363–376.

Conger, M., McMullen, J. S., Bergman Jr, B. J., & York, J. G. (2018). Category membership, identity control, and the re-evaluation of prosocial opportunities. *Journal of Business Venturing, 33*(2), 179–206.

Cornwall, J. R. (1998). The entrepreneur as a building block for community. *Journal of Developmental Entrepreneurship, 3*(2), 141–149.

Dacin, M. T., Dacin, P. A., & Tracey, P. (2011). Social entrepreneurship: A critique and future directions. *Organization Science, 22*(5), 1203–1213.

Davis, G. F., & White, C. J. (2015). *Changing your company from the inside out: A guide for social intrapreneurs*. Boston, MA: Harvard Business Review Press.

Deci, E. L., & Ryan, R. M. (2000). The 'what' and 'why' of goal pursuits: Human needs and the self-determination of behavior. *Psychological Inquiry, 11*(4), 227–268.

Dees, J. G. (1998). *The meaning of social entrepreneurship*. Retrieved from www.redalmarza.cl/ing/pdf/TheMeaningofsocialEntrepreneurship.pdf.

Dees, J. G., & Anderson, B. B. (2006). Framing a theory of social entrepreneurship: Building on two schools of practice and thought. *Research on Social Entrepreneurship: Understanding and Contributing to an Emerging Field: ARNOVA Occasional Paper Series, 1*(3), 39–66.

Di Domenico, M., Haugh, H., & Tracey, P. (2010). Social bricolage: Theorizing social value creation in social enterprises. *Entrepreneurship Theory and Practice, 34*(4), 681–703.

Ditlev-Simonsen, C. D. (2015). The relationship between Norwegian and Swedish employees' perception of corporate social responsibility and affective commitment. *Business & Society, 54*(2), 229–253.

Germak, A. J., & Robinson, J. A. (2014). Exploring the motivation of nascent social entrepreneurs. *Journal of Social Entrepreneurship, 5*(1), 5–21.

Girschik, V. (2020). Shared responsibility for societal problems: The role of internal activists in reframing corporate responsibility. *Business & Society, 59*(1), 34–66.

Glavas, A., & Kelley, K. (2014). The effects of perceived corporate social responsibility on employee attitudes. *Business Ethics Quarterly, 24*, 165–202.

Godkin, L. (2015). Mid-management, employee engagement, and the generation of reliable sustainable corporate social responsibility. *Journal of Business Ethics, 130*, 15–28.

Grayson, D., McLaren, M., & Spitzeck, H. (2014). *Social intrapreneurism and all that jazz.* Sheffield: Greenleaf.

Halme, M., Lindeman, S., & Linna, P. (2012). Innovation for inclusive business: Intrapreneurial bricolage in multinational corporations. *Journal of Management Studies, 49*(4), 743–784.

Haski-Leventhal, D. (2013). Employee engagement in CSR: The case of payroll giving in Australia. *Corporate Social Responsibility and Environmental Management, 20*(2), 113–128.

Haski-Leventhal, D. (2018). *Strategic corporate social responsibility: Tools and theories for responsible management.* London: Sage.

Haski-Leventhal, D., Roza, L., & Meijs, L. C. (2017). Congruence in corporate social responsibility: Connecting the identity and behavior of employers and employees. *Journal of Business Ethics, 143*(1), 35–51.

Hemingway, C. A. (2005). Personal values as a catalyst for corporate social entrepreneurship. *Journal of Business Ethics, 60*(3), 233–249.

Höchstädter, A. K., & Scheck, B. (2015). What's in a name? An analysis of impact investing understandings by academics and practitioners. *Journal of Business Ethics, 132*(2), 449–475.

Jenkins, B. (2018). Cultivating the social intrapreneur. *Stanford Social Innovation Review.* Retrieved from https://ssir.org/articles/entry/cultivating_the_social_intrapreneur.

Kacperczyk, A. J. (2012). Opportunity structures in established firms: Entrepreneurship versus intrapreneurship in mutual funds. *Administrative Science Quarterly, 57*(3), 484–521.

Kahn, W. A. (1990). Psychological conditions of personal engagement and disengagement at work. *Academy of Management Journal, 33*, 692–724.

Kickul, J., & Lyons, T. S. (2016). *Understanding social entrepreneurship: The relentless pursuit of mission in an ever changing world.* New York: Routledge.

Kistruck, G. M., & Beamish, P. W. (2010). The interplay of form, structure, and embeddedness in social intrapreneurship. *Entrepreneurship Theory and Practice, 34*(4), 735–761.

Kuratko, D. F., Hornsby, J. S., & McMullen, J. S. (2011). Corporate entrepreneurship with a purpose: Exploring the antecedents to corporate social entrepreneurship. *Academy of Management Annual Meeting Proceedings*, 1–6. Retrieved from https://doi.org/10.5465/AMBPP.2011.65869702.

Kuratko, D. F., McMullen, J. S., Hornsby, J. S., & Jackson, C. (2017). Is your organization conducive to the continuous creation of social value? Toward a social corporate entrepreneurship scale. *Business Horizons, 60*(3), 271–283.

Lee, L. (2010). Corporate volunteering: Considering multiple stakeholders. *Third Sector Review, 16*(1), 87–104.

Macey, W. H., & Schneider, B. (2008). The meaning of employee engagement. *Industrial and Organizational Psychology, 1*(1), 3–30.

Mair, J., & Martí, I. (2006). Social entrepreneurship research: A source of explanation, prediction, and delight. *Journal of World Business, 41*(1), 36–44.

Margolis, J. D., & Walsh, J. P. (2003). Misery loves companies: Rethinking social initiatives by business. *Administrative Science Quarterly, 48*(2), 268–305.

Mirvis, P., & Googins, B. (2017). The new business of business: Innovating for a better world. *The Conference Board.* Retrieved from www.conference-board.org/retrievefile.cfm?filename=TCB-GT-V2N1-The-New-Business-of-Business1.pdf&type=subsite.

Mirvis, P., & Googins, B. (2018). Engaging employees as social innovators. *California Management Review, 60*(4), 25–50.

Mirvis, P., Herrera, M. E. B., Googins, B., & Albareda, L. (2016). Corporate social innovation: How firms learn to innovate for the greater good. *Journal of Business Research, 69*(11), 5014–5021.

Myler, L. (2013). Beyond employee engagement: Why one intrapreneur is worth a hundred 'engaged' employees. *Forbes.* Retrieved from www.forbes.com/sites/larrymyler/2013/09/13/beyond-employee-engagement-why-one-intrapreneur-is-worth-a-hundred-engaged-employees/#38649ea7736c.

Rich, B. L., LePine, J. A., & Crawford, E. R. (2010). Job engagement: Antecedents and effects on job performance. *Academy of Management, 53*, 617–635.

Rodell, J., Breitsohl, H., Schröder, M., & Keating, D. J. (2016). Employee volunteering: A review and framework for future research. *Journal of Management, 42*(1), 55–84.

Rosenzweig, W. (2004). *Double bottom line project report: Assessing social impact in double bottom line ventures.* Retrieved from https://escholarship.org/uc/item/80n4f1mf.

Rupp, D. E., Shao, R., Skarlicki, D. P., Paddock, E. L., Kim, T.-Y., & Nadisic, T. (2018). Corporate social responsibility and employee engagement: The moderating role of CSR-specific relative autonomy and individualism. *Journal of Organizational Behavior, 39*(5), 559–579.

Ryan, R. M., & Deci, E. L. (2000). Self-determination theory and the facilitation of intrinsic motivation, social development, and well-being. *American Psychologist, 55*(1), 68–78.

Saks, A. M. (2006). Antecedents and consequences of employee engagement. *Journal of Managerial Psychology, 21*(7), 600–619.

Santos, F. (2013). The rise of the social intrapreneur. *INSEAD Knowledge.* Retrieved from https://doi.org/10.1126/science.aab1422.

Shane, S., & Venkataraman, S. (2000). The promise of entrepreneurship as a field of research. *Academy of Management Review, 25*(1), 217–226.

Shen, J., & Benson, J. (2016). When CSR is a social normal: How socially responsible human resource management affects employee work behavior. *Journal of Management, 42*, 1723–1746.

Shepherd, D. A., & Patzelt, H. (2011). The new field of sustainable entrepreneurship: Studying entrepreneurial action linking 'what is to be sustained' with 'what is to be developed'. *Entrepreneurship Theory and Practice, 35*(1), 137–163.

Sonenshein, S., DeCelles, K. A., & Dutton, J. E. (2014). It's not easy being green: The role of self-evaluations in explaining support of environmental issues. *Academy of Management Journal, 57*, 7–37.

Tracey, P., & Stott, N. (2017). Social innovation: A window on alternative ways of organizing and innovation. *Innovation, 19*(1), 51–60.

Vanclay, F. (2003). *International principles for social impact assessment.* Retrieved from www.docente.unicas.it/useruploads/000507/files/2012-13/social_ia.pdf.

Venn, R., & Berg, N. (2013). Building competitive advantage through social intrapreneurship. *South Asian Journal of Global Business Research, 2*(1), 104–127.

Wang, H., Tong, L., Takeuchi, R., & George, G. (2016). Corporate social responsibility: An overview and new research directions. *Academy of Management Journal, 59*(2), 534–544.

Weller, J., Boyd, M., & Cumin, D. (2014). Teams, tribes and patient safety: Overcoming barriers to effective teamwork in healthcare. *Postgraduate Medical Journal, 90*(1061), 149–154.

Wickert, C., & De Bakker, F. G. (2018). Pitching for social change: Toward a relational approach to selling and buying social issues. *Academy of Management Discoveries, 4*(1), 50–73.

Wry, T., & Haugh, H. (2018). Brace for impact: Uniting our diverse voices through a social impact frame. *Journal of Business Venturing, 33*(5), 566–574.

Wrzesniewski, A., & Dutton, J. E. (2001). Crafting a job: Revisioning employees as active crafters of their work. *Academy of Management Review, 26*, 179–201.

York, J. G., & Venkataraman, S. (2010). The entrepreneur–environment nexus: Uncertainty, innovation, and allocation. *Journal of Business Venturing, 25*(5), 449–463.

Part 4
Impacts

8 Global Pro Bono Service: Implications for Employees, Companies and the Communities Served

Philip Mirvis, Amanda MacArthur, Marieka Walsh,
and Tanya Gapeka

Overview

Increasing numbers of corporate employees are engaged in global pro bono (GPB) programmes, where they provide managerial and technical assistance to organisations addressing human needs in emerging markets and under-served communities. Drawing on data collected from over 25 firms sponsoring GPB programmes (2010–2018), this chapter examines: (1) the varieties of and participants in GPB programmes, (2) companies' motivations for investing in GPB and how programmes are managed, (3) how employees experience service assignments, and (4) the impact of GPB on employees, companies and the communities served. Attention is then paid to critical success factors in GPB programmes and to areas for their continued improvement.

Learning objectives

By the end of this chapter, readers should be able to:

- introduce the variety and scope of corporate global pro bono (GPB) programmes
- consider what motivates companies to invest in GPB and where they send employees
- explain what volunteers do on GPB assignments, how they help their clients and what they learn from the experience
- examine the impact of GPB on employees, their companies and the clients served
- assess the limits on and issues within these programmes and how companies might address them.

Introduction: Global pro bono service

A new era of international corporate volunteerism and service is taking shape. A growing number of companies have devised an innovative way to simultaneously develop employees' leadership skills, advance corporate social responsibility (CSR) and expand business knowledge and opportunities in emerging markets. They are implementing service programmes that enable their employees to provide managerial and technical assistance to small businesses, not-for-profit organisations, government agencies and universities around the world through *global pro bono* (GPB) programmes.

The case has been made that these programmes are a win-win-win proposition: companies, their employees and the organisations served all benefit from the partnerships developed, new skills learned and assistance provided (Caligiuri, Mencin, & Jiang, 2013; Mirvis, Thompson, & Gohring, 2012; Pless, Maak, & Stahl, 2011). Companies gain from staff with greater knowledge of countries important to business expansion and from an enhanced reputation as a global corporate citizen. Employees in service assignments are schooled in how to operate in complex, multi-stakeholder environments, how to get things done with limited resources and how to navigate another culture. Finally, local recipient organisations (clients) benefit from improved processes, enhanced staff performance and new networks and external relationships.

Still, questions abound as to the purposes, operations and sustainable impact of GPB programmes. For instance, what motivates companies to sponsor these programmes? One aim of engaging employees through CSR is to attract and retain millennial-generation employees, many of whom want to participate in socially responsible activities in their companies (Bhattacharya, Sen, & Korshun, 2008; Deloitte, 2016). Are GPB programmes all about 'winning the war for talent' or do they serve a broader strategic purpose? What segments of employees participate in them?

Who runs GPB programmes in companies? A familiar critique of CSR initiatives is that they are 'bolt on' rather than 'built in' to the business (Grayson & Hodges, 2004). Another rap on CSR initiatives is that many of them aim at 'brand building' to enhance the image of a company more so than achieve significant social impact (Mirvis, 2011). Evidence is needed as to what extent GPB connects with corporate strategy and whether or not firms take seriously the social impact of their GPB programmes.

Many have called for more systematic research on employee volunteering and the impact of corporate volunteer initiatives on employees, companies and the communities served (Haski-Leventhal, Roza, & Meijs, 2017; Rodell, Breitsohl, Schröder, & Keating, 2016). Surveys of employers, such as those by Deloitte (2017) and the Committee Encouraging Corporate Philanthropy (CECP and Conference Board, 2018), provide a profile of corporate volunteering. The consultancies Taproot (2019) and Emerging World (2017) have conducted studies specifically of companies and employees involved in GPB efforts. This chapter adds to this database the results of longitudinal surveys (2010–2018) from over 25 companies on their GPB programmes, collected by PYXERA Global (2014, 2016, 2018), an international nongovernmental organisation (NGO) that matches corporate employees with service clients around the world.

Our chapter examines the characteristics of GPB programmes in operation today, companies' motivations for and management of these programmes, the employee 'experience' on service assignments, and the reported impact on companies, local clients and employees. We conclude the chapter by identifying key considerations in GPB's strategic and operational issues for firms and managers to consider, and topics for further study.

Pro bono programmes

Companies are doing many things to engage their employees through volunteerism. Recent years have seen an increase in traditional forms of corporate volunteerism – supporting employees who mentor schoolchildren, care for the homeless, elderly or disadvantaged, participate in disaster relief, build community playgrounds or habitat-for-humanity housing, and so on – along with more 'skill-based' engagements wherein employees use their technical and commercial know-how to address social concerns (Deloitte, 2017). Select firms have launched project-based service learning and GPB programmes (Hills & Mahmud, 2007; Wankel & DeFillippi, 2005).

What do we know about volunteer programmes involving service and learning? The literature on service learning involving university- and school-sponsored programmes reports that such experiences can stretch students' skills and emotional intelligence, make them more aware of diversity and social issues, and enhance their sense of civic and social responsibility (Haski-Leventhal et al., 2019). These and other skill-building and pro-social benefits have also been documented in service learning with corporate volunteers (Grant, 2012; Muthuri, Matten, & Moon, 2009; Rodell et al., 2016). Studies specifically concerned with GPB, though fewer in number, report high levels of personal learning for participants and, in select cases, in their development as globally responsible leaders (Caligiuri, Mencin, Jayne, & Traylor, 2019; Gitsham, 2012; Mirvis, Thompson, & Marquis, 2010; Pless & Borecká, 2014).

As for companies, the documented benefits of service learning and GPB programmes include greater staff engagement, talent attraction and retention, and new knowledge about doing business in unfamiliar countries (Guarnieri & Kao, 2008; MacArthur, 2014). And while many client organisations surely benefit from GPB programmes, there are corporate assessments of GPB initiatives but no independent, multi-company findings of social impact beyond those to be reported here.

Method: PYXERA Global surveys on GPB

In 2003, Pfizer deployed its employees into emerging markets to strengthen health systems as part of its Global Health Fellows programme. In 2008, IBM piloted its Corporate Service Corps, a team-based pro bono model (Marquis & Kanter, 2009). In 2010, PYXERA Global began formally tracking companies sponsoring GPBs by surveying 10 firms about their motivations, operations and experiences. Assessments have continued to date: in 2013 (26 companies), 2014 (27), 2016 (21) and 2018 (26). These corporate surveys are typically completed by the executive in charge of GPB. The sample of firms across each of these waves varies to some extent (as companies new to GPB joined the study and others discontinued their participation). Some 11 firms have participated annually since 2014.

To gather data directly from GPB participants and clients, PYXERA Global developed common performance indicators and to date has surveyed the views of 1040 GPB volunteers, from 46 countries, and 300 GPB client organisations. In-depth interviews of participants and case studies of projects were conducted in select instances (Walsh & Gapeka, 2018). Findings from these several investigations enable us to answer key questions raised about GPB programmes.

Findings: programme design and participation

Companies that sponsor GPB programmes are typically large, have global reach, employ a largely professional workforce and concentrate in sectors like banking, high technology, finance and pharma. Yet, there is considerable variation in how these firms design their global service programmes – in terms of the length and type of service assignments and the makeup and number of participants (Pless & Borecká, 2014).

IBM's Corporate Service Corps (CSC) is modelled on the US Peace Corps, deploying over 500 people annually and engaging teams of volunteers in three months of pre-work: one month in-country and two months in post-service where they harvest insights for themselves and their business. Ernst & Young's fellows programme is much smaller and focuses exclusively on improving small business in Latin America. But its volunteers spend three months in direct service – giving them more time to deliver tangible results. Accenture Development Partnership operates as a not-for-profit organisation housed within a profit-making business. The parent company forgoes its margin and covers pro bono overhead; the client pays a small fee; and the employee takes a salary reduction while serving clients in need.

Some pharmaceutical companies have built their volunteerism on the model of Doctors Without Borders (Médecins Sans Frontières). Pfizer's Global Health Fellows programme, for example, has the company 'loan' individual employees to NGOs to address local health care needs. To date, over 230 Pfizer fellows have worked with 30 NGO partners, primarily in Asia and Africa. By contrast, the great majority of companies deploy teams of employees, often employees from different functions and geographies, in GPB assignments or use a combination of team and individual service models. Where do these volunteers serve?

Global, local and virtual

PYXERA Global's first few surveys (2010–2014) report that participating companies' GPB programmes were targeted at emerging markets and involved *in situ* service by employees. More recently, several companies have adapted and applied the model to domestic service. GlaxoSmithKline (GSK), for instance, has about half of its volunteers serve in emerging markets while the other half share their health care expertise closer to 'home'. The local option enables employees to serve society while still fulfilling work, family and child-rearing responsibilities.

The 2019 survey, representing 47 programmes run by 26 companies (and one multi-company initiative), found that over half (51%) of the programmes continue to feature on-the-ground global service assignments. Over the past four years, Africa, Latin America and Asia have hosted the lion's share of

Figure 8.1.   **Regions hosting global pro bono 2013–19**

programmes, with an uptake in global assignments to Central and Eastern Europe and the Middle East (see Figure 8.1).

The rationale for companies focusing on emerging markets is straightforward. A report on IBM and Dow's GPB service in Africa says it plainly:

> The pro bono approach to accelerating market entry in Africa has two primary benefits. First, it accelerates a dynamic understanding of the potential in these markets, providing insight to the company as to how it might engage the community long term with a more sustainable approach to business that creates shared value – an element often absent from business in the African context. At the same time, a pro bono team of consultants can enhance the social well-being of communities where such companies seek to operate, authentically raising the profile of the corporate brand amongst their key stakeholders. (Litow, Hawkins, & White, 2014, p. 3)

Some 17% of the programmes studied in 2018 have a domestic focus, where employees aid underserved domestic communities in their home nation or region. Consider JP Morgan Chase's investments in Detroit, Michigan. Over the past five decades, Detroit's population has declined significantly, from a peak of 1.5 million in the 1970s to less than 700,000 today, causing a large drop in the city's tax base and decimating city services. In June 2013, Detroit filed for Chapter 9 bankruptcy, with estimated debts of more than $18 billion. A year later, the city emerged from bankruptcy but nearly 80,000 buildings, or 30% of the city's total stock, were empty.

In early 2014, JP Morgan Chase made a $100 million commitment to the city of Detroit. The firm coupled this financial investment with sending in employee volunteers – in the form of their Detroit Service Corps. In November 2014, its first team partnered with four local not-for-profit organisations to support neighbourhood and workforce development. To date, nearly 100 employees have helped 21 Detroit organisations to improve their capabilities and strengthen community outreach. The combination of financial support and employee assistance from Morgan Chase enabled these local organisations to provide training and career education to nearly 15,000 Detroiters, and technical assistance to 18,000 entrepreneurs and small businesses, yielding more than 700 jobs. Recently, JP Morgan Chase offices expanded its local GPBs and grants to Chicago, New York, London, Paris and Hong Kong.

In addition, several companies now feature 'virtual' GPB programmes (13% of total programmes) or 'hybrids' (19% of the total) that combine on-site and online engagement. To illustrate, Dow's Leadership in Action programme has employees consult five months virtually with their client organisations, then spend one week in-country, working with them side by side.

Participation

PYXERA Global reports a 90% increase in the number of GPB participants in the companies it has studied from 2013 to 2018. Clearly, the idea is spreading. But a common mistake is to assume that corporates based in the USA and Europe are primarily sending their domestic employees on these emerging market initiatives. On the contrary, in its first 10 years of operation, IBM engaged over 4,000 volunteers from 62 different countries. SAP's cumulative 1050 participants represent 56 different nationalities.

It is also apparent that GPB participants are not just young people seeking to contribute to society. Indeed, one-third of participants are classified as executives in their companies, the majority being managers or individual contributors, and only 16% are in junior posts. Digging into the GPB participant profiles of a smaller sample of five companies, Emerging World (2017) finds a near 50/50 split between men and women volunteers, with 43% of the participants under the age of 35 and 57% over 35.

Most companies conduct a formal orientation session to prepare their people for service – either in person (36%), virtually (39%) or both (14%) – with an average of three days in length (11% do not do an orientation). There has been an increase in the length of in-person training from 2013 to today and, in the Emerging World sample, nearly three-quarters of volunteers surveyed report being well prepared for their GPB assignments.

Corporate motivations and interests

Beyond their philanthropic intent, an important motivation for GPB programmes in their first incarnation was to attract talent and engage employees. Yet, companies like GSK and IBM also saw the potential of GPB assignments for leadership development (Mirvis et al., 2010). Pro bono activity provides an ideal milieu for developing future leaders – it affords them global exposure, project-based service learning, immersion in an unfamiliar culture and the gratification of doing socially rewarding work (Ayas & Mirvis, 2005; MacArthur & Bonner Ness, 2013). In its 2013 survey, PYXERA Global found staff engagement and leadership development to be the top motivations for GPB programmes.

Fast-forward to today and employers now report that a major reason to invest in GPB programmes is to generate sustainable social impact (cited by 82%). Leadership development and staff satisfaction/retention (each cited by 57%) are no longer the dominant motivators. To an extent, this may reflect the broader integration of CSR into the business visions and strategies of large companies today. Indeed, 90% of the companies surveyed in 2018 say that they align their GPB programmes to corporate strategy.

Programme scope and management

The size and scope of GPB programmes is quite variable. Some 22% of companies have comparatively large programmes and send over 150 employees annually on assignments. SAP, for example, has dramatically scaled its pro bono programme, SAP Social Sabbatical, over the past few years, from 30 employees in 2012 to 220 employees in 2018, in a combination of global and local programmes. The programme aligns strategically with SAP's emphasis on social innovation (Van der Ploeg & White, 2014). SAP began work in this space in 2013 when its employees partnered with Barclays to host Start-up@RISE Africa where South African tech entrepreneurs participated in training to develop prototypes using the SAP HANA Cloud® technology. Over the next few years, teams of SAP employees were sent on assignments to consult with innovation hubs, incubators, academic centres, and the like, to reach many more social entrepreneurs and their enterprises. SAP employees have, to date, assisted nearly 350 NGOs and social businesses. Closer to HQ, SAP employees staff Social Impact Labs in Berlin, Hamburg and other German cities for social entrepreneurs that are set to scale.

By comparison, 37% of companies send fewer than 30 volunteers on assignment per year (15% send 31–50 volunteers; 19% send 51–100; 7% send 101–150). Why the differences in size? SAP is big, has global reach and has made its GPB programme a centrepiece of its leadership development strategy and a vehicle to enhance its connections and reputation in developing markets. Firms that operate small programmes rely on other vehicles to develop future leaders and tend to have less business-related, more eleemosynary motivations.

The corporate responsibility function (57%) oversees and manages GPB service in the majority of companies, with human resources (17%) in charge in select firms. On this count, there are no notable differences between CSR- versus HR-led GPB programmes in terms of corporate motivation and strategic intent.

Service focus

Ten years ago, the majority of GPB programmes were targeted at education, with only pharmaceuticals working in health care. Recent years have seen more diversification in the challenges addressed by company volunteers. Figure 8.2 shows the sectors served by GPB programmes, as of 2017, focused on the millennial development goals. And, while over 60% of programmes concern education, large numbers of them are aimed at entrepreneurship, health care and economic/workforce development.

Pro bono service centred on women's empowerment (SDG 5) illustrates how programmes can have multiple foci. PYXERA Global identified 179 distinct GPB projects, involving 150 client organisations, targeting women's empowerment – in 35 countries overall but with over a third based in India. Most of these women-aimed projects are in areas of entrepreneurship and employment (37%) or health and nutrition (36%). A joint project between IBM and Vasavya Mahlilia Mandali (VMM), a female-led not-for-profit that trains women to become community leaders, illustrates a dual focus. The IBMers helped VMM draft a new strategic plan and introduced staff to tools for stakeholder analyses, needs assessment and risk management. They assisted VMM in launching two new social enterprises addressing maternal and child health and in drafting grant proposals for international donors and foundations, yielding nearly $250,000 in new funding. VMM estimates that this will enable it to reach an additional 400,000 women and 200,000 children.

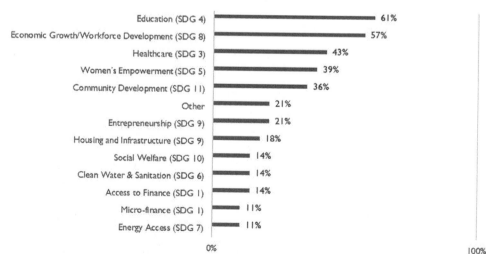

Figure 8.2.   **Pro bono assignments by sector**

The pro bono experience

Studies find that the benefits of participating in socially relevant activities at work include personal satisfaction, an enriched sense of meaning and purpose on the job and, in certain cases, the development of problem-solving and leadership skills (Glavas, 2016; Grant, 2012; Pless & Maak, 2008). GPB adds the intrinsic challenges of working with front-line clients to addressing, with limited resources, serious economic, social and environmental problems.

IBMer Matt Berry faced a complex challenge on his GPB assignment: reducing road traffic in Lagos, Nigeria, whose population will grow from 21 million today to 40 million by 2030. He reported:

> This project was unlike anything I ever had a chance to work on in my career. We had three short weeks to analyse the problem, meet with a dozen government agencies, navigate political issues, understand the technical solutions available, survey commuters, factor in economic and social issues, and build a strategic transportation roadmap for one of the fastest growing cities in the world.

Of course, challenge and the chance to be creative are earmarks of projects of all types. The social relevance of pro bono work gives employees the chance not only to use their talents and abilities, but also to do something useful for society. This can be a source of meaning for socially conscious employees and enhance their sense of purpose on the job. As another GPB volunteer explained: 'Plucked away from the comforts of our environment with a zeal to share our knowledge and working practices, our quest for giving became the prime function.'

Life on the ground

What do corporate volunteers do on their assignments? Bonnie Glick, volunteering with a local NGO in Brazil through IBM's Corporate Service Corps (CSC), helped to develop a funding strategy for a community-based organisation, *Aprendiz*, which works to keep disadvantaged youth off the streets in the slums of São Paulo. Participants in PWC's Ulysses programme have, in turn, produced a professional evaluation of the growth and income-generation potential of the eco-tourism sector in Belize; worked with the United Nations Development Programme on the Lokoho Rural Electrification Project in Madagascar; and contributed to the Recovery, Employment and Stability (RESPECT) effort in conflict-ridden East Timor by setting up a system to ensure the accountability of all stakeholders involved.

Taproot (2019) queried GPB participants on what kinds of skills they employ on their assignments. The responses included management and data analysis (cited by 84%), communications, technology and marketing/branding (72% in each category), finance/accounting and strategy (68% each), and HR and customer sales/service (60% each).

MacArthur (2014) finds that by working collaboratively within a team of peers, and confronting clients' complex social challenges, executives take on new roles, experiment with new behaviours and see markets and societies from a new vantage point. As noted, the majority of companies send employee teams on global service assignments and most of these teams are diverse in their racial-ethnic makeup, age, geography, functional areas and work experience. By working in a diverse team, participants learn about the work styles and cultures of their team members. They learn, too, about practice in functions different from their own, and junior- and senior-level employees are able to share their respective experiences in management and in the use of new technologies. On this count, IBM's CSC participants report that the opportunity to work in a diverse team was one of the most beneficial parts of their assignment.

Programme impact

Surveying some 1040 GPB participants, from seven sponsoring companies, PYXERA Global finds that over 90% of GPB participants acquired or improved their skills as a result of their assignment and gained a better understanding of the role of business in society. Other benefits cited included heightened cultural awareness (80%), improved communication (74%) and problem-solving (71%) skills, and greater adaptability (52%).

Several companies conduct surveys of their participants. Surveys of alumni of GSK's GPB PULSE programme from 2009 to 2015 found that the vast majority had developed leadership skills and competencies (90%) and had made positive changes in their work (83%) after returning from their assignments. GSK also surveyed participants' managers and colleagues on programme impact, who reported that PULSE volunteers had developed their interpersonal skills (94%), taken on increased leadership responsibilities (71%) and brought reinvigorated energy, spirit, motivation and morale to GSK (83%). Former PULSE programme leader, Ahisya Posner Mencin, reports that many of its GPB participants have a 'life-changing experience' and return to GSK 'as leaders with greater passion, energy, confidence, creativity, gratitude and practical knowledge of how to do more with less' (Kassi-Vivier, Pawlowski, & Guttery, 2012, p. 19).

In its study, Emerging World (2017) asked 688 pro bono participants about what had happened to them after their service assignment. While nine-in-ten continued to work for the company that had sponsored their pro bono experience, over 75% had changed roles since their assignment. Note, too, that 47% moved to roles with more responsibility and 52% said that their pro bono experience had contributed to their change in role.

Company benefits

Companies that institute GPBs benefit from staff with greater knowledge of countries important to business expansion, and they often see an increase in staff retention and performance. Companies also benefit from an enhanced reputation in those countries where programmes are implemented – which improves their ability to win new business – and from being seen world-wide as a global corporate citizen.

Pfizer and GSK, for instance, report that their 'license to operate' in several African countries has improved due to relationships developed with governments, universities and throughout the health care sector. IBM's work in Calabar, capital of the Cross River State in Nigeria, was at the request of and in partnership with Governor Liyel Imoke. One project funded by the World Bank provided support to pregnant women and children under 5. Governor Imoke was so impressed by the work that he personally asked IBM to continue in a commercial way as project managers. This led to a $1.2m services deal – IBM's first in West Africa.

Beyond the immediate rewards, companies also cite the 'social capital' that flows from their global service. Corporate websites featuring blog postings and videos produced by volunteers tackling significant economic, social and environmental problems around the world, instil a sense of pride in the workforce overall and also attract the interest of job candidates, students and the media. Meanwhile, programme alumni often stay in touch with one another and with their clients via email and Skype chats.

Social impact

Companies are increasingly interested in assessing the social impact of their GPB. PYXERA Global's surveys show that 97% of some 300 GPB clients surveyed are satisfied with their programme, and 92% say that GPB participants served as a 'change agent' for their organisation. Local organisations report operational benefits in areas of stakeholder management, leadership and governance, marketing and external relationships, and training and development. In addition, clients testify to benefits from improved processes and enhanced staff performance yielding increased revenues. GPB services received have been valued at over $7.5 million, with 2,000 client organisation staff helped by programmes and over 57 million touched by the work of GPB service teams (see Figure 8.3).

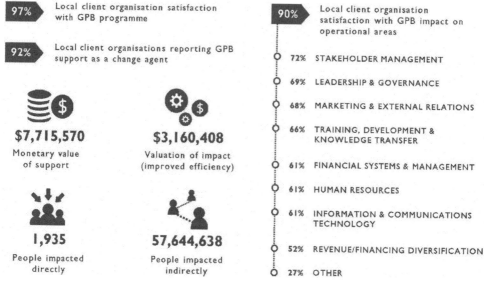

Figure 8.3.   Client impact of global pro bono programmes

As a small example, Becton, Dickinson, and Company (BD) sent 13 company employees, in partnership with Heart to Heart International, a medical aid humanitarian organisation, to earthquake-devastated Haiti. The BD volunteers and partners worked with the National Lab of Haiti to devise a 'lab in a box' for clinics in rural areas to increase access to quality care, and created patient education materials on proper hygiene, nutrition and sexually transmitted diseases to help reduce the spread of disease.

On a larger scale, John Deere's pro bono morphed into a long-term partnership with a community in India. The Joint Initiative for Village Advancement (JIVA) programme, supported by Deere's Foundation in three rural villages of the Rajasthan, takes an integrated approach to community development. Deere employees run 'train the trainer' programmes to enable farmers to spread knowledge across villages, to teach and mentor in village schools and to work hand in hand with locals on infrastructure development, including on the construction of toilets, wash basins and the like. The effort is managed through a strategic plan, replete with targets and key performance indicators (KPIs) for both the villagers and Deere's pro bono contributors.

Implications for practice

Several features of GPB differentiate it from traditional corporate volunteer programmes and require thoughtful consideration in design and operation. On this count, companies report several 'success factors' in meeting pro bono project objectives, as follows.

Partnering

Few firms have the appropriate staff, resources and know-how to operate in this space on their own and, in any case, may lack legitimacy with local communities to do so. Indeed, PYXERA Global finds that over 80% of companies work with an NGO implementing partner that helps to identify client organisations, establish the scope of work, place employees and handle logistics. On this count, a study by Austin and colleagues (2005) finds NGOs to be far more knowledgeable about social needs and more effective at planning social action than businesses. Partnering with NGOs also eases a company's access to foreign governments and social service organisations in developing countries (Mirvis & Googins, 2018a).

Selection

Firms use two methods to recruit and select volunteers. Nearly half rely on supervisor nominations to identify GPB candidates, while the rest call for self-nominations or depend on recommendations from their talent development or HR functions. Typically, candidates either complete a survey or submit an essay expressing their interest in and aim for GPB service. Many companies follow up applications with a telephone (44%) or in-person (26%) interview. Reported selection criteria include: (1) a strong track record within the company; (2) high potential for leadership advancement; (3) personal motivation, flexibility, resilience and a demonstrated service ethic; and (4) project-relevant technical, managerial or cross-cultural skills. The selection process can be daunting. For example, when IBM launched its CSC in 2008, it expected 500 applications and received 1000. A few years later, it got over 30,000 applications, with the largest number from its employees in Asia.

Strategic alignment

We have seen the increased connection of GPB programmes to company strategy. This is likely a sign that more firms are engaged in strategic philanthropy and seek business benefits from their social investments (Porter & Kramer, 2006, 2011). As evidence of this, survey analysis finds that companies who take a strategic approach to GPB are more likely to measure their business benefits than firms who don't take this approach. Second, there is increased emphasis on achieving 'sustainable social impact' and many more companies are measuring the social impact of GPB programmes. This may indicate that companies are taking CSR more seriously today and giving attention to measurement and accountability concerning the results of their social investments (Henderson, 2018).

Positioning

We have seen how GPB is housed within the corporate responsibility or HR functions of most companies surveyed. The attendant risk is that it can be marginalised from the mainstream business. To counter this, PYX-ERA Global found (in 2018) that many GPB programme heads are actively engaged with 'internal stakeholders' in their companies, including business units, marketing and R&D. Interestingly, survey analyses show that GPB programmes that are linked to corporate strategy feature greater alignment and collaboration between corporate CSR, HR, talent development, marketing/communication and business units. In addition, the survey finds that GPB programmes get top-level support via either the CEO (52%), a vice-president (18%) or others in the C-suite (26%). This is important not only for the success of GPB programmes but also to employee volunteers. On this point, Emerging World (2017) finds that participants report having learned more from GPB programmes championed by top management (versus those not championed by them) and being more apt to support corporate efforts to act as a 'force for good'.

Issues and areas for improvement

What else should companies consider when undertaking GPB programmes? One criticism of such programmes is that corporate teams parachute in to help clients solve social problems and then, in short order, return to their business – leaving the clients to handle any implementation challenges on their own. In response, companies today are increasing the length of their services assignments, with some 46% having employees serve three weeks or more – a substantial increase on two years ago when only 18% featured assignments of three weeks or more. Furthermore, many GPB teams stay in touch with their clients through virtual coaching and some companies send clients a subsequent pro bono team to 'pick up the ball'. At present, however, there has been no systematic study of how the length of GPB assignments, or the addition of virtual coaching or follow-up teams, relates to improvements in client organisations – a topic for future research.

Harvesting lessons

Another critique is that relatively few companies conduct a structured debriefing of participants on completion of their GPB assignment. This makes the harvesting of lessons learned and their application to business needs episodic and haphazard. To illustrate, Emerging World reports that, although 92% of the GPB participants it surveyed say that they acquired new knowledge and skills from their assignment, only 56% felt they had made a positive business impact on their organisation as a result of their insights and learning.

GSK is tackling this problem in its revamped GPB programme. Historically, GSK Pulse volunteers were given a briefing, before embarking on their assignment, that covered only the logistics of their placement, methods of community support and areas for personal development. In its new version, Pulse+ TRACK, volunteers are educated on GSK's strategic priorities by various business leaders before they go into the field, and are encouraged to think of themselves as intrapreneurs and to be on the lookout for ideas that may apply to company priorities. Upon their return, they are expected to brief the management team on what they learned and propose innovative new ways of doing things (GSK, 2015).

Employee learning

While employees' passion for and learning from GPB work is well documented, it is uncertain how much of this enthusiasm and learning is retained once they return to their work 'cubicles'. To address this matter, Merck has partnered with Cornell University to develop an action learning programme for its GPB fellows, based on four characteristics of entrepreneurial leadership: curiosity, commitment, collaboration and connectivity. Before their assignment, Merck participants are given reading tasks and must complete a leadership self-assessment and participate in an interactive two-day workshop focused on team development and the setting of personal leadership goals. Halfway through the assignment, a check-in provides participants with the opportunity to self-reflect, revisit their goals and consider lessons learned and how these could benefit the company. On return to Merck, their three-month assignment complete, participants attend two follow-up discussion sessions, one after 90 days and the other after six months, to mark progress against their goals and share learning across the alumni community.

In other companies, GPB programme alumni have formed communities of practice where they relive their volunteer experience and share day-to-day challenges on the job. It seems that many companies, too, are making use of alumni to support their GPB efforts overall. Of the companies surveyed, over half have alumni serve as mentors to GPB participants and nearly as many assist in participant training. Roughly 30% of firms engage alumni in participant selection.

Innovation and continuous improvement

Recent years have seen innovations in GPB programmes. To expand opportunities, reduce costs and include those who, due to personal or family responsibilities, are unable to travel abroad, several companies have also set up 'local' pro bono service options so that employees can serve in-country. SAP, which sponsors both global and local GPB programmes, finds that ratings of employee and client satisfaction are comparable in the two kinds of programmes. Certainly, the local option has increased substantially the number of SAP's GPB volunteers. Still, we need to know more about the comparative advantages and disadvantages of global versus local programmes and of virtual volunteering.

Several companies have joined forces to form multi-company GPB teams. IBM, for example, has invited a number of its clients, including FedEx, John Deere and JP Morgan Chase, to collaborate and join IBM CSC teams. Global Health Corporate Champions (GHCC) – developed by USAID, the Public Health Institute and PYXERA Global – is a GPB programme that includes employee volunteers from PIMCO, PricewaterhouseCoopers (PwC), Dow Chemical Company, SAP and WE Communications. In 2016 and 2017, this diverse group of leaders leveraged their business and operational expertise on projects related to clean water and sanitation, food and nutrition, security, health system strengthening and/or gender inclusion and empowerment in Ghana, Rwanda and Senegal.

What are the benefits of this multi-company model? Asiala (2018) reports that multi-company participants not only learned from their engagements with clients but also from their interactions with peers. As one manager from Dow reports:

> Another important aspect ... was the corporate culture learning. I really want to stress this, because the culture between Dow, PIMCO, and PwC was so obviously different. I saw strengths in Dow that clearly came out, but I also saw strengths in those other corporate cultures, for which I now have new appreciation and respect.

Conclusion

This chapter has shown how GPB programmes have taken hold in select global companies over the past decade or so, have become more fully integrated into the strategy and operations of these firms, and produced tangible benefits for employees, companies and the clients served. Nonetheless, comparatively few large companies are sponsoring GPB programmes and many run small programmes with fewer than 50 volunteers annually. This reminds us that the 'market for virtue' varies across firms and industries as well as employment markets (Vogel, 2006). The firms hosting GPB programmes studied here are all global, employ a largely professional workforce and operate in competitive talent markets (in professional services, IT and pharma who have competitors that feature GPB programmes). Certainly, these factors are relevant for executives to consider when judging whether or not GPB is right for their firm.

There are, of course, many other ways to engage employees in socially relevant service, including on the job (Mirvis, 2012). Growing numbers of employees today are involved in sustainable supply chain management, cause-related marketing and green business initiatives. That said, employee volunteerism in the USA, Australia and other nations has historic roots. Recognition that many more employees today want to be engaged in the CSR efforts of their companies is a key driver in the increased emphasis given to volunteerism generally and to the addition of local and virtual GPB programmes in the firms studied here. Beyond this, there are many ways of combining GPB-type service and learning with the on-boarding of new employees, with corporate education programmes and even with developing new strategies, products and services.

Mirvis and Googins (2018b) contrast the strengths and weaknesses of GPB programmes with other types of engagement platforms in companies, including in employee innovation contests and hackathons, partnerships with social entrepreneurs and company-wide social innovation efforts. Certainly, companies have a choice about how to engage their employees in socially meaningful and strategically relevant work. We see from the data reported here that there is a strong business case for investing in GPB, but how does it compare with other worthwhile ways to engage employees in CSR?

Questions for students

1. Have you ever had an extended volunteer experience? How did it contribute to your development as a leader?
2. Why are companies sending volunteers to emerging markets and underserved communities in their home country? Consider the benefits but also the expense and risks!
3. Pick a big company you are interested in. Would you recommend it launch a GPB programme? What would be its aims, who should participate and where would volunteers serve?
4. Some argue that the USA and other countries should have national service programmes where high school graduates contribute to society before going on to work or college. What do you think about this idea?

References

Asiala, L. (2018). *Taking global pro bono to the next level.* Retrieved from www.PYXERAglobal.org/taking-global-pro-bono-next-level.
Austin, J., Leonard, H., Reficco, E., & Wei-Skillern, J. (2005). Social entrepreneurship: It's for corporations, too. In A. Nicholls (Ed.), *Social entrepreneurship: New paradigms of sustainable social change.* Oxford: Oxford University Press.

Ayas, K., & Mirvis, P. H. (2005). Educating managers through service learning projects. In C. Wankel & R. DeFillippi (Eds.), *Educating managers through real world projects*. Greenwich: IAP.

Bhattacharya, C. B., Sen, S., & Korschun, D. (2008). Using corporate social responsibility to win the war for talent. *MIT Sloan Management Review, 49*(2), 37–44.

Caligiuri, P., Mencin, A., Jayne, B. & Traylor, A. (2019). Developing cross-cultural competencies through international corporate volunteerism. *Journal of World Business, 54*(1), 14–23.

Caligiuri, P., Mencin, A., & Jiang, K. (2013). Win–win–win: The influence of company sponsored volunteerism programs on employees, NGOs, and business units. *Personnel Psychology, 66*(4), 825–860.

CECP and Conference Board (2018). *Giving in numbers*. Retrieved from http://cecp.co/home/resources/giving-in-numbers.

Deloitte (2016). *The 2016 Deloitte millennial survey: Winning over the next generation of leaders*. Retrieved from www2.deloitte.com/content/dam/Deloitte/global/Documents/About-Deloitte/gx-millenial-survey-2016-exec-summary.pdf.

Deloitte (2017). *Volunteerism survey*. Retrieved from www2.deloitte.com/content/dam/Deloitte/us/Documents/about-deloitte/us-2017-deloitte-volunteerism-survey.pdf.

Emerging World (2017). *2017 CISL impact benchmark study*. Retrieved from www.emergingworld.com/wp-content/uploads/2019/04/2017-cisl-impact-benchmark-study-443.pdf.

Gitsham, M. (2012). Experiential learning for leadership and sustainability at IBM and HSBC. *Journal of Management Development, 31*(3), 298–307.

Glavas, A. (2016). Corporate social responsibility and employee engagement: Enabling employees to employ more of their whole selves at work. *Frontiers in Psychology, 7*, 796. Retrieved from https://doi.org/10.3389/fpsyg.2016.00796.

Grant, A. M. (2012). Giving time, time after time: Work design and sustained employee participation in corporate volunteering. *Academy of Management Review, 37*(4), 589–615.

Grayson, D., & Hodges, A. (2004). *Corporate social opportunity! 7 steps to make corporate social responsibility work for your business*. Sheffield: Greenleaf.

GSK (2015). *Intrapreneurship: Keeping our fingers on the PULSE*. Retrieved from www.gsk.com/en-gb/responsibility/our-people/employee-engagement/intrapreneurship-keeping-our-fingers-on-the-pulse.

Guarnieri, R., & Kao, T. (2008). Leadership and CSR – a perfect match: How top companies for leaders utilize CSR as a competitive advantage. *People and Strategy, 31*(3), 34–41.

Haski-Leventhal, D., Paull, M., Young, S., MacCallum, J., Holmes, K., Omari, M., Scott, R., & Alony, I. (2019). The multidimensional benefits of university student volunteering: Psychological contract, expectations, and outcomes. *Nonprofit and Voluntary Sector Quarterly, 49*(1), 113–133.

Haski-Leventhal, D., Roza, L., & Meijs, L. C. (2017). Congruence in corporate social responsibility: Connecting the identity and behavior of employers and employees. *Journal of Business Ethics, 143*(1), 35–51.

Henderson, R. M. (2018). More and more CEOs are taking their social responsibility seriously. *Harvard Business Review, 12*, 2–5.

Hills, G., & Mahmud, A. (2007). *Volunteering for impact: Best practices in international corporate volunteering*. Boston, MA: FSG Social Impact Advisors.

Kassi-Vivier, Y., Pawlowski, J., & Guttery, C. (2012). *Demonstrating the business value of pro bono service*. Taproot Foundation and Pro Bono Lab.

Litow, S., Hawkins, N. & White, D. (2014). *Accelerating market entry in Africa*. Retrieved from www.PYXERAglobal.org/white-paper-accelerating-market-entry-africa.

MacArthur, A. (2014). *The state of global pro bono*. Retrieved from www.conference-board.org/retrievefile.cfm?filename=TCB-GT-V1N8-State_of_Global_Pro_Bono1.pdf&type=subsite.

MacArthur, A., & Bonner Ness, A. (2013). Skills-based volunteering: The new executive training ground. *Stanford Social Innovation Review*. Retrieved from https://ssir.org/articles/entry/skills_based_volunteering_the_new_executive_training_ground#.

Marquis, C., & Kanter, R. M. (2009). IBM: The corporate service corps. *Harvard Business School Case*, No. 409-106. Retrieved from www.hbs.edu/faculty/Pages/item.aspx?num=37178.

Mirvis, P. (2011). Reputation and corporate social responsibility: A global view. In G. Martin, C. Cooper, & R. Burke (Eds.), *Corporate reputation: Managing threats and opportunities*. London: Gower.

Mirvis, P. (2012). Employee engagement and CSR: Transactional, relational, and developmental approaches. *California Management Review*, 54(4), 93–117.

Mirvis, P., & Googins, B. (2018a). Catalyzing social entrepreneurship in Africa: Roles for Western universities, NGOs and corporations. *Africa Journal of Management*, 4(1), 57–83.

Mirvis, P., & Googins, B. (2018b). Engaging employees as social innovators. *California Management Review*, 60(4), 25–50.

Mirvis, P., Thompson, K., & Gohring, J. (2012). Toward next-generation leadership: Global service. *Leader to Leader*, 2012, 20–26.

Mirvis, P., Thompson, K., & Marquis, C. (2010). Preparing next generation business leaders. In R. Burke & M. Rothstein (Eds.), *Self-management and leadership development*. Cheltenham, UK: Edgar Elgar.

Muthuri, J. N., Matten, D., & Moon, J. (2009). Employee volunteering and social capital: Contributions to corporate social responsibility. *British Journal of Management*, 20(1), 75–89.

Pless, N. M., & Borecká, M. (2014). Comparative analysis of international service learning programs. *Journal of Management Development*, 33(6), 526–550.

Pless, N. M., & Maak, T. (2008). Responsible leaders as agents of world benefit: Learnings from 'Project Ulysses'. *Journal of Business Ethics*, 85(1), 59–71.

Pless, N. M., Maak, T., & Stahl, G. K. (2011). Developing global leaders through international service learning programs: The Ulysses experience. *Academy of Management Learning & Education*, 10(2), 237–260.

Porter, M. E., & Kramer, M. R. (2006). The link between competitive advantage and corporate social responsibility. *Harvard Business Review*, 84(12), 78–92.

Porter, M. E., & Kramer, M. R. (2011). Creating shared value. *Harvard Business Review*, January–February, 1–17.

PYXERA Global (2014). *Benchmarking survey – Corporate global pro bono: State of the practice*. Retrieved from www.pyxeraglobal.org/corporate-global-pro-bono-state-practice.

PYXERA Global (2016). *Global pro bono: State of practice*. Report on the 7th Global Pro Bono Benchmarking Survey. Retrieved from www.PYXERAglobal.org/global-pro-bono-state-practice-survey-2017.

PYXERA Global (2018). *Global pro bono: State of practice*. Retrieved from www. pyxeraglobal.org/wp-content/uploads/2019/06/PYXERAGlobal_8thGlobalProBono_ StateofthePracticeReport.pdf.

Rodell, J. B., Breitsohl, H., Schröder, M., & Keating, D. J. (2016). Employee volunteering: A review and framework for future research. *Journal of Management*, *42*(1), 55–84.

Taproot (2019). *State of pro bono*. Retrieved from https://k1sxsm5s8y-flywheel. netdna-ssl.com/wp-content/uploads/2019/02/Taproot_State_of_ProBono_Corp.pdf.

Van der Ploeg, A., & White, D. (2014). Social sabbaticals and the new face of leadership. *Stanford Innovation Review*. Retrieved from https://ssir.org/articles/ entry/social_sabbaticals_and_the_new_face_of_leadership.

Vogel, D. (2006). *The market for virtue: The potential and limits of corporate social responsibility*. Washington, DC: Brookings Institution Press.

Walsh, M., & Gapeka, T. (2018). *Benchmarking global pro bono's impact on investment*. Retrieved from www.pyxeraglobal.org/wp-content/uploads/2018/04/ CPICaseStudies_03.pdf.

Wankel, C., & DeFillippi, R. (Eds.) (2005). *Educating managers through real world projects*. Greenwich, CT: IAP.

Attractiveness of CSR in Job Choice Decisions: The Case of India

9

9

Femida Handy, Lesley Hustinx, and Katharina Spraul

Overview

Corporate social responsibility (CSR) has become increasingly attractive to job-seekers. Monetary incentives and the nature of the job notwithstanding, superior talent is also attracted by the company's reputation for being a good citizen. This chapter reports on the attractiveness of employers' engagement with and commitment to CSR practices to job-seekers in India. We examine attitudes towards CSR and investigate the compensation job-seekers are willing to forgo to work at a corporation with the desired CSR practices. Our findings suggest that, in the Indian context, the educational content may play a minor role in explaining the attractiveness of CSR-practising employers. Furthermore, different forms of employee volunteering may invoke different employee reactions. Finally, in recruiting talent, companies with a desirable CSR reputation may be successful, even with offers of lower monetary wages.

Learning objectives

By the end of this chapter, readers should be able to:

- explain that CSR is important to job-seekers in many countries, including India
- show that job-seekers are interested in working for companies with good CSR records
- demonstrate how even students with little exposure to CSR in their field of study find CSR attractive in future employers
- implement CSR as a means to attract job-seekers.

Introduction

Attracting and retaining superior talent are key issues for firms seeking to maintain a competitive advantage. Monetary incentives notwithstanding, superior talent is also attracted by the nature of the job and other organisational characteristics (Montgomery & Ramus, 2011). When potential applicants consider where they might want to work, they often have limited knowledge of employing organisations (Barber, 1998; Turban, 2001), which may be based on an organisation's image as an employer, its role in the community (CSR programmes) and its position in the economy – each of which is found to be a strong predictor of applicants' attraction after an initial interview (Lievens & Highhouse, 2006). Findings in the literature suggest that perceptions of a firm's corporate social responsibility (CSR) programmes indeed matter to job applicants when they are making job-choice decisions (Jones, Willness, & Madey, 2014; Rupp, Shao, Thornton, & Skarlicki, 2013).

Why is CSR attractive to job applicants? There is a well-established theoretical rationale and concomitant empirical findings linking CSR and job-applicant attraction based on the following rationale: firms adopting CSR programmes signal a more positive image of a caring employer, making them more attractive as an employer and thereby attracting a higher number of high-quality applicants. As signals in one cultural context may not have the same signalling power in other contexts (Spence, 1978), many of the previous studies of the attractiveness of CSR conducted in the West cannot be easily generalised to the Indian context. Indeed, recent government policies have mandated CSR undertakings by large companies in India (Singh & Verma, 2014). This chapter seeks to establish whether CSR is attractive to job-seekers in India, and their commitment to CSR practices.

Studies on the attractiveness of CSR to job applicants are usually undertaken by examining students studying in the business programme who primarily seek jobs in corporations. However, these findings cannot be generalised to all employees being recruited by corporations such as engineers, computer scientists, researchers, chemists, and so on, all of whom may also be influenced by the CSR practices of their employer. As students are likely to self-sort themselves into study programmes, they may also have different expectations and attitudes in general (Borkowski & Ugras, 1998), and may not react in the same way to the CSR practices of their employer. Thus, it is useful to see if the attractiveness of CSR in job-choice decisions is influenced by the study of different programmes.

In this chapter we ask: What is the attractiveness of CSR to students in their job-seeking decisions in India? We include study programme (business or engineering), individual-level factors found in the literature that could impact on the attractiveness of CSR, such as exposure to CSR and personal job expectations, and the importance the students ascribe to profitability as the goal of business in society (Wong, Long, & Elankumaran, 2010).

We measure the attractiveness of CSR to future job-seekers in two ways: compensation foregone and commitment, as described below:

- The compensation respondents are willing to forgo to work at a corporation practising CSR suggests a good proxy measure of the commitment to CSR (Montgomery & Ramus, 2011). The willingness to work for a lower monetary wage as a trade-off was suggested by the literature on not-for-profit employees who were willing to work at lower wages for social causes important to them (Frank, 1996; Handy, Mook, Ginieniewicz, & Quarter, 2007; Haski-Leventhal, Pournader, & McKinnon, 2017).
- Another measure of commitment to CSR, as suggested by Aguilera, Rupp, Williams, and Ganapathi (2007), is engagement with employers' CSR efforts, such as corporate volunteering programmes.

Context of the study: India

While there exists a plethora of literature about the attractiveness of CSR to job-seekers in developed western countries, less is known about what transpires in the developing world. Due to increasing global influences and the proliferation of multinational companies, it is likely that job-seekers have similar perspectives on CSR as those in developed countries. Our study is based in India where there is a long tradition of corporate philanthropy (Kassam, Handy, & Janson, 2016; Sharma, 2009). However, CSR, as it is now known, is a relatively new phenomenon due to India's late entry into the market economy. There has been a shift in expectations among job-seekers in recent decades, largely due to easily available information on the internet about CSR practices globally, with many firms (especially multinationals) utilising CSR programmes to attract talent in India (Ardichvili, Jondle, Kowske, Cornachione, Li, & Thakadipuram, 2012; Tymon, Stumpf, & Doh, 2010). With recent government initiatives requiring large companies in India to undertake CSR activities (Singh & Verma, 2014), the discourse of CSR has changed from being voluntary to mandatory for a small segment of large and profitable businesses, and has further changed expectations among stakeholders in the years preceding its final passage by the legislature.

Methods

This study surveyed business and engineering students, soon to be job-seekers, at a large university in South India. Using a sample of convenience, we avoided biases inherent in large classroom settings and ensured students across the faculties were part of the sample by distributing the surveys at various locations, including libraries, small classrooms and student cafeterias, over a period of three weeks. In general, most students, when requested, filled out the surveys, which took roughly 10–12 minutes to complete and were written in English, the language of instruction at the university. Less than 5% of students refused to fill out the survey, and there were no incentives given to complete them. We concluded our survey collection after we received completed surveys from 400 business and engineering graduate students.

We note that there exists a mandatory course on Corporate Governance and Ethics in the second semester for business students, while there is no such requirement for engineering students at the university where the survey was conducted. We also note that the university is located in Karnataka, where ample job opportunities in IT and other sectors exist and high economic growth has been recorded (from 5.5% in 1999 to 10.4% in 2010) (Paul, Sridhar, Reddy, & Srinath, 2012). There is a high demand for talent, which creates a competitive market and gives business and engineering students the ability to choose employment best suited to their preferences.

Measures

Dependent variables

Attractiveness of CSR as a job applicant: participants were asked to indicate the attractiveness of CSR in their job choice. We asked, 'How important would it be to you that your future employer is engaged in CSR activities?' Responses on the Likert-type five-point scale ranged from 'Not important' to 'Very important'. This single-item measure was used following Backhaus, Stone and Heiner (2002, p. 303), who found a high correlation in their four-item measure, suggesting a single-measure criterion to reduce respondent fatigue.

Engagement with CSR: respondents were asked, 'Would you find it acceptable if your future employer expects you to volunteer on behalf of the company?' with responses measured on a five-point Likert-type scale. We further differentiated the responses by introducing whether the volunteering was *'on company time'* versus *'in your free time'*; based on the findings of employee volunteering literature (Meijs, Tschirhart, Ten Hoorn, & Brudney, 2009; Meinhard, Handy, & Greenspan, 2010; Rodell, Breitsohl, Schröder, & Keating, 2016; Van Der Voort, Glac, & Meijs, 2009), companies often choose different strategies in engaging employees. These strategies had differing personal costs to the employee.

Commitment to CSR: we measured the wage trade-off for CSR used by Montgomery and Ramus (2011) and asked students to select a range of their earnings (a percentage from 0% to more than 10%) that they would be willing to forgo ('if you knew your company was engaged in CSR activities you agreed with?').

Independent variables

Job expectations: we asked 22 questions derived from the scales used in the literature (Hurst & Good, 2009). Through an exploratory factor analysis (maximum likelihood estimation, varimax rotation), we obtained a two-factor solution with a simple structure. The first factor (Alpha Cronbach .81) refers to '*extrinsic job expectations*' and includes 10 items such as 'work that offers appropriate pay', 'promotion possibilities in the workplace', 'making a lot of money' and 'being able to afford a good standard of living'. The second factor (Alpha Cronbach .79) refers to '*intrinsic job expectations*' and consists of eight items, including 'making the world a better place through my work', 'helping people in need', 'having the opportunity to do something worthwhile for society' and 'having good relationships with my colleagues'.

Primary goal of business: this variable estimated students' view on what the primary goal of a business is, as suggested by Wong et al. (2010). We measured the extent to which students think that the primary goal of business is 'to make profit for its owners' or 'to provide social, cultural and economic benefits for the community'. In both cases, the possible responses ranged from 1 = strongly disagree to 5 = strongly agree.

CSR-related education: respondents differed in their exposure to CSR-related education. Building on the work of Evans and Davis (2011), we asked students to rate the extent to which they learned about CSR at their university on a five-category scale, ranging from 'not at all' to 'in all my courses'.

Study programme: students were coded as 'business' or 'engineering' for their self-reported study programme.

Control variables: gender, age and family income were also measured, as these have been used as control variables in previous studies (Greening & Turban, 2000).

Analytical model

We examined the influence of the study programme, CSR-related education, job expectations and what was perceived as the primary goal of business on the students' evaluation of the attractiveness of CSR as a job applicant

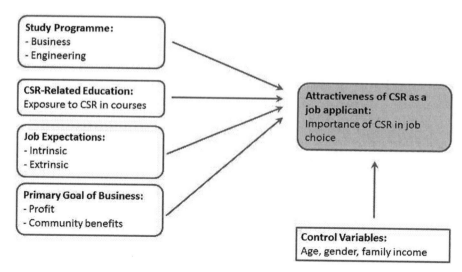

Figure 9.1.   Model on the attractiveness of CSR

(Figure 9.1). Next, we assessed the influence of these independent variables on students' engagement with and commitment to CSR as future employees. We added the attractiveness of CSR as a job applicant to the model to examine its effect on the students' engagement with and commitment to CSR as future employees (Figure 9.2, Models A and B). We used simple linear regression models to assess the net effect of the explanatory variables on each of the dependent variables.

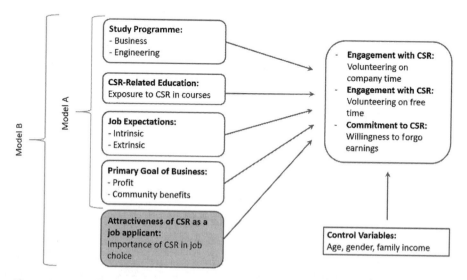

Figure 9.2.   Model A & B Engagement with CSR and commitment to CSR

Sample characteristics

In our sample of 400 students, there was a slight overrepresentation of males (57.1%). This was likely caused by the overrepresentation of males among business students (63.3% male). Among the engineering students in our sample, there was a more balanced gender distribution (51.0% male). The age of the respondents ranged from 18 to 34 years, with an average of 21.7 years. The mean age was 22.9 years (business students) and 21.6 years (engineering students). Most respondents came from a middle-income class (85.4%). In engineering, there were slightly more students from a higher income class (13.1%) than in business (8.0%), but the difference was not statistically significant. Interestingly, and maybe contrary to prevailing views of business students compared to students from other disciplines, both groups expressed similar job expectations, valuing both extrinsic and intrinsic job expectations equally strongly (4.25 and 4.44 on a five-point Likert scale), and both groups saw the community benefits of business as more of a primary goal than just making profit (4.23 and 4.03 on a five-point Likert scale).

Given the likely influence of exposure to CSR education on how students evaluate a future employer's CSR practices, it is important to note that business and engineering students in our sample significantly ($p<.000$) differed in the extent to which they had learned about CSR on their course, with 39.5% of business students indicating that CSR was a topic in most to all of their courses, as compared to 13.4% of engineering students. Moreover, more business students than their engineering counterparts rated their exposure to CSR-related courses as very important (44.4% versus 24.9%, $p<.000$). Descriptive analysis, however, indicates that, in spite of these differences, students' engagement with and commitment to CSR did not vary depending on the study programme. On average, students expressed a slightly higher interest in volunteering on company time than in volunteering in their free time if a future employer required them to volunteer on behalf of the company (3.88 and 3.64 on a five-point Likert scale). Furthermore, students on average were willing to forgo between 1% and 6% of their income to work for a company with a CSR policy they found attractive.

Findings

Correlational analysis of key variables

Table 9.1 reports on the bivariate correlations among our key variables. First, with respect to CSR-related education, we found a positive, albeit relatively weak, association with the attractiveness students attach to a future employer's engagement in CSR activities ($r = .16$). Surprisingly, a much

Table 9.1.   Pearson correlations among key variables

1. CSR-related education	–								
2. Attractiveness of CSR	.16**	–							
3. Job expectations: extrinsic	.10	.21**	–						
4. Job expectations: intrinsic	.02	.23**	.49**	–					
5. Primary goal of business = profit	.22**	.11*	.19**	.13*	–				
6. Primary goal of business = community benefits	.04	.21**	.17**	.22**	.12*	–			
7. Engagement with CSR: volunteering on work time	.13*	.33**	.11*	.05	.17**	.08	–		
8. Engagement with CSR: volunteering in free time	.11*	.33**	-.09	.17**	.11*	.08	.09	–	
9. Commitment to CSR: willingness to forgo earnings	.02	.05	-.24**	-.06	.07	.06	.07	.19**	–

Notes: *Correlation is significant at the 0.05 level (2-tailed); **Correlation is significant at the 0.01 level (2-tailed).

stronger positive correlation (r = .22) existed between CSR-related education and students' view that the primary goal of a company is to make profit for its stakeholders. Further, the more students were exposed to CSR-related education, the more willing they were to volunteer on company time and in their free time. However, no significant association existed for the willingness to work for less salary in support of a company's CSR policy.

Compared to CSR-related education, the job expectations of students were more strongly correlated with the attractiveness of an employer's CSR, and, surprisingly, this was the case for both extrinsic and intrinsic job expectations (r = .21 and r = .23 respectively). This suggests that there was no contradiction between the more material and non-material value orientations of students (considering that both intrinsic job expectations and the attractiveness of CSR are part of a non-material value pattern), which is indicated by the strong, significant positive correlation between both sets of job expectations (r = .49). This observation is further supported by the positive significant correlation that exists between the attractiveness of an employer's CSR and what job applicants consider to be the primary goals of a business (r = .11 for making profit and r = .21 for benefiting the community). There is a significant positive correlation between both primary goals (r = .12), which are also positively correlated with both types of job expectations. In other words, no mutually exclusive relationship exists between a material, profit-oriented outlook and a non-material, community benefit-oriented outlook.

Finally, students' job expectations, extrinsic and intrinsic, are also associated with their engagement with CSR through employee volunteering and their commitment to CSR; however, clear differences exist.

While both extrinsic and intrinsic job expectations were positively correlated (r = .33) with the attractiveness of CSR, extrinsic job expectations correlated positively with a willingness to volunteer on company time (r = .11), but negatively with a willingness to forgo earnings (r = .24). Intrinsic job expectations were not associated with volunteering on company time, but were positively correlated with employee volunteering in one's free time (r = .17). Thus, in terms of students' personal engagement with CSR, we seem to be measuring separate phenomena and it appears to be dependent on their job expectations.

This is further supported by the lack of association between the three indicators. A positive correlation existed between willingness to volunteer in one's free time and willingness to work for less money in support of a company's CSR activities (r = .19), but no significant correlation was found between employee volunteering on company time and employee volunteering in one's free time or working for less money. Thus, volunteering on company time and in one's free time, while both part of the 'employee volunteering' CSR programme, were not correlated, suggesting they were perceived as separate phenomena by students.

Regression analyses

In a second step in the analysis, we examine the influence of the study programme, CSR-related education, job expectations and perceptions of the primary goal of business on the students' evaluation of the attractiveness of CSR as a job applicant (Figure 9.1 above). Table 9.2 shows the results of the simple linear regression.

First, no significant difference exists between business and engineering students with regard to the attractiveness of CSR as job-seekers, even when controlling for covariates. Furthermore, the exposure to CSR-related education on their courses did not predict the attractiveness of CSR. Albeit a positive relationship, it was only marginally significant (p = .055). However, students' personal value orientations, manifested in job expectations, were important. Intrinsic job expectations significantly increased the attractiveness of CSR to a job applicant. In addition, if students perceived the primary goal of a company to be benefits to the community, they were also more likely to attach attractiveness to their future employer.

In the next three simple linear regression models, based on Figure 9.2, we examined the three dependent variables for job applicants' potential engagement with CSR: volunteering on company time – Model 1; volunteering in one's free time – Model 2; and willingness to forgo earnings – Model 3 (in Table 9.3). For each of these three models, we tested a basic model (Figure 9.2, Model A) and then examined the additional effect of

Table 9.2. Dependent variable: attractiveness of CSR

	Attractiveness of CSR
Gender (ref = male)	.05
Age	−.02
Family income: high (ref = middle or low)	.001
Study programme: Engineering (ref = business)	−.04
CSR-related education – most or all courses (ref = in fewer courses)	.11
Job expectations:	
Extrinsic	.07
Intrinsic	.19**
Primary goal of business = profit	.07
Primary goal of business = community benefits	.17**
R-Square	.14
Adjusted R-Square	.12

Note: Linear regression model, standardised beta-coefficients significance: *p<.05; **p<.01

Table 9.3. Dependent variables: engagement with CSR and commitment to CSR

Model	1. Engagement with CSR: volunteering on company time		2. Engagement with CSR: volunteering in free time		3. Commitment to CSR: willingness to forgo earnings	
	Model A1	Model B1	Model A2	Model B2	Model A3	Model B3
Gender (ref = male)	−.10	−.12*	−.08	−.09	−.03	−.04
Age	.03	.03	−.04	−.03	.06	.06
Family income:						
High (ref = middle or low)	.02	.2	.01	.02	.05 ̄	.05
Study programme: Engineering (ref = business)	.05	.06	.04	.04	.06	.06
CSR-related education – most or all courses (ref = in fewer courses)	.08	.05	.12*	.12	−.01	−.02
Job expectations:						
Extrinsic	.11	.09	−.21**	−.20***	−.27***	−.27***
Intrinsic	−.07	−.12	.25***	.22***	.06	.05
Primary goal of business = profit	.12	.09	.11	.09	.16**	.15*
Primary goal of business = community benefits	.04	−.01	.09	.03	.16**	.15*
Attractiveness of CSR		.30***		.33**		.07
R-Square	.05	.13	.10	.13	.11	.11
Adjusted R-Square	.02	.10	.07	.10	.08	.08

Note: Linear regression model, standardised

the attractiveness of the CSR of the employer on the dependent variables (Figure 9.2, Model B).

We now discuss the findings across the models for the independent variables:

Control variables: of all the control variables (gender, age and family income), only gender played a role. In Model B1 (volunteering on company time), when controlling for the attractiveness of CSR, females were less inclined than males to volunteer on company time.

Study programme: whether students pursued business or engineering did not affect their engagement with and commitment to CSR as a future employee in all models.

CSR-related education: among the three models, CSR-related education had only a positive effect on employee volunteering in one's free time (Model A2); however, this effect is insignificant when controlling for the attractiveness of CSR (Model B2). This suggests that CSR-related education raised interest and support for CSR which then had an additional effect on students' commitment to CSR by way of volunteering in one's free time (Table 9.2). It however should be noted that we did not find a significant net effect of CSR-related education on the attractiveness of CSR in one's future employer (Table 9.2).

Job expectations: intrinsic and extrinsic job expectations had no significant influence on employee volunteering on company time (Model A1), but played a significant role in Model A2 and Model A3. Stronger extrinsic (material) job expectations were negatively associated with volunteering in one's free time (Model A2) and with earning less (Model A3). Intrinsic (non-material) job expectations were positively associated with a willingness to perform employee volunteering in one's free time (Model A2), but had no effect on forgoing earnings. These effects remain stable when adding the attractiveness of CSR (Models B1, B2, B3).

Primary goal of the company: a strong belief in the primary goal of the business being either to make profit or to provide community benefits, was positively related to students' willingness to forgo earnings, even when controlling for the attractiveness of CSR (Model B3).

Attractiveness of CSR: the stepwise addition of the attractiveness of CSR in the regression model had a strong positive effect on volunteering both on company time (Model B1) and in one's free time (Model B2), but not on the willingness to forgo earnings in support of CSR (Model B3).

Scenario

An IT company based in Bangalore has trouble finding a new employee to head up its corporate volunteering programme after the previous person responsible for it has left the company. The HR manager, Akriti, is thinking about whether she should suggest to the board that they use the allocated salary instead of giving a bonus to the best employees. This would fit with the firm's talent management strategy to attract the best university graduates and recognise their hard work. On the other hand, Akriti does not want to compromise on the company's CSR strategy, which puts a lot of emphasis on giving back to the local community in terms of an elaborate corporate volunteering programme based on the individual skills and values of employees. So, she has the company's employees come up with a corporate volunteering programme and, as a prize, will offer the successful employee one year of paid leave from their current job at the company to take up the new position of implementing their award-winning programme. Akriti has read that good CSR programmes, such as corporate volunteering, both attract and retain employees. She uses her ideas and the research she has read and prepares a presentation for the board with the headline 'Attracting and retaining talent – via CSR expenditure or higher earnings?'

Discussion

This chapter has examined the attractiveness of employers' engagement with and commitment to CSR practices to job-seekers in India. Our analysis reveals that neither the study programme nor CSR-related education have an influence on the attractiveness of CSR-practising employers. Instead, students' job expectations and their view on the primary goal of a business are of importance, albeit with varying effects on different types of CSR involvement.

First, contrary to our expectations, we found that any self-selection that occurred in students choosing between business and engineering did not affect their potential engagement with and commitment to CSR. This was underscored by the fact that in both groups there was no influence of CSR-related education on perceptions of the attractiveness of CSR, future engagement with CSR in terms of volunteering (Models A1/B1) on company time (Models A2/B2) and volunteering on free time, or on commitment to CSR in terms of willingness to forgo earnings (Models A3/B3). This suggests that students in the same age cohort have similar perceptions of CSR, given the discourse on public policy, and that their choice of career does not influence CSR perceptions. Most end up working for corporations and hence may not be dissimilar in their attributes.

Despite the fact that most of the business students are exposed to and interested in CSR educational content, CSR-related education did not have a significant influence on either the perceived attractiveness of CSR-practising employers or the students' potential engagement with and commitment to CSR. Perhaps university-based CSR education is not internalised and consequently does not show up in individual decisions. Indeed, the findings of a survey of CSR-related courses across business schools in India by

Srinivasan, Srinivasan, and Anand (2012) showed that the 'pedagogy itself poses a challenge due to lack of available Indian cases' (p. 18) due to a lack of faculty training and the limited indigenous course materials.

It is likely that the attractiveness of CSR-involved employers comes not from the students' exposure to CSR-related courses but from the growing social norm of CSR in the larger, more successful companies in India (Gautam & Singh, 2010), as well as from governmental influence and discourse in the regulatory arena on CSR (Singh & Verma, 2014). Thus, the counterintuitive finding on the influence of CSR-related education can be explained by looking at prevailing CSR social norms among corporations, expectations and changes in public policy regarding CSR and the influence of the media (Dash, 2012). We consider this finding to be of both theoretical and practical importance. The students were quite aware of CSR regardless of their study programme or the extent of exposure to CSR within their course; there may be a deep socialisation process among students regarding the role of corporations in society, that is not restricted to business majors.

We found no differences among students on the business programme or the engineering programme. Ruling out any a priori self-sorting into different programmes, our findings indicate a sorting of students with respect to job expectations. Those individuals with intrinsic job expectations, regarded as being more altruistic, see their employment as a means to 'making the world a better place through my work', 'helping people in need' and 'having the opportunity to do something worthwhile for society'. Thus, altruistic students differed from those with more self-interested job expectations; they were more likely to engage in their future employer's CSR efforts even at their own cost, while students with extrinsic job expectations were more likely to participate if volunteering was done at the employer's cost. This brings into focus the importance of developing CSR practices that engage both employees with more extrinsic job expectations and those with more intrinsic ones.

Furthermore, commitment to CSR, in terms of the amount of salary students were willing to forgo, showed a negative and significant correlation only with extrinsic job expectations. This finding is consistent with experimental evidence that a value fit between students and employers has a mediating effect on the attractiveness of CSR (Jones et al., 2014).

Interestingly, we found counterintuitive findings: regardless of whether students believed that profit-making or societal goals were the primary objective of the corporation, they were equally likely to forgo part of their earnings to work for companies with CSR practices they valued. There are different interpretations of these findings. As CSR is currently a strong societal expectation and became mandatory for large, profitable companies, students wishing to be employed by such companies can reconcile making profits with the goal of community benefits through CSR practices.

On CSR-related courses, as well as in the popular press and media, students often learn that profitability and CSR go hand in hand and can reinforce one another. Thus, when companies generate profits, the need to 'compensate' society with CSR activities is elevated. From another perspective, CSR activities may be strategically chosen to enhance profits (Friedman, 2010), and students who see profit-making as a primary goal may also value CSR as it strengthens profits.

From both perspectives, the trade-off between profitable and socially beneficial employers is seen by students to establish a virtuous cycle, hence their commitment to CSR as employees. Thus, it is not surprising to find a positive correlation between CSR and profit, as it is also an educational effect: where CSR education and the popular media promote the idea that CSR makes good sense and greater profits (Chandler, 2016).

Limitations and research outlook

Like all cross-sectional studies, our study is limited and we cannot comment on the causality of our results. Future research using experimental designs may overcome this limitation. Furthermore, the survey used in this study focused on the behavioural intention of students as future employees. Thus, another limitation of our study is that students' intended behaviour after graduating may alter if some contextual variables change, such as there being greater demand in the labour market or regulation requiring companies to engage in CSR. To overcome this limitation, future research could use data collected over a period of time to understand the impact of such contextual variables.

Although our comparison of business and engineering students did not show significant differences, it could be useful to look at students in other fields such as nursing, education and public services, where the talent search is also competitive.

Finally, our study is situated in India, thereby adding an international perspective to the literature by including research done in an emerging economy, with recently mandated CSR policies and relatively poor educational opportunities in CSR training. Further research could investigate these questions a few years post-regulation to see if there are any changes among job-seekers' evaluation of and commitment to CSR.

Further studies should examine similar questions in other developing countries as commenced by Marika, Magutu and Munjuri (2017) in Kenya. This would give insight into how job-seekers in politically unstable environments, or under corrupt regimes, value the reputation of companies practising CSR. These findings would be crucial to multinationals recruiting local talent in such countries.

Our findings show that potential employees are cognisant of the costs they need to bear for employee volunteer programmes; and they find companies attractive only if the costs are borne by the company and not by themselves. In order to get buy-in from employees, it is necessary to examine how CSR programmes are perceived by employees; do employees ascribe costs to themselves or to their employers? As the willingness to volunteer in one's free time for CSR activities may be affected by demographic variables such as marital status, personal norms and values, self-efficacy and volunteering behaviour, further studies could include these variables, thereby increasing the predictive power of our models.

Companies should question whether employees are willing to shoulder some of the costs of CSR initiatives, especially if these initiatives are linked with CSR outcomes valued by employees. Further research is needed to better understand the interrelations between the attractiveness of CSR, the commitment to CSR, the engagement with CSR activities and the design of CSR activities in different contexts (the particular sector, whether it is a local company or a multinational, etc.), as employee expectations may differ.

Practical implications

There are several implications of our findings, which we address by first examining our results on the attractiveness of CSR to students who will soon be in the job market as potential employees. The attractiveness of CSR-practising employers may result from socialisation processes and education. Although we found no influence of education in our study, further studies need to disentangle the nature of CSR education from its influence – for example, the quality and relatedness of the CSR materials to the cultural practices, the training received by teachers in using local materials, and so on. Another unresolved question is whether cultural and social norms regarding the CSR practices of employers are moderated by the influence of CSR education.

Second, our findings are of interest to companies designing CSR practices involving employees. In a study based on 990 Canadian companies (Basil, Runte, Easwaramoorthy, & Barr, 2009), employers were aware that employee volunteer programmes increased their attractiveness and helped ameliorate damaged reputations. However, as our study suggests, companies designing CSR employee volunteering programmes should be aware of how different forms of employee volunteering evoke different reactions. The likelihood of participation depends on whether volunteering is done on company time versus in employees' own free time. For (future) employees, volunteering on company time carries a cost for the company, whereas volunteering in one's own free time costs the employee his/her time.

Their interpretation of the different forms of employee volunteering may be that employers are paying 'lip service' to the concept of employee volunteering as CSR in general, assuming that in practice the costs are borne by the employee (Basil et al., 2009).

Third, with respect to commitment to CSR in terms of willingness to forgo earnings, our results suggest that companies should be aware of the potential effects of recruiting graduates with extrinsic job expectations. Both business and engineering students, who have extrinsic job expectations, were less willing to give up a small percentage of their wages to work for a company practising CSR they valued. Students with extrinsic job expectations, which are related to a more materialistic outlook on life, are less likely to make sacrifices in the name of CSR. This finding is in line with that of Handy and Katz (1998), who propose that offering lower wages may serve as a sorting mechanism to attract employees who are not solely concerned with achieving personal goals.

In the case of India where there is rampant corruption (Sharma, 2018), companies with a good CSR record may be perceived by job-seekers to be less corrupt and exploitative of employees (Rodriguez, Siegel, Hillman, & Eden, 2006). Thus, the willingness to forgo income to work for an employer with valued CSR practices may also reflect a choice of working for an employer that is not corrupt.

Conclusion

Our study contributes to the literature examining the attractiveness of CSR to job applicants in two different ways. First, we examined not only the determinants of CSR attractiveness to potential job applicants, but also the interrelation between CSR attractiveness and three probable types of engagement with and commitment to the CSR of potential employees. These results extend our knowledge of the antecedents and consequences of the attractiveness of CSR and its impact on potential employees' engagement with companies' CSR activities.

Second, while previous research has focused mainly on business students, this study extends the scope of the findings to include engineering students. We did this to understand the potential differences between students on different programmes in their responses to potential employers' CSR efforts.

Questions for students

1. What main factors are found in this research to be related to the attractiveness of CSR?
2. What other factors do you think may be related to the attractiveness of CSR?
3. Do you believe that CSR practices make a company more profitable? Why or why not?
4. What implications could be drawn from this study for the design of CSR programmes?
5. What are the important factors to consider in designing effective programmes in different contexts (e.g., types of employees, industries, countries)?
6. Should employees be obliged to participate in corporate volunteering programmes as part of a firm's CSR policy?
7. Would it make a difference if the corporate volunteering takes place within or outside of paid working hours?

References

Aguilera, R. V., Rupp, D. E., Williams, C. A., & Ganapathi, J. (2007). Putting the S back in corporate social responsibility: A multilevel theory of social change in organizations. *Academy of Management Review, 32*(3), 836–863.

Ardichvili, A., Jondle, D., Kowske, B., Cornachione, E., Li, J., & Thakadipuram, T. (2012). Ethical cultures in large business organizations in Brazil, Russia, India, and China. *Journal of Business Ethics, 105*(4), 415–428.

Backhaus, K. B., Stone, B., & Heiner, K. (2002). Exploring the relationship between corporate social performance and employer attractiveness. *Business and Society, 41*(3), 292–318.

Barber, A. E. (1998). *Recruiting employees: Individual and organizational perspectives*. Thousand Oaks, CA: Sage.

Basil, D. Z., Runte, M. S., Easwaramoorthy, M., & Barr, C. (2009). Company support for employee volunteering: A national survey of companies in Canada. *Journal of Business Ethics, 85*(2), 387–398.

Borkowski, S. C., & Ugras, Y. J. (1998). Business students and ethics: A meta-analysis. *Journal of Business Ethics, 17*(11), 1117–1127.

Chandler, D. (2016). *Strategic corporate social responsibility: Sustainable value creation (5th edition)*. Thousand Oaks, CA: Sage.

Dash, A. K. (2012). Media impact on corporate governance in India: A research agenda. *Corporate Governance: The International Journal of Business in Society, 12*(1), 89–100.

Evans, W. R., & Davis, W. D. (2011). An examination of perceived corporate citizenship, job applicant attraction, and CSR work role definition. *Business and Society, 50*(3), 456–480.

Frank, R. H. (1996). What price the moral high ground? *Southern Economic Journal, 63*(1), 1–17.

Friedman, M. (2010). The social responsibility of business is to increase its profits. In P. Griseri & N. Seppala (Eds.), *Corporate ethics and corporate governance* (pp. 173–178). Berlin: Springer.

Gautam, R., & Singh, A. (2010). Corporate social responsibility practices in India: A study of top 500 companies. *Global Business and Management Research: An International Journal, 2*(1), 41–56.

Greening, D. W., & Turban, D. B. (2000). Corporate social performance as a competitive advantage in attracting a quality workforce. *Business and Society, 39*(3), 254–280.

Handy, F., & Katz, E. (1998). The wage differential between nonprofit institutions and corporations: Getting more by paying less? *Journal of Comparative Economics, 26*(2), 246–261.

Handy, F., Mook, L., Ginieniewicz, J., & Quarter, J. (2007). The moral high ground: Perceptions of wage differentials among executive directors of Canadian nonprofits. *Philanthropist, 21*(2), 109–127.

Haski-Leventhal, D., Pournader, M., & McKinnon, A. (2017). The role of gender and age in business students' values, CSR attitudes, and responsible management education: Learnings from the PRME international survey. *Journal of Business Ethics, 146*(1), 219–239.

Hurst, J. L., & Good, L. K. (2009). Generation Y and career choice: The impact of retail career perceptions, expectations and entitlement perceptions. *Career Development International, 14*(6), 570–593.

Jones, D. A., Willness, C. R., & Madey, S. (2014). Why are job-seekers attracted by corporate social performance? Experimental and field tests of three signal-based mechanisms. *Academy of Management Journal, 57*(2), 383–404.

Kassam, M., Handy, F., & Janson, E. (2016). *Philanthropy in India: Practice and promise.* New Delhi: Sage.

Lievens, F., & Highhouse, S. (2006). The relation of instrumental and symbolic attributes to a company's attractiveness as an employer. *Personnel Psychology, 56*(1), 75–102.

Marika, N. M., Magutu, J. M., & Munjuri, M. G. (2017). Corporate social responsibility and employer attractiveness among business students at the University of Nairobi, Kenya. *International Journal of Arts and Commerce, 6*(2), 71–88.

Meijs, L. C. P. M., Tschirhart, M., Ten Hoorn, E. M., & Brudney, J. L. (2009). Effect of design elements for corporate volunteer programs on volunteerability. *The International Journal of Volunteer Administration, 26*(1), 23–32.

Meinhard, A., Handy, F., & Greenspan, I. (2010). Corporate participation in the social economy: Employer-supported volunteering programs. In L. Mook, J. Quarter, & S. Ryan (Eds.), *Researching the social economy* (pp. 245–266). Toronto: University of Toronto Press.

Montgomery, D. B., & Ramus, C. A. (2011). Calibrating MBA job preferences for the 21st century. *Academy of Management Learning and Education, 10*(1), 9–26.

Paul, S., Sridhar, K. S., Reddy, A. V., & Srinath, P. (2012). *The state of our cities: Evidence from Karnataka.* Oxford: Oxford University Press.

Rodell, J. B., Breitsohl, H., Schröder, M., & Keating, D. J. (2016). Employee volunteering: A review and framework for future research. *Journal of Management, 42*(1), 55–84.

Rodriguez, P., Siegel, D. S., Hillman, A., & Eden, L. (2006). Three lenses on the multinational enterprise: Politics, corruption, and corporate social responsibility. *Journal of International Business Studies, 37*(6), 733–746.

Rupp, D. E., Shao, R., Thornton, M. A., & Skarlicki, D. P. (2013). Applicants' and employees' reactions to corporate social responsibility: The moderating effects of first-party justice perceptions and moral identity. *Personnel Psychology, 66*(4), 895–933.

Sharma, A. (2018). New brooms and old: Sweeping up corruption in India, one law at a time. *Current Anthropology, 59*(S18), S72–S82.

Sharma, S. G. (2009). Corporate social responsibility in India: An overview. *The International Lawyer, 43*(4), 1515–1533.

Singh, A., & Verma, P. (2014). From philanthropy to mandatory CSR: A journey towards mandatory corporate social responsibility in India. *European Journal of Business and Management, 6*(14), 146–152.

Spence, M. (1978). Job market signaling. In P. Diamond & M. Rothschild (Eds.), *Uncertainty in economics* (pp. 281–306). New York: Academic Press.

Srinivasan, P., Srinivasan, V., & Anand, R. V. (2012). *Status of ethics, corporate governance, CSR and environment education in business schools in India: An exploratory study.* Working Paper No. 362. Retrieved from http://ssrn.com/abstract=2116274.

Turban, D. B. (2001). Organizational attractiveness as an employer on college campuses: An examination of the applicant population. *Journal of Vocational Behavior, 58*(2), 293–312.

Tymon Jr., W. G., Stumpf, S. A., & Doh, J. P. (2010). Exploring talent management in India: The neglected role of intrinsic rewards. *Journal of World Business, 45*(2), 109–121.

Van Der Voort, J. M., Glac, K., & Meijs, L. C. (2009). 'Managing' corporate community involvement. *Journal of Business Ethics, 90*(3), 311–329.

Wong, A., Long, F., & Elankumaran, S. (2010). Business students' perception of corporate social responsibility: The United States, China, and India. *Corporate Social Responsibility and Environmental Management, 17*(5), 299–310.

10 Corporate Political Activism and Employee Responses

Daniel Korschun and Zoë Godfrey

Overview

Companies are increasingly making public statements on political issues, elections and government legislation. This chapter examines an overlooked potential consequence of such corporate political activism – employee engagement. We present a framework that identifies three facets which drive employee reactions to activism: the stated rationale of the political position, the extremity of the position, and perceived manager support for activism. The framework distinguishes between ideological engagement and functional engagement, and delineates which facets of corporate political activism affect which form of engagement. Each form of engagement subsequently drives distinct consequences. The chapter concludes with implications for theorists and practitioners.

Learning objectives

By the end of this chapter, readers should be able to:

- identify three key facets of corporate political activism as they pertain to employee engagement
- understand the distinction between ideological and functional engagement
- explain the ways the ideological or functional engagement leads to diverse employee behaviours inside and outside of work
- detail the ways in which companies might implement this knowledge to engage employees.

Introduction

Companies are increasingly becoming politically active in the public sphere. For example, Nike launched a campaign in 2018 in which it featured the former National Football League player Colin Kaepernick, who became the centre of controversy when he began kneeling during the national anthem at games in order to draw attention to police brutality against minorities in the USA. Nike's campaign immediately drew both praise and criticism from consumers; many consumers lauded the company on social media, while some posted videos in which they set their Nike shoes on fire. Analogous customer reactions to corporate political activism of this sort have been documented anecdotally (e.g., Smith & Korschun, 2018) and to some extent in scholarly research (Chatterji & Toffel, 2016).

Managers and scholars have put most of their attention on consumers and have largely overlooked an equally important group of stakeholders – employees (Hambrick & Wowak, 2019). This oversight is consequential because the actions of the corporation are arguably most salient to employees, who spend considerable time, effort and emotional resources on the job. For example, the literature suggests that employees can be quite sensitive to non-market strategies of the company (McWilliams & Siegel, 2001). Some employees must also serve as representatives of the company with customers, suppliers and other corporate constituents (Korschun, 2015). In these cases, they may be asked about corporate political activism while trying to accomplish other tasks (Edinger-Schons, Lengler-Graiff, Scheidler, & Wieseke, 2019). In sum, there is a need to understand how employees respond to corporate political activism.

In this chapter, we present a framework for researchers who wish to study this burgeoning phenomenon. The framework describes how key dimensions of corporate political activity contribute to both ideological and functional engagement, which subsequently lead to several forms of employee behaviour. We contribute to theory on this topic by identifying key dimensions of corporate political activism for employees that have not yet been revealed in prior research: the expressed rationale for the activism, the extremity of the activism and managerial support for the activism. Identifying these specific dimensions delves into deeper theoretical territory than the literature to date, moving beyond the question of whether employees will respond favourably or unfavourably to corporate activism. We also contribute by uncovering the psychological mechanism through which corporate activism may drive employee engagement. The framework reveals a key tension between ideological and functional engagement, of which each have distinct antecedents and consequences. We also introduce the notion of pressure to conform, which, we argue, mitigates the degree to which corporate activism may negatively contribute to ideological engagement yet increase functional engagement. Finally, we contribute by identifying those consequences which are not typically associated with engagement. On the ideological side, we explain that corporate activism may heighten motivation to engage in political participation, such as voting or attending political demonstrations; on the functional side, we explain that when corporate activism contributes to functional goals, it may motivate a more transactional form of engagement, whereby an employee will invest more in their work.

In the next section, we describe those dimensions of corporate activism which are most relevant to employee engagement. We then present a series of propositions which predict how and under what conditions these dimensions contribute to ideological and functional goals, and finally downstream forms of employee engagement. We end the chapter by outlining the implications of our framework for both theorists and managers.

Facets of corporate political activism

When is political activity by a company considered activism? We define *corporate political activism* as a public appeal for action by an organisation or its executives on a political issue, election or government legislation. We contend that such activism has at least two defining characteristics. First, corporate political activism is public. In contrast to traditional political lobbying, which often takes place behind the scenes (e.g., Hillman & Hitt, 1999; Sethi, 1982), corporate political activism has at least some component in which the organisation openly discloses or even promotes a political agenda in an attempt to sway public opinion or affirm a company's stated corporate values. Second, it is designed to change the status quo by drawing attention to an unsettled political issue. Typically, it goes beyond supporting existing laws to include what future legislation should look like. Thus, corporate political activism often involves putting pressure on legislators or other public officials by swaying public opinion or by increasing media attention on a political issue. Although still unusual, a few companies describe themselves as activist companies; for example, Patagonia uses the term prominently in its corporate social responsibility and sustainability reporting.

Corporate political activism shares some conceptual territory with corporate social responsibility (CSR) in that both involve directing corporate attention or resources to address pressing social or environmental issues. Yet, corporate political activism differs from CSR in some notable ways. For example, the goal of CSR is to improve lives or the environment, usually by directly impacting beneficiaries through corporate programmes (Pomering & Dolnicar, 2009). However, corporate political activism explicitly targets the political process as a mechanism to indirectly change the social, economic or environmental landscape and thereby benefit society. Thus, a company which touts its reduction of carbon emissions would be engaging in CSR or sustainability, while a company arguing that the USA should be part of The Paris Agreement on climate change is engaging in activism. Another way in which CSR tends to differ from corporate political activism is in the type of issues it addresses. While both address important social or environmental challenges, corporate political activism not only addresses issues such as immigration, gun control, abortion, welfare programmes or taxes, but also advocates for the best means to tackle that issue, which may align with a political party or viewpoint (e.g., reducing gun violence by promoting either gun control or gun rights). Thus, corporate political activism often involves choosing a side on an unsettled and contentious issue (Nalick, Josefy, Zardkoohi, & Bierman, 2016). Overall, we view corporate political activism as multifaceted and conceptually distinct from CSR. Moreover, we identify several facets of corporate political activism that are likely to influence employee engagement. These are rationale for the political activism, the extremity of the company position and the degree to which management is believed to support the company's political position. We now discuss each of these in turn.

Rationale for political activism

Companies that engage in political activism are often subject to inquiries from the press and other stakeholders as to their motivation (Korschun, Rafieian, Aggarwal, & Swain, 2019). Some companies may claim that a stand was announced because a policy or law would have a substantial impact on financial performance. For example, Ryanair CEO Michael O'Leary stated that his airline opposed Brexit because it would make fares more expensive and harm the performance of companies in the industry (Meredith, 2018). In contrast, Disney opposed a restrictive abortion law in Georgia on purely moral grounds, stating that it would reconsider filming in the state if the law is enacted (Denning, 2019).

We contend that employees respond differently to political activism depending on whether the justification for that activism is based on moral or performance reasoning. This is consistent with Smith and Korschun (2018), who distinguish between the moral and performance motives of companies taking a stand.

Extremity of company position

Political opinions among the general public may be becoming less centrist and more extreme. A Pew Research Center study (2014) finds that the political views of Democrats and Republicans have diverged over the past few decades, leaving the USA more polarised than ever. Such a trend reveals variance in the extremity of views among the general public, and these are reflected in the varied political positions of companies.

Several methods have been used to define and measure the extremity of a political position. For example, Jost, Napier, Thorisdottir, Gosling, Palfai, and Ostafin (2007) asked respondents to indicate their ideological extremism using a 1 to 9 scale, with 1 being extremely liberal and 9 being extremely conservative. They measured extremism by calculating the distance of each response from the midpoint (i.e., the absolute value of the score subtracted by the midpoint value). Other studies use analogous methods to capture the extremism of a political view (i.e., Fernbach, Rogers, Fox, & Sloman, 2013; Toner, Leary, Asher, & Jongman-Sereno, 2013). This distance from the middle allows for unique comparisons and is separate from the scales that utilise left or right directional measurement to capture the liberality or conservativeness of respondents.

Based on this prior work, we conceptualise political views on an issue as residing on a spectrum from extreme right (conservative) to extreme left (liberal); a political position would be considered more moderate if residing closer to the middle or mainstream, and more extreme as it approaches either pole (Abelson, 1995). Thus, we contend that employees may attend not only to which side of the political spectrum a position is on (i.e., left versus right) but also the extent to which that stand diverges from a more mainstream and ostensibly centrist view.

Manager support of political position

Upper management shapes employee experiences at work (e.g., Albert & Whetten, 1985) and employees are aware of these views (Kennedy, Goolsby, & Arnould, 2003; Kirca, Jayachandran, & Bearden, 2005). Some literature suggests that employees form impressions not only of their views about operations and critical business functions, but also of their views about CSR (Korschun, Bhattachary, & Swain, 2014). We extend this to the political realm, suggesting that when a company takes a political position, employees routinely assess the degree to which the position is shared across management. Employees use these construals to determine how they fit in with the company's most prototypical members (i.e., managers and executives). Thus, employees not only evaluate the political position itself, but also the extent to which the company's stated view is uniform across the organisation's management.

When an organisation begins engaging in political activism, an employee may perceive that much of management, including their immediate supervisor, is united in the political position. For example, when Microsoft announced its position on Deferred Action for Childhood Arrival (DACA) in the USA, it did so by having multiple executives appear in near unison on television broadcast networks. They committed to defending DACA-protected employees in court. In such cases where multiple managers are vocal in their activism on behalf of the company, employees may see the support of the activism as prototypical behaviour which is shared by the majority of organisational members. Thus, we contend that employees will assess the diffusion of manager support for the corporate activism as a means to evaluate their role (Hackman & Oldham, 1976; La Rocco & Jones, 1978) and fit (Cable & Judge, 1996; Kristof, 1996) in the organisation.

How corporate political activism drives employee engagement

Our proposed framework explains how and when corporate activism drives employee engagement (see Figure 10.1). Previous literature defines engagement broadly as the 'cognitive, emotional, and behavioural components that are associated with individual role performance' (Saks, 2006, p. 602). However, the political realm reveals a form that goes beyond individual role performance. Our framework distinguishes between two different kinds of engagement: functional and ideological. Functional engagement is more consistent with traditional descriptions of general employee engagement, which occurs when an employee is immersed in individual role performance (Kahn, 1990). For example, a factory worker may enjoy and be highly engaged in the activity of production. A second, parallel form of engagement is more ideological. Such ideological engagement occurs when an employee becomes physically, cognitively and emotionally immersed in aspects of their job that contribute to the company's ideological goals. Such ideological engagement thus involves a similar psychological process, yet a broader orientation towards how one's role may affect society. For example, an employee in the coffee industry who is deeply immersed in their job due to its positive impact on the lives of suppliers would be ideologically engaged. Importantly, our conceptualisation enables us to demarcate those elements of engagement that are extra-role

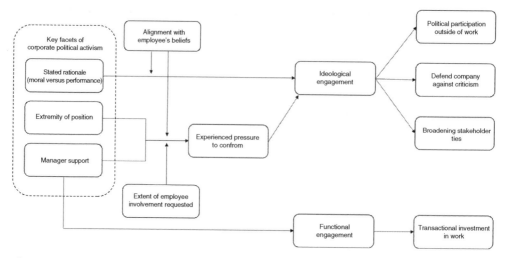

Figure 10.1.   The corporate political activism and employee engagement model

and may inculcate motivations for societal impact. It is also consistent with prior research, such as that of Du, Bhattacharya, and Sen (2015), who argue that employees respond to CSR based on how much it fulfils either developmental or ideological needs. We build upon this view, distinguishing between two different forms of engagement: ideological and functional.

The framework focuses on ideological and functional engagement as the consequences of three key dimensions of corporate activism for employees: the expressed rationale for corporate political activism, the extremity of the activism and managerial support for the activism. Our framework ties these dimensions to employees' ideological engagement. In essence, a moral rationale for the activism has a direct effect on an employee's ideological engagement, while the extremity of corporate activism and managerial support for the activism have an indirect effect through experienced pressure to conform, which has a negative effect on ideological engagement. Ideological and functional engagement in turn have respective outcomes; ideological engagement leads to political participation outside of work and defence of the company when criticised, while functional engagement leads to greater personal investment in work. We now provide the logical reasoning for each link in the model in more detail.

Stated rationale for corporate political activism and ideological engagement

We propose that when a company uses a moral (as opposed to performance-based) justification for its corporate political activism, it will drive ideological engagement. Prior research (Holzer, 2010; Smith & Korschun, 2018) suggests that companies may use either distinction. We argue that an employee's degree of ideological engagement will vary based on the type of justification provided. For example, we argue that a moral rationale will make the moral and ethical aspects at work more salient for an employee, and thus may encourage them to frame their workplace experience in terms of moral values. Thus, a moral rationale for corporate political activism may lead employees to connect their work behaviours to a superordinate purpose based on societal or moral concerns, thereby facilitating ideological engagement. On the other hand, a performance-based rationale will not engage moral and ideological elements of the employee's sense of self and will therefore be less likely to drive ideological engagement.

The moderating influence of alignment with employees' beliefs

Employees must reconcile company actions with their personal beliefs. The ideological alignment between an employee and their employer's political activism will influence the degree to which such activities will encourage the employee's ideological engagement. We envision the alignment of activism with employee beliefs as a moderator on the relationship between the stated rationale for corporate political activism and ideological engagement. That is, the more corporate beliefs are aligned with employee beliefs, the stronger the relationship between the stated rationale of the activism (whether moral or performance-based) and the ideological engagement should become.

When an employee becomes aware that their employer is expressing similar beliefs to their own through corporate political activism, the employee may feel freer to express those personal thoughts through their job. That is, to the extent that the company's stand matches that of the employee, it may signal that expressing those views in the workplace is acceptable and appropriate. An employee may begin to view his job as a means of ideological expression and become more cognisant of his work's ideological benefits. In contrast, a mismatch between the company's stand and the personal view of the employee may signal that the employee must inhibit that same expression, lest they expose a moral conflict with the company (Haski-Leventhal, Roza, & Meijs, 2017). For example, if a company takes a strong stand on the issue of abortion that is not in alignment with an employee's beliefs, the employee is likely to refrain from sharing those beliefs freely at work. We predict that such an employee's reluctance to openly disagree with their employer will reduce ideological engagement at work, resulting in less likelihood that they will engage in political participation outside of work, defend the company against criticism and broaden stakeholder ties.

In the previous section, we discussed the notion that moral rationales should induce greater ideological engagement than performance-based justifications for corporate political activism. The greater the alignment with employee beliefs and the activism, the more the rationale (whether moral or performance-based) should result in ideological engagement. This is presented in the framework (Figure 10.1) as an interaction between a stated rationale for corporate activism and alignment with employees' beliefs. Moral (versus performance-based) justification should have a positive effect on ideological engagement, and the effect is stronger when aligned with the political position of the employee.

Extremity of corporate activism and experienced pressure to conform

Prior research finds that employees sometimes create false representations of the self in order 'to appear as if they embrace organizational values' (Hewlin, 2003, p. 633). Employees engage in such a facade to the extent that they experience pressure – whether real or perceived – to conform to the values or goals of the organisational collective. We argue that a company making its political positions public may provide fertile ground for this to take place. In particular, we propose that more extreme activism stances by companies will cause employees to experience increased pressure to conform. Some businesses make strong statements for or against social issues, expressing extreme left or extreme right viewpoints rather than the traditionally 'safer' moderate stance. The starkness of extreme stances can make even the most complicated issue seem black and white, providing little grey area in which allowances may be made for varying opinions. Even if differences are not obvious to onlookers, employees are likely to critically evaluate their own views in relation to those expressed by the company.

An employee may normally experience increased pressure to conform to extreme activism, but this pressure dissipates the more that the political position is agreeable to the employee. In other words, we expect that the greater the alignment with an employee's beliefs, the less the extremity of the corporate activism will result in experienced pressure to conform. If an employee and an employer are already in agreement ideologically, an extreme political stance carries minimal pressure for conformity. When misalignment occurs between the employee beliefs and activism, the effect of an extreme stance is heightened, resulting in greater pressure to conform. If employees do not agree ideologically with the company, an extreme stance should result in even greater experienced pressure to conform.

Manager support of corporate political activism and experienced pressure to conform

Employees may experience pressure to conform in a variety of ways. Whether or not it is intended, employees may feel that they are missing out on opportunities for career advancement, networking or socialising if they do not share the views expressed by their employers. Manager support of corporate political activism is expected to make a significant impact on how the activism is perceived by employees. Whether a team leader, department head or CEO, we consider managers at every level to have the potential to impact employees' experience regarding activism. The greater the degree of manager support of the activism, the more we expect an employee to experience pressure to conform.

In a traditional workplace, the management is responsible for carrying out and overseeing the organisation's initiatives. If management does not uniformly support a political initiative, it may not be highly prioritised, strictly adhered to or enforced. Therefore, employees will not feel much effect of the activism and will experience little pressure to conform. Alternatively, if management strongly supports corporate political activism, employees may feel increased pressure to conform because managers have so much influence over their day-to-day work and career advancement.

Manager support for corporate political activism should have an impact on an employee's experienced pressure to conform (van Schie, Gautier, Pache, & Güntert, 2019). This impact should be especially strong if the corporate political activism and employee's personal beliefs are misaligned. If an employee shares the beliefs of the company, then extra support from the manager should not induce pressure to conform; they are already in agreement. Alternatively, if an employee disagrees with the activism, manager support of the activism should result in much greater experienced pressure to conform; the company and manager support a view in opposition to the employee.

We expect that manager support for a political initiative can produce either explicit or implicit pressure for employees to conform. Explicit pressure to conform may be found in conspicuous actions, such as an internal memo that promotes or lauds the activism initiatives of the company. Implicit pressure to conform may be found in subtler ways, such as the assumption that everyone in an office shares the same viewpoint on a topic.

The moderating influence of the extent of employee involvement requested

Another factor that will impact employee reactions to corporate political activism is the degree to which they are asked personally, and visibly, to be involved in carrying it out. For example, a manager may announce that the office will be given the afternoon off to attend a political rally. While attendance is not mandatory, non-compliance is highly visible and would thus result in increased pressure to conform. Another example is that a co-worker is praised for their financial contribution to the activism initiative. Again, involvement is only requested, but it is obvious to the group who is involved and who is not. The extent of involvement requested is key to understanding this phenomenon: how much is the company asking of its employees? Hertel-Fernandez (2017) examined the extent to which employees had 'voted in the 2014 election, contacted a lawmaker, made a political donation, volunteered for a political cause, or attended a political meeting' (p. 109), and the correlation between these actions and the involvement requested by employers. Another study, by Hertel-Fernandez (2016), revealed that approximately one in four survey respondents had experienced 'some form of political contact with the top managers at their main jobs' (p. 413). The survey revealed that political messages from employers included topics such as the following: policy issue or bill, turning out to vote, registering to vote, presidential candidates, state candidates, contacting a legislator, house candidates, senate candidates, donating to a candidate and other topics.

Employees experience pressure to conform to the extent that they believe that they are not aligned with a social group (Hewlin, 2003). We posit that the effects of extremity of the political position and manager support for the corporate political activism on experienced pressure to conform will become more acute the more an employee is requested to be involved in the political activism. The extent of employee involvement requested can further amplify pressure because becoming involved in activities will make the views of both the individual employee and the group more apparent. This additional salience will underscore the differences between the employee and others in his or her social network at the company. Moreover, when an employee is asked to participate in political activism on behalf of the company, it signals that managers not only care about it themselves, but also that activism is important for the organisation. Therefore, we propose that the extent of employee involvement requested moderates both the relationship between the extremity of corporate activism and experienced pressure to conform, and the relationship between manager support of activism and experienced pressure to conform.

Experienced pressure to conform and ideological engagement

Pressure to conform arises out of discomfort or dissonance (Brehm & Cohen, 1962; Festinger, 1957) between employer activism and employee beliefs. We expect that an increase in experienced pressure to conform will result in a decrease in employee ideological engagement. The more pressure to conform employees experience, the less they will be able to engage ideologically through their work. Ideological engagement is a form of creative self-expression, and pressured conformity makes one feel that one's opinions are of little value. Therefore, when employees experience pressure to conform, they are less likely to prioritise ideological engagement because their employer does not appear to value their viewpoint.

Ideological engagement and political participation outside of work

We expect that ideological engagement in the workplace will lead to greater political participation outside of work. The more an employee feels that their work is connected to their moral self, the more that employee will feel empowered to share their views elsewhere. This may be because the issues are at the forefront of employees' minds due to company activism. This increased salience of the activism makes employees more apt to notice other opportunities for political involvement in other settings. We acknowledge that political participation outside of the company may be on a broad range of issues that may not even relate to the employer's activism. If the activism of the company results in the high ideological engagement of an employee, this is likely to spark political participation from that employee on a range of issues.

Ideological engagement and defending the company against criticism

The more ideological engagement experienced by an employee, the more we expect that employee to defend their employer against criticism. While the largest criticism we foresee could come from those who oppose the activism, there could be broader implications, with employees feeling the need to defend their employer against non-political criticism as well. We posit that employees who are highly ideologically engaged will not only share beliefs with their employer, but also understand the reasoning behind the employer activism. This provides a personal connection with the company's support of the cause and the ability to provide a reasoned defence against critics. We envision that if a criticism is conveyed to a highly ideologically engaged employee about his place of employment, that criticism could be viewed as a personal attack due to the deep connection the employee feels to his employer's ideology. We envision these acts in defence of the company as taking place in the physical as well as virtual worlds. For example, in conversation with a friend, an employee may find herself defending the recent actions of her employer. Social media is another setting that allows employees to share views and defend company actions easily. Some applications and websites offer even more anonymity, such as the forum 'Blind' which allows industry professionals to post and reply in an anonymous forum. Employees may feel more comfortable expressing or defending opinions on corporate political activism on a social media platform than they would in a face-to-face conversation.

Ideological engagement and broadening of stakeholder ties

Greater ideological engagement may strengthen corporate ties with employees in multiple ways. Our framework provides for the effects of ideological engagement on ties with employees as stakeholders in the company. We propose that the more an employee is ideologically engaged, the more that employee will broaden stakeholder ties with the company. Besides fulfilling their job description, employees can interact with their place of employment as stakeholders in many ways (Freeman, 1984; Korschun, 2015). Employees are likely to enact their roles as stakeholders by either consuming the goods or services of the company or investing in the company. We believe that the greater ideological engagement experienced by an employee at work, the broader and stronger the ties between corporation and employee will become outside of work (Bhattacharya & Korschun, 2008, 2019; Bhattacharya, Korschun, & Sen, 2009). That is, as an employee's work becomes an expression of themselves, the more an employee will be apt to invest themselves (and their financial resources) in the company.

Manager support of corporate activism and functional engagement

In addition to ideological engagement, the outcomes of employee functional engagement should be considered as well. Functional engagement is the extent to which employees enjoy their work and believe they are advancing their careers. Whereas ideological engagement includes employees' contributions to society via their work, functional engagement has to do with the benefits employees gain from the work itself. We believe that if a manager supports corporate political activism, this can lead to greater functional engagement for employees. The key factor for increased functional engagement to occur is managerial support of the activism because the manager has control over career advancement. Therefore, by taking part in the activism, employees believe they are boosting their careers. If a manager does not support the activism, the employee is unlikely to experience functional engagement as a result of it.

Functional engagement and transactional investment in work

The greater the functional engagement experienced by an employee, the greater transactional investment we expect the employee to make in their work. The more the employee sees that work as rewarding and functionally engaging, the more their career path develops. In turn, we expect that they will be more likely to fully invest in their career path. This outcome is reflexive; the more benefits the employee reaps from hard work, the more likely they will be to again invest in their work. Even if one is not ideologically engaged, it is still possible to invest much time and effort in one's place of employment because of the potential career rewards.

Implications for practice

Our framework describes a pathway through which corporate political activism affects employee engagement and, subsequently, employee behaviour. We identify three critical facets of such activism and trace their effects on two forms of engagement as well as subsequent behavioural outcomes. In essence, we propose that some facets of corporate political activism can drive ideological engagement, while others may reduce it by creating perceived pressure for the employee to conform to the values of the organisation. We also posit that, under some circumstances, activism can stimulate functional engagement by providing opportunities to be recognised by managers at the company. Each form of engagement – ideological and functional – has distinct consequences. The framework has implications for both theorists and practitioners, which we describe below.

Corporate political activism

Some prior authors on corporate political activism have pointed to the dangers of companies becoming too political (Hertel-Fernandez, 2017). Others suggest that a values overlap is the key ingredient in whether employees embrace or reject such activism (Hambrick & Wowak, 2019). We delve deeper, first delineating key facets of corporate political activism from the employee's point of view, and second, exploring how it affects employees' engagement. Our framework suggests that responses to corporate political activism are far from uniform and that different facets of these activities may engender different responses from employees. A theoretical implication of our framework is that corporate political activism may present conflicts for employees that they must resolve in the course of their work. While we identify some of these tensions in this chapter, we also acknowledge that an employee's interpretation of these tensions and their coping response may be idiosyncratic. We call for future research that examines how potentially conflicting signals, and even potentially conflicting motivations within employees, might affect employee outcomes.

Ideological versus functional engagement

Our framework distinguishes between ideological and functional engagement. While prior research has characterised employee engagement as a single holistic concept reflecting the overall immersion of the self into the job or job role, we argue that an employee may become immersed in their job role (functional engagement) or in the societal consequences of their job (ideological engagement). Moreover, we argue that a company can stimulate ideological engagement by explaining the motivation behind a political activism stand. Although our conceptualisation of functional engagement shares much with previous research, our proposal regarding ideological engagement goes beyond what appears (at least explicitly) to date. It is somewhat reminiscent of research on the purpose of meaning of work (Grant, 2008). However, our framework extends that literature, proposing variance in the degree to which an employee may be engaged in making the psychological connection between their work and collective societal goals. Our framework provides a number of likely contributors to ideological engagement; however, we acknowledge that it is far from comprehensive. We call for additional research on whether other, more traditional job characteristics (c.f., Hackman & Oldham, 1976) may contribute to or reduce such engagement. For example, one might predict that task significance will lead to ideological engagement more than functional engagement, while other job characteristics such as task complexity should have stronger effects on functional engagement.

Experienced pressure to conform

We argue that the extremity of the political stand, as well as the extent to which managers support the stand, can create the conditions under which an employee will experience pressure to conform to those stated organisational beliefs or values. This suggests a notable tension in the framework. While corporate political activism may enable ideological engagement by making the company's and the employee's values more salient and central to the job, there is also a darker side, where an employee may feel social pressure from managers and fellow employees to express the same values as those of the organisation. We predict that such experienced pressure to conform can threaten ideological engagement by preventing the employee from expressing themselves fully on the job. This suggests that employees must sometimes navigate social settings which can cause work-related stress, as it simultaneously provides avenues for self-expression. Future research may investigate more longitudinally how employees adjust to these social pressures over time.

Implications for practitioners

Our framework provides actionable insight for practitioners. Many managers already acknowledge the importance of employee engagement for business performance, and measurement of the concept is already widely diffused. We distinguish between ideological and functional engagement and explain how each drives distinct types of behaviour. We are agnostic on which is more important for any individual business. Our only prescription is that companies encourage either form of engagement based on the ultimate behaviours they wish to motivate among employees, or groups of employees. Some companies may wish to encourage employees to prioritise the needs of external stakeholders (requiring more ideological engagement), while, for others, a more transactional relationship focused on efficiency and efficacy of job tasks (requiring functional engagement) may be more appropriate. For those companies that wish to encourage ideological engagement, managers must also consider the potential danger that, in doing so, they may unintentionally induce employees to experience a pressure to conform ideologically with the organisation, which could harm the very engagement they are attempting to foster. Therefore, managers should use caution in embarking upon this route.

Our framework also calls attention to the fact that each employee interprets corporate political activities with their personal situation in mind. Thus, managers need to take into account not only how involved employees are (Beatty, Homer, & Kahle, 1988) in the political issue, but also how embedded they might already be in the company's network. For example, our framework implies that closely monitored employees who work on site may be more susceptible to work pressures to conform from managers and other employees than contract employees who are more autonomous. We recommend that managers remain cognisant of these differences when shaping their political engagement strategies.

Finally, companies that are successful at engendering employee participation may be able to generate feedback loops which can reinforce the effects as part of a virtuous cycle. For example, employees who take part in political activities after work may subsequently bring that enthusiasm to the workplace, influencing the facets of corporate political activism that will continue to shape outcome effects for themselves and other employees. For example, Patagonia encourages employees to be highly engaged in environmental issues. As more employees and managers participate outside of the corporate sphere, it may reinforce their ideological engagement and desire for the company to become more active.

How corporate political activism affects employees remains an understudied yet important topic for theorists. Our proposed framework provides a theory-based view of how employees interpret and respond to such activism, which we hope will serve as a springboard for future discovery.

Conclusion

Corporate political activism, once a rarity, is becoming increasingly common. Yet, employee response to corporate political activism remains an understudied topic. Our proposed framework provides a theory-grounded view of how employees interpret and subsequently respond to such activism. While our approach breaks new theoretical ground, it is not intended to be comprehensive. Our framework is intended to be an early step in understanding the complex and often idiosyncratic linkages between companies, employees and the political realm, linkages that until recently were presumed to be largely separate. We, therefore, view the topic as ripe for additional studies that delve deeper into the psychological reactions behind employee responses to corporate political activism.

Questions for students

1. Is it possible to simultaneously drive ideological and functional engagement?
2. Can you think of an instance where increased pressure to conform would produce a positive result?
3. Discuss instances where having an extreme position would be a good or bad idea.

References

Abelson, R. (1995). Attitude extremity. In R. Petty & J. Krosnick (Eds.), *Attitude strength: Antecedents and consequences* (pp. 25–41). Mahwah, NJ: Lawrence Erlbaum.

Albert, S., & Whetten, D. A. (1985). Organizational identity. In L. L. Cummings & B. M. Staw (Eds.), *Research in organizational behavior* (Vol. 7). Greenwich, CT: JAI Press.

Beatty, S. E., Homer, P., & Kahle, L. R. (1988). The involvement–commitment model: Theory and implications. *Journal of Business Research, 16*(2), 149–167.

Bhattacharya, C. B., & Korschun, D. (2008). Stakeholder marketing: Beyond the four Ps and the customer. *Journal of Public Policy & Marketing, 27*(1), 113–116.

Bhattacharya, C. B., & Korschun, D. (2019). Motivating boundary-spanning employees to engage external stakeholders: Insights from stakeholder marketing. In J. Harrison, J. Barney, R. Freeman, & R. Phillips (Eds.), *The Cambridge Handbook of Stakeholder Theory* (pp. 147–162). Cambridge: Cambridge University Press.

Bhattacharya, C. B., Korschun, D., & Sen, S. (2009). Strengthening stakeholder–company relationships through mutually beneficial corporate social responsibility initiatives. *Journal of Business Ethics, 85*(2), 257–272.

Brehm, J. W., & Cohen, A. R. (1962). *Explorations in cognitive dissonance.* Hoboken, NJ: John Wiley & Sons Inc.

Cable, D. M., & Judge, T. A. (1996). Person–organization fit, job choice decisions, and organizational entry. *Organizational Behavior and Human Decision Processes, 67*(3), 294–311.

Chatterji, A. K., & Toffel, M. W. (2016). Do CEO activists make a difference? Evidence from a field experiment. *Harvard Business School Working Paper,* No. 16-100, March.

Denning, S. (2019). Netflix and Disney speak out against Georgia's pending abortion law. *Forbes,* 30 May. Retrieved from www.forbes.com/sites/stephaniedenning/2019/05/30/netflix-and-disney-speak-out-against-georgias-pending-abortion-law/#43e1da807cd5.

Du, S., Bhattacharya, C. B., & Sen, S. (2015). Corporate social responsibility, multi-faceted job-products, and employee outcomes. *Journal of Business Ethics, 131*(2), 319–335.

Edinger-Schons, L. M., Lengler-Graiff, L., Scheidler, S., & Wieseke, J. (2019). Frontline employees as corporate social responsibility (CSR) ambassadors: A quasi-field experiment. *Journal of Business Ethics, 157*(2), 359–373.

Fernbach, P. M., Rogers, T., Fox, C. R., & Sloman, S. A. (2013). Political extremism is supported by an illusion of understanding. *Psychological Science, 24*(6), 939–946.

Festinger, L. (1957). *A theory of cognitive dissonance* (Vol. 2). Redwood City, CA: Stanford University Press.

Freeman, R. E. (1984). *Strategic management: A stakeholder approach.* Boston, MA: Pitman.

Grant, A. M. (2008). The significance of task significance: Job performance effects, relational mechanisms, and boundary conditions. *Journal of Applied Psychology, 93*(1), 108–124.

Hackman, J. R., & Oldham, G. R. (1976). Motivation through the design of work: Test of a theory. *Organizational Behavior and Human Performance, 16*(2), 250–279.

Hambrick, D. C., & Wowak, A. (2019). CEO sociopolitical activism: A stakeholder alignment model. *Academy of Management Review.* Retrieved from https://doi-org.eur.idm.oclc.org/10.5465/amr.2018.0084.

Haski-Leventhal, D., Roza, L., & Meijs, L. C. (2017). Congruence in corporate social responsibility: Connecting the identity and behavior of employers and employees. *Journal of Business Ethics, 143*(1), 35–51.

Hertel-Fernandez, A. (2016). How employers recruit their workers into politics: And why political scientists should care. *Perspectives on Politics, 14*(2), 410–421.

Hertel-Fernandez, A. (2017). American employers as political machines. *The Journal of Politics, 79*(1), 105–117.

Hewlin, P. F. (2003). And the award for best actor goes to…: Facades of conformity in organizational settings. *Academy of Management Review, 28*(4), 633–642.

Hillman, A. J., & Hitt, M. A. (1999). Corporate political strategy formulation: A model of approach, participation, and strategy decisions. *Academy of Management Review, 24*(4), 825–842.

Holzer, B. (2010). *Moralizing the corporation: Transnational activism and corporate accountability.* Northampton, MA: Edward Elgar Publishing.

Jost, J. T., Napier, J. L., Thorisdottir, H., Gosling, S. D., Palfai, T. P., & Ostafin, B. (2007). Are needs to manage uncertainty and threat associated with political conservatism or ideological extremism? *Personality and Social Psychology Bulletin, 33*(7), 989–1007.

Kahn, W. A. (1990). Psychological conditions of personal engagement and disengagement at work. *Academy of Management Journal, 33*, 692–724.

Kennedy, K. N., Goolsby, J. R., & Arnould, E. J. (2003). Implementing a customer orientation: Extension of theory and application. *Journal of Marketing, 67*(4), 67–81.

Kirca, A. H., Jayachandran, S., & Bearden, W. O. (2005). Market orientation: A meta-analytic review and assessment of its antecedents and impact on performance. *Journal of Marketing, 69*(2), 24–41.

Korschun, D. (2015). Boundary-spanning employees and relationships with external stakeholders: A social identity approach. *Academy of Management Review, 40*(4), 611–629.

Korschun, D., Bhattacharya, C. B., & Swain, S. D. (2014). Corporate social responsibility, customer orientation, and the job performance of frontline employees. *Journal of Marketing, 78*(3), 20–37.

Korschun, D., Rafieian, H., Aggarwal, A., & Swain, S. D. (2019). *Taking a stand: Consumer responses when companies get (or don't get) political*, 3 July. Retrieved from https://dx.doi.org/10.2139/ssrn.2806476.

Kristof, A. L. (1996). Person–organization fit: An integrative review of its conceptualizations, measurement, and implications. *Personnel Psychology, 49*(1), 1–49.

La Rocco, J. M., & Jones, A. P. (1978). Co-worker and leader support as moderators of stress-strain relationships in work situations. *Journal of Applied Psychology, 63*(5), 629–634.

McWilliams, A., & Siegel, D. (2001). Corporate social responsibility: A theory of the firm perspective. *Academy of Management Review, 26*(1), 117–127.

Meredith, S. (2018). Risk of a no-deal Brexit grounding flights across Europe is being 'underestimated', warns Ryanair boss. *CNBC*, 12 September. Retrieved from www.cnbc.com/2018/09/12/ryanair-ceo-warns-of-a-no-deal-brexit-says-risk-being-underestimated.html.

Nalick, M., Josefy, M., Zardkoohi, A., & Bierman, L. (2016). Corporate sociopolitical involvement: A reflection of whose preferences? *Academy of Management Perspectives, 30*(4), 384–403.

Pew Research Center (2014). *Political polarization in the American public.* Retrieved from www.people-press.org/2014/06/12/political-polarization-in-the-american-public.

Pomering, A., & Dolnicar, S. (2009). Assessing the prerequisite of successful CSR implementation: Are consumers aware of CSR initiatives? *Journal of Business Ethics, 85*(2), 285–301.

Saks, A. M. (2006). Antecedents and consequences of employee engagement. *Journal of Managerial Psychology, 21*(7), 600–619.

Sethi, S. P. (1982). Corporate political activism. *California Management Review, 24*(3), 32–42.

Smith, N. C., & Korschun, D. (2018). Finding the middle ground in a politically polarized world. *MIT Sloan Management Review, 60*(1), 1–5.

Toner, K., Leary, M. R., Asher, M. W., & Jongman-Sereno, K. P. (2013). Feeling superior is a bipartisan issue: Extremity (not direction) of political views predicts perceived belief superiority. *Psychological Science, 24*(12), 2454–2462.

van Schie, S., Gautier, A., Pache, A. C., & Güntert, S. T. (2019). What keeps corporate volunteers engaged: Extending the volunteer work design model with self-determination theory insights. *Journal of Business Ethics, 160*(3), 693–712.

Part 5
Discussion

11 Discussion and Conclusion: Moving Forward from Here

Debbie Haski-Leventhal, Lonneke Roza, and Stephen Brammer

This book on corporate social responsibility (CSR) and employee engagement aimed to bring forward contemporary and cutting-edge knowledge at the micro-level of CSR. While there is a vast amount of research and many publications on CSR, mainly developed over the last two decades, the micro-level of CSR is still understudied (Aguinis & Glavas, 2012). We aimed to shed light on employee involvement in CSR as well as on employee engagement through CSR. To do so, the book focused on three related areas: the antecedents of employee engagement in CSR; the processes through which employees can get involved; and the impacts of CSR on employees and other stakeholders.

Antecedents, processes and impacts of CSR and employee engagement: book summary

The first part of the book examined the **antecedents** of CSR and what can assist companies in (further) involving their employees in their social and environmental responsibility. Glavas and Willness (Chapter 2) discussed the antecedents to employee engagement in CSR, while also exploring what could lead to disengagement. They emphasise that employees vary by so many variables that there cannot be a one-size-fits-all solution when engaging them in CSR. Subsequently, without examining the individual determinants that lead to CSR engagement, companies may end up with many disengaged employees. Kidd et al. (Chapter 3) offered an overall review of CSR and employee engagement, exploring the role of employees as implementers and leaders of CSR. For example, this chapter demonstrates that values and value congruence play a vital role in engaging employees in

CSR, and how the desire for meaningfulness can lead to these results. An important antecedent of CSR is employee gender, which is discussed in the following chapter, written by Schulz and Rupp (Chapter 4). Their review showed that women tend to support, and participate in, CSR more than men, and that CSR and employee engagement can include gender equity as a matter of social responsibility and a way to further engage employees.

The second part of the book focused on 'how' – the **processes** that can be used to enhance employee engagement in CSR. When we designed the book, we, the editors, thought this part would include chapters on corporate volunteering and payroll giving, but the result is somewhat different and more innovative. Van der Heijden and Cramer (Chapter 5) discussed how companies can use employees as change agents in their long-term CSR engagement strategies. Doing so will not only increase employee involvement, but also provide them with a sense of ownership. This can be an effective way of using word of mouth and peer pressure to engage more employees in CSR. The authors' longitudinal research within 18 pioneering companies distinguished four engagement strategies that change agents developed and used over time. Wagner, Roza, and Haski-Leventhal (Chapter 6) used a qualitative study to discuss the importance of internal communication as a process of engaging employees and overcoming their passivity. Finally, the last chapter in this part on processes is by Haski-Leventhal, Glavas, and Roza (Chapter 7). It discusses social intrapreneurship as a new horizon for employee engagement in CSR. It shows that social intrapreneurship occurs when employees lead innovative solutions to social problems while working for an established organisation. As such, social intrapreneurship can connect CSR and employee engagement, if companies see it as an opportunity and address the related challenges.

The third and last part of this book examines the possible results and **impacts** of employee engagement in CSR. Chapter 8, by Mirvis, MacArthur, Walsh, and Gapeka, examines the idea of global pro bono service (also known as international corporate volunteering). Using the results of a large-scale, international survey, the authors examine the varieties of participants in these programmes, the company's motivations for investing in them and the impact on employees, companies and the communities served. Handy, Hustinx and Spraul show in Chapter 9 how CSR can be used to attract students and graduates to potential employers. Based on a study in India, the chapter shows that companies with a desirable CSR reputation may be successful even when offering lower-than-average monetary wages. This part of the book concludes with Chapter 10 by Korschun and Godfrey, who bring us the novel idea of corporate political activism and discuss the impacts of such work on employees. They do so by identifying three facets which drive employee reactions to activism: the stated rationale of the political position, the extremity of the position, and perceived manager support for activism.

Insights

Reading the book in its entirety can provide several significant insights into employee engagement, CSR and the integration of the two. The rich information in all the chapters of the book and the variety of thought-provoking and innovative angles some of the authors have taken, may inspire further research and practical implementation while also instigating a conversation on this topic.

First, together, the chapters of this book demonstrate that employee engagement in CSR is a complex issue, with antecedents, processes and impacts. We cannot discuss the outcomes of CSR on employee engagement without diving into the notion of processes, nor can we discuss antecedents without a vision of impact. These three aspects of employee engagement in CSR are important, each with its own weight, but it is the integration of the three that truly helps us understand the depth and breadth of CSR and of employee engagement. Some of the chapters only touched on the one aspect, the part of the book that this chapter belonged to. However, most chapters included aspects of all three: antecedents, processes and impacts. This is because addressing CSR holistically requires a good understanding and implementation of all three.

Second, the chapters of this book show that there is no unified way of implementing CSR, and this is also true for employee engagement in CSR. Different companies will have different approaches on how to address their social and environmental responsibilities, and the rich examples, case studies and vignettes in this book demonstrate this well. Furthermore, as asserted by several authors here, different employees may have different motivations and needs which can be addressed through CSR, and it is important to offer a variety of ways for employees to be involved. Some employees, such as females or millennials, might be more inclined towards social and environmental issues, while others might view it more as a means to an end and join for personal motives. Some employees prefer to take a more passive role in CSR, while others desire to lead their own CSR initiatives and even become social intrapreneurs (see Chapter 7).

Third, as a book written by authors from all around the world, we show the importance of culture, norms and values in the context of employee engagement and CSR. The book includes studies from Europe, the USA, Australia and India, while some chapters include examples from a number of countries. As CSR is affected by the local culture (Aguinis & Glavas, 2012), so too is the manner in which companies involve employees in it. For example, in India (see Chapter 9) corporate philanthropy is compulsory for large companies. On the one hand, this might impact the number of companies that are involved. On the other hand, the CSR Act only refers to giving money and, as such, there may be less effort made to involve employees. Corporate political activism (Chapter 10) has become a widespread phenomenon in the last few years, but mainly in the USA. It is possible that the current regime and presidency have evoked this political action by companies.

Finally, several chapters in this book exemplify the most recent trends in employee engagement in CSR. In the initial stages of CSR, a couple of decades ago, most CSR was done top-down, led by executive management or the marketing department (Haski-Leventhal, 2018). At the second stage, companies realised that they could involve their employees in CSR through corporate volunteering and payroll giving, not only to do more for the community, but also to create positive outcomes for employees and the company. In the current, third stage, employees take a lead in some companies, through employee-led CSR and social intrapreneurship. Furthermore, companies innovate on how they involve their employees, for example via global pro bono programmes (Chapter 8) or as change agents (Chapter 5). For many companies, particularly in the USA and Europe, CSR is manifesting itself gradually in the more mainstream value chain too. Where CSR had been considered as peripheral for a long time, it is increasingly being seen as an 'everyday practice' and part of the in-role behaviour of employees (Aguinis & Glavas, 2013). For instance, Chapter 5 clearly shows the various CSR journeys that companies may take through time and how they relate to in-role behaviour. Even if CSR is considered extra-role (e.g., corporate volunteering or community involvement), we can see that there is an increasing link with organisational and in-role behaviour. As a result, CSR is balancing out between being peripheral and integrated. As Aguinis and Glavas (2013) show, both have advantages for the business, employees and the community. Finding a proper balance is key.

Future research

This book is one of the first to fully focus on employee engagement in CSR, including antecedents, processes and impacts. Its focus on the micro-level of CSR helps to shed light on an understudied aspect of social responsibility and sustainability. However, more empirical research and theoretical development are needed to enable us to create the required body of knowledge and managerial tools.

First, we suggest the development of a comprehensive model or even a theory on CSR and employee engagement. While many writers on this topic use existing theories, such as motivation, identification or behavioural theories (e.g., the theory of planned behaviour; see Ajzen, 1991), developing such a (combined) model and theory will assist writers in the field. There are a few models, such as the CSR congruence model (Haski-Leventhal, Roza, & Meijs, 2017), which specifically look at the dynamics between the antecedents, processes and outcomes of employee engagement in CSR, but additional models are needed.

We also believe that a special, scholarly attention needs to be given to the issue of motivation. First, we need to better understand what motivates employees to partake in the CSR activities, programmes and approach of their employer. It is imperative to collect data on how background variables, such as gender, age, managerial position, education and experience, affect these motivations. Studies might also look at the relationship between self-transcendence values and pro-social attitudes and motivations. Furthermore, empirical research is required on how these motivations impact the actions and behaviour of employees.

Second, research is needed on the motivations of companies. Aguilera, Rupp, Williams, and Ganapathi (2007) asserted that companies are involved in CSR for moral, instrumental and relational reasons, and it is important to understand how corporate motivations affect the level and manner of employee engagement in these issues. It is also important to assess the motivation congruence between employees and employers and the outcomes of this alignment, or lack thereof.

Furthermore, we suggest another direction for future research based on the outcomes and impacts of employee engagement in CSR. This can be done as a multilevel analysis, considering the micro-, meso- and macro-levels. At the micro-level, future research might look at the impact of employee engagement in CSR on employees – their well-being and happiness, as well as on their job-related outcomes, such as job satisfaction, affective commitment, intention to stay and actual retention. While there is some existing research on these research questions (e.g., Brammer, Millington, & Rayton, 2007; Glavas, 2016; Mirvis, 2012), it would be beneficial to focus on the most recent trends of employee engagement in CSR, such as social intrapreneurship, to assess their impact on employees. As many studies on the micro-level seem to solely focus on the positive effects of CSR, we would also like to stimulate critical research at the micro-level that unravels the potential negative consequences, such as absenteeism, leaving the organisation or even job loss. Lastly, we might also think about how CSR can be used to stimulate reflection on the current worldviews of employees, and how they might use this critical reflection to change their behaviour both inside and outside the workplace.

In addition, at the meso-level, researchers might examine the multiple impacts on and outcomes for the organisation – from reputation and performance to their impact-generation capacity and stakeholder integration. There is literature showing that organisations that involve their employees in their CSR yield benefits (e.g., Bučiūnienė & Kazlauskaitė, 2012; Story & Neves, 2015; Tang, Hull, & Rothenberg, 2012), but we need to also look at their ability to further lead with responsibility and sustainability. In addition, we would encourage more research on how employee engagement in

CSR can change organisational behaviour. Employee-led initiatives that foster a diverse and inclusive workplace can impact the organisation's mission, values, goals and business practices (Ashong-Lamptey, Welbourne, Lewis, Mills, Beaver, Monneuse, & England, 2019).

Finally, on the macro-level, it is important to examine the impact of employee engagement in CSR on the community and society. We often assume that employee engagement in CSR leads to higher levels of social impact, simply because of the additional working hands enabling us to do more. However, we need to create indicators for mid-term outcomes and long-term impacts to establish the ways that employee engagement in CSR may benefit society at large. Demonstrating such an impact could also establish a strong rationale for continuing to involve employees in CSR. Further research is needed to explore how employee engagement in CSR can help achieve the SDGs and raise awareness of them in the public mind.

Contribution

In addressing the micro-level of CSR, the book contributes to the emerging knowledge on CSR. Based on stakeholder theory (Freeman, 1984), the chapters of this book demonstrate how companies can improve their stakeholder integration, for example by including their internal stakeholders (employees) in their efforts to be more sustainable and responsible. Some of the chapters further contribute to motivation theory and engagement theory (e.g., Chapters 2, 3 and 7), by showing how CSR can help to motivate and engage employees. For example, Chapter 7, on social intrapreneurship, discusses how this might help employees meet their autonomy, competence and relatedness needs based on self-determination theory (Ryan & Deci, 2000), while other chapters (2 and 3) touch on Khan's theory of employee engagement. More specifically, the book contributes to the emerging knowledge on concepts such as corporate volunteering (e.g., Chapter 3); social intrapreneurship (Chapter 7); corporate political activism (Chapter 8); and global pro bono programmes (Chapter 9). Furthermore, the book contributes to the need to do multidisciplinary research that does justice to the complexity of employee engagement in and through CSR. The authors of the book have backgrounds in behavioural psychology, organisational behaviour, economics and sociology. This is reflected in the extensive use of a breadth of theories that together shed light on the complexity of the concepts at hand.

The book also provides an important contribution to managerial practice. First, it can assist CSR managers and directors in developing new programmes, initiatives and prospects for CSR, as CSR has shifted from focusing solely on corporate philanthropy to a more holistic approach, embedding various approaches in all aspects of the company and beyond. When a company uses all its resources, people, talent, skills and intellect to create a positive impact, there is no limit to what can be achieved (Haski-Leventhal, 2018). As some of the authors in this book claim, CSR can include global programmes, political activism and social entrepreneurship and intrapreneurship, to name a few.

Second, the book offers new ways of involving employees in CSR. Some of the chapters here show that employees can also lead and initiate CSR and innovative ways of addressing society's most pressing problems. Chapter 5 includes various strategies that a company might adopt to transform into a more sustainable and socially responsible firm.

Third, the book can help companies and managers build a strong rationale (a business case) for CSR, as several chapters, particularly in Part 3, show the positive impacts of CSR. In an era where so many employees are disengaged or actively disengaged (Gallup, 2018), CSR offers an outstanding way of engaging and motivating employees, thus increasing performance and employee attraction and retention (Aguinis & Glavas, 2012; Collier & Esteban, 2007). Finally, involving employees in the company's CSR can help it to increase its social impact and community outreach, and become more sustainable, responsible, impactful and purposeful.

References

Aguilera, R. V., Rupp, D. E., Williams, C. A., & Ganapathi, J. (2007). Putting the S back in corporate social responsibility: A multilevel theory of social change in organizations. *Academy of Management Review, 32*(3), 836–863.

Aguinis, H., & Glavas, A. (2012). What we know and don't know about corporate social responsibility: A review and research agenda. *Journal of Management, 38*(4), 932–968.

Aguinis, H., & Glavas, A. (2013). Embedded versus peripheral corporate social responsibility: Psychological foundations. *Industrial and Organizational Psychology: Perspectives on Science and Practice, 6*, 314–332.

Ajzen, I. (1991). The theory of planned behaviour. *Organizational Behavior and the Human Decision Process, 50*, 179–211.

Ashong-Lamptey, J., Welbourne, T. M., Lewis, W., Mills, M., Beaver, G. R., Monneuse, D., & England, K. (2019). Building inclusion through grass-roots efforts: The case for employee resource groups. *Academy of Management Proceedings, 1*.

Brammer, S., Millington, A., & Rayton, B. (2007). The contribution of corporate social responsibility to organizational commitment. *The International Journal of Human Resource Management, 18*(10), 1701–1719.

Bučiūnienė, I., & Kazlauskaitė, R. (2012). The linkage between HRM, CSR and performance outcomes. *Baltic Journal of Management, 7*(1), 5–24.

Collier, J., & Esteban, R. (2007). Corporate social responsibility and employee commitment. *Business Ethics: A European Review, 16*(1), 19–33.

Freeman, R. E. (1984). *Stakeholder management: Framework and philosophy.* Mansfield, MA: Pitman.

Gallup (2018). *Employee engagement.* Retrieved from https://news.gallup.com/poll/241649/employee-engagement-rise.aspx.

Glavas, A. (2016). Corporate social responsibility and employee engagement: Enabling employees to employ more of their whole selves at work. *Frontiers in Psychology, 7,* 796.

Haski-Leventhal, D. (2018). *Strategic corporate social responsibility: Tools and theories for responsible management.* London: Sage.

Haski-Leventhal, D., Roza, L., & Meijs, L. C. (2017). Congruence in corporate social responsibility: Connecting the identity and behavior of employers and employees. *Journal of Business Ethics, 143*(1), 35–51.

Mirvis, P. (2012). Employee engagement and CSR: Transactional, relational, and developmental approaches. *California Management Review, 54*(4), 93–117.

Ryan, R. M., & Deci, E. L. (2000). Self-determination theory and the facilitation of intrinsic motivation, social development, and well-being. *American Psychologist, 55*(1), 68–78.

Story, J., & Neves, P. (2015). When corporate social responsibility (CSR) increases performance: Exploring the role of intrinsic and extrinsic CSR attribution. *Business Ethics: A European Review, 24*(2), 111–124.

Tang, Z., Hull, C. E., & Rothenberg, S. (2012). How corporate social responsibility engagement strategy moderates the CSR–financial performance relationship. *Journal of Management Studies, 49*(7), 1274–1303.

Appendix

Table 1. Individual Factors that Influence Employee Engagement in CSR (listed are both theoretical and empirical publications)

Topic Area	Publications
General Engagement Themes:	
a. Values	Values (Jones, Willness, & Madey, 2014; Swanson, 1995); other-regarding values (Evans, Davis, & Frink, 2011); values fit (i.e., CSR-Induced Intrinsic Attributions) (Vlachos, Panagopoulos, & Rapp, 2013) • Employees' own harmonious environmental passion (Robertson & Barling, 2013) • Individual concern (Bansal, 2003; Bansal & Roth, 2000; Graves et al., 2013; Mudrack, 2007) • Importance of CSR (Peterson, 2004); salience of CSR issues to employee (Bansal & Roth, 2000)
b. Meaningfulness/ Purpose	Employees believe that if they engage in CSR that their work will be more meaningful (Aguinis & Glavas, 2019; Du et al., 2015; Glavas, 2016; Glavas & Kelley, 2014); project meaningfulness (Caligiuri et al., 2013)
c. Organisational Support	Perceived organisational support (Ditlev-Simonsen, 2015; Glavas & Kelley, 2014; Shen & Benson, 2016); Employee self-centered CSR attributions (i.e., expected benefit to employee from CSR) (De Roeck, & Delobbe, 2012)

d. Self-evaluation	This is a more complex view of the self that is situated with contexts in which both self-assets and self-doubts can lead to engagement or disengagement (Sonenshein et al., 2014). Related articles:
	• Identity – which can social (i.e., identification with organisation and with external beneficiaries) and person identity which can be based on a person's morals and or competencies (e.g., an individual sees themselves as a good person) (Opoku-Dakwa et al., 2018)
	  ○ Environmental identity (Sparks & Shepherd, 1992)
	  ○ Virtue identity, which is a type of identity in which a person sees themselves as being a good person (Dutton, Roberts, & Bednar, 2010)
	  ○ Conscience, such as being a good person (Costas & Kärreman, 2013); consciousness around CSR (Tsai et al., 2014)
	  ○ Moral identity (Rupp, Shao, Thornton, & Skarlicki, 2013); moral reflectiveness (Kim et al., 2014); moral outrage (Hafenbrädl & Waeger, 2017)
	  ○ Sense of responsibility, duty (Bansal & Roth, 2000)
	  ○ Self-perception as a change agent (Wickert & De Bakker, 2018)

Table 1.   Individual Factors that Influence Employee Engagement in CSR (listed are both theoretical and empirical publications) (Continued)

Topic Area	Publications

Other Common Themes Found in the Literature:	• Organisational identification (De Roeck et al., 2016; De Roeck & Farooq, 2018; El Akremi et al., 2015; Farooq et al., 2016)
	• Multiple needs of justice (cf. Cropanzano, Byrne, Bobocel, & Rupp, 2001) applied to CSR which are instrumental, relational, and moral drivers (Gond et al., 2017); employee psychological needs (Aguilera, Rupp, Williams, & Ganapathi, 2007; Rupp, 2011; Rupp & Bell, 2010; Treviño, Weaver, & Reynolds, 2006)
	• Individual differences such as age (Wiernik et al., 2013); personality traits such as conscientiousness (Kim et al., 2014); gender (Brammer, Millington, & Rayton, 2007; Hatch & Stephen, 2015); independent self-construal (Simpson et al., forthcoming); individualism (Rupp et al., 2018); personal orientations such as a humane orientation (Mueller et al., 2012)
	• Affective commitment (El Akremi et al., 2018; Farooq et al., 2014; Vlachos et al., 2014)
	• Benefits of engaging in CSR – socialisation (Hejjas et al., 2019); perceived social support (Caligiuri et al., 2013); skill development (Bode & Singh, 2018; Caligiuri et al., 2013; Hejjas et al., 2019); financial incentives (Merriman et al., 2016)
	• Perceptions of CSR – i.e., that one's company is involved in CSR, which then sends cues regarding the importance of CSR (De Roeck & Farooq, 2018)
	   o Evaluations summarised in Gond et al. (2017) in that employees have different affective and cognitive processes of evaluating the organisation. For example, the work on attributions shows that employees might engage more in CSR if they perceive it to be substantive or authentic compared to symbolic or insincere (Donia et al., 2017; Donia &Tetrault Sirsly, 2016; Vlachos, Panagopoulos, & Rapp, 2013)
	   o Positive perceptions of CSR (Simpson et al., forthcoming)

Other Themes:	The following are important areas of study; however, they have not been studied as much in the micro CSR literature: • Advocacy within work groups (Kim et al., 2014) • Dissatisfaction with status quo (Wickert & De Bakker, 2018) • Attendance at CSR conferences (Johnson & Greening, 1999; Weaver et al., 1999a, 1999b)

Table 2.   Organisational Factors that Influence Employee Engagement in CSR (listed are both theoretical and empirical publications)

Topic Area	Publications
Values and Culture:	• Organisational values (Bansal, 2003; Merriman et al., 2016; Maignan et al., 1999; Marcus & Anderson, 2006). • CEO emphasis on stakeholder values (Sully de Luque, Washburn, Waldman, & House, 2008) • CEO values (Agle, Mitchell, & Sonnenfeld, 1999) • Organisational culture (Bansal & Roth, 2000; Hejjas et al., 2019; Morsing & Oswald, 2009)
Organisational Practices:	• CSR training (Stevens, Steensma, Harrison, & Cochran, 2005) • Communication – signals of organisational encouragement (e.g., policies, published statements) (Ramus & Steger, 2000) and job seekers perception of potential value fit, expected treatment, and anticipated pride and prestige (Jones et al., 2014)

Support from Organisation and Leadership:	• Management commitment (Erdogan et al., 2015; Weaver, Treviño, & Cochran, 1999a, 1999b)
	 • Organisational support of CSR (Opoku-Dakwa et al., 2018)
	 • Support from middle managers (Vlachos et al., 2014)
	 • Supervisor support:
	    o Manager's own implementation of a deliberative strategy, and their leadership style (i.e., non-directive leadership style) (Vlachos et al., 2014);
	    o Employee perceptions of leadership – i.e., ethical (De Roeck & Farooq, 2018);
	    o Signals of supervisor support for CSR such as innovation, competence building, communication, information dissemination, rewards and recognition, management of goals and responsibilities (Ramus & Steger, 2000);
	    o Leader green behaviour (Kim et al., 2014);
	    o Supervisor commitment to CSR (Buehler & Shetty, 1976; Greening & Gray, 1994; Muller & Kolk, 2010; Ramus & Steger, 2000)
	    o Leaders' workplace pro-environmental behaviours – i.e., leaders' environmental descriptive norms predicted their environmentally-specific transformational leadership and their workplace pro-environmental behaviours, both of which predicted employees' harmonious environmental passion (Robertson & Barling, 2013)

Table 3.   Factors that Influence Employee Disengagement in CSR (listed are both theoretical and empirical publications)

Individual factors: Individual differences, attitudes, preferences, or employee behaviours	*Organisational factors:* Organisational actions / characteristics of CSR initiatives / implementation of CSR
• Perceived corporate citizenship has a negative influence on OCB for those with lower other-regarding value orientation (Evans et al., 2011) • Citizenship negatively affects altruism and courtesy dimensions of OCB (Lin et al., 2010) • When CSR is perceived as important, symbolic CSR is negatively related to perceptions of fit with the organisation (Donia et al., 2017) • Social cynicism associated with perceiving benefit from company practices that benefit the employee, rather than CSR that seems to benefit others (West et al., 2015) • Some portion of employees for whom CSR is associated with cynicism, stress, frustration, and discomfort in their work (Onkila, 2015) • Small percentage of job seekers were unaffected by or reacted negatively towards CSR for reasons that suggested scepticism or cynicism (Jones, Willness, & Heller, 2016) • Machiavellian employees are less attracted to companies that are high in CSR (Zhang & Gowan, 2012)	• Higher levels of CSR related to higher turnover to other law firms, but not related to overall turnover rates (Carnahan et al., 2017) • CSR not adequately embedded (Aguinis & Glavas, 2013); a lack of strategic alignment of CSR to business/personal objectives, or conflict between CSR and business practices are impediments to CSR engagement (Slack et al., 2015) • When CSR is extra-role it negatively affects employees (Glavas, 2016) • If seen as disingenuous or inauthentic (Beckman et al., 2009; McShane & Cunningham, 2012) • Symbolic CSR has a negative effect on person–organisation fit and self-reported performance (Donia et al., 2017) • 'Egoistic' motives negatively influence trust in the organisation (Vlachos et al., 2010) • Inconsistency between internal (employee directed) and external (philanthropic) CSR is linked to perceptions of corporate hypocrisy, emotional exhaustion, and ultimately higher turnover (intentions and behaviours) (Scheidler et al., 2018) • Tension between perceptions of how employees are treated versus investments in CSR that presumably benefit others (Brunton et al., 2015; Rodrigo & Arenas, 2009) • Employee perceptions of external legitimacy without internal legitimacy (that CSR is supported by colleagues and managers) attenuates CSR authenticity, which had a 'negative net effect' on organisational identification and attachment (Lee & Yoon, 2018) • Incongruence between employee's and organisation's CSR orientation associated with decreases in satisfaction (Singhapakdi et al., 2015) • When POS is high, employees' OBCs towards the environment and management commitment to the environment were inversely related (Erdogan et al., 2015) • When employees are pressured to be involved in CSR (Hejjas et al., 2019) • When justice climate is perceived as unfair and CSR is favorable, it can lead to more deviant behaviours (Thornton & Rupp, 2016)

Index

Page numbers in *italics* refer to figures; page numbers in **bold** refer to tables.

Made in the USA
Middletown, DE
05 February 2023